You Can Write a Song

Joel Hirschhorn

SIMON AND SCHUSTER · NEW YORK

2 3 4 5 6 7 8 9 10

Library of Congress Cataloging in Publication Data

Kasha, Al.
    If they ask you, you can write a song.

    Includes index.
    1. Music, Popular (Songs, etc.)—Writing and
publishing.   I.   Hirschhorn, Joel, joint
author.   II.   Title.
MT67.K37   784'.028   79-10089
ISBN 0-671-24149-4

The authors gratefully acknowledge permission from the following to quote song lyrics:
    "After the Thrill is Gone," by Don Henley and Glenn Frey. Copyright © 1976 by WB Music Corporation. All rights reserved. Used by permission.
    "Ain't Nothin' like the Real Thing," by Nicholas Ashford and Valerie Simpson. Copyright © 1967, 1968, and 1974 by Jobete Music Company, Inc. All rights reserved. Reprinted by permission.
    " 'A' My Name Is Alice," by Al Kasha and Joel Hirschhorn. Copyright © 1976 by Fox Fanfare Music, Inc., 20th Century Music Corporation and Caseyem Music. All rights reserved. Used by permission.
    "Bill of Sale," by Al Kasha and Joel Hirschhorn. Copyright © 1976 by Walt Disney Music Company and Wonderland Music Company, Inc. Reprinted by permission. All rights reserved.
    "Candle on the Water," by Al Kasha and Joel Hirschhorn. Copyright © 1976 by Walt Disney Music Company and Wonderland Music Company, Inc. Reprinted by permission.
    "Can't Get Enough of Your Love, Babe," by Barry White. Copyright © 1974 by Sa-Vette Music Company and Six Continents Music Publishing, Inc. (BMI) Used by permission. All rights reserved.
    "Charlie Brown," by Jerry Leiber and Mike Stoller. Copyright © 1959 by Hill and Range Songs, Quintet Music, Inc., and Freddy Bienstock Music Company. All rights administered by Unichappell Music, Inc. (Belinda Music, publisher.) Used by permission.

(continued on page 337)

To Harriet Wasser
for bringing us together

Acknowledgments

We would like to express special thanks to: Happy Goday for his unwavering belief; Ceil, Dana, and Larry Kasha for their love and support; Evelyn and Irving Hirschhorn and Madeleine Woolsey for their constant encouragement.

To the following people, all of whom were instrumental in shaping our career with their realistic and creative direction: Roy Acuff, Stanley Adams, Paul Adler, Barney Ales, Irwin Allen, Wayne Allwine, George Alpert, Nick Alphin, Ken Anderson, Neil Anderson, Paul Anka, Ron Anton, Harry Archinal, Fred Astaire, Bob Austin, Charles Aznavour, Burt Bacharach, Tom Bahler, Paul Baratta, Shirley Bassey, Bee Gees, Jerry Belson, Dianne Bennett, Dick Berg, Mel Bly, Alan and Marilyn Bergman, Spence Berland, Chuck Berry, Freddie Bienstock, Sonny Bono, Ernest Borgnine, David Braun, Leon Brettler, Artie Butler, Red Buttons, John Cacavas, Charles Calello, Marvin Cane, Frank Capra, Jr., Johnny Cash, Tom Catalano, Stanley Catron, Cher, Sal Chiantia, Don Costa, Jerome Courtland, Kimberly Coy, Ed Cramer, Mike Curb, Flo Daniels, Ron Dante, Tad Danz, Bobby Darin, Hal David, Clive Davis, Sammy Davis, Jr., Merrill Dean, Walter Dean, Lord Bernard Delfont, Joel Diamond, Neil Diamond, Luther Dixon, Marion Dougherty, Lamont Dozier, Bob Dylan, Herb Eiseman, Mama Cass Elliott, Ahmet Ertegun, Nesuhi Ertegun, Bob Esposito, Marion Evans, Wes Farrell, Howard Fast, Jerry Fielding, Jim Fitzgerald, Henry Fonda, Four Evers, Four Tops, Aretha Franklin, Chuck Fries, Al Gallico, David Garland, Snuff Garrett, George Garvarentz, Bob Gaudig, Gerry Goffin, Jack Gold, Wally Gold, Billy Goldenberg, George Goldner, Jerry Goldsmith, Gene and Harry

Goodman, Roger Gordon, Berry Gordy, Jr., Joe Green, Florence Greenberg, Harold Greenberg, Howard Greenfield, Ken Greengrass, Vic Guder, Burt Haber, Roy Halee, Bob Halley, Arthur Hamilton, Marvin Hamlisch, John Hammond, Yip Harburg, Ira Howard, Sal Ianucci, Bob Jackman, Arthur Jacobs, Jack Jones, Phil Kahl, David Kapralik, Casey Kasem, Harriet Katz, Howard Keel, Gene Kelly, Evelyn Kennedy, Bob King, Carole King, Don Kirshner, Eugene Klein, Mal Klein, Joe Kolsky, Charles Koppelman, Mark Koren, Irwin Kostal, Gary Krisel, Jules Kurz, Larry Kusik, Len Latimer, Steve Lawrence, Jerry Leiber, Goddard Leiberson, Paul Leka, Tommy Leonetti, Irv Levin, Michael Lloyd, Jay Lowy, Arlene Ludwig, Irving Ludwig, Bruce Lundvall, John Mahan, Barry Mann, Irving Mansfield, Paul Marks, Garry Marshall, Ed Matthews, Irwin Mazur, Maureen McGovern, Mike Medavoy, Johnny Mercer, Georges Meyerstein, Ron Miller, Stanley Mills, Ulpio Minucci, Artie Mogull, Ivan Mogull, Charles Monk, Mike Nadel, Ronald Neame, Al Nevins, Anthony Newley, Lionel Newman, Wayne Newton, Tim O'Brien, Tony Orlando, The Osmonds, Marty Ostrow, Horace Ott, Frank Paris, Sid Parnes, Richard Perry, Emile Petrone, Marilyn Mark Petrone, David Picker, George Pincus, Irwin Pincus, Vini Poncia, Jane Powell, Norm Prescott, Elvis Presley, Theron Raines, Helen Reddy, Russ Regan, Nelson Riddle, Artie Ripp, Gerry Robinson, Irwin Robinson, Richard Rodgers, Johnny Rodriguez, Brian Rohan, Donny Rubin, Ronnie Rubin, Dave Rubinson, Ray Ruff, Carole Bayer Sager, Al Schlesinger, Aaron Schroeder, Irwin Schuster, Jack Schwartzman, Ben Scotti, Carol Curb Scotti, Tony Scotti, Neil Sedaka, Norman and Gayle Sedawie, Ned Shankman, Bill Sheppard, Paul Sherman, Lester Sill, Ed Silvers, Carly Simon, Frank Sinatra, Nancy Sinatra, Joe Smith, Rick Smith, Abe Somer, Bert Sommer, Stephen Sondheim, Dennis C. Stanfill, Phil Steinberg, Ray Stevens, Jimmy Stewart, Malcolm Stewart, Mike Stewart, Mike Stoller, Barbra Streisand, Gordon Stulberg, Jacqueline Susann, James Taylor, Elliot Tiegel, Frankie Valli, Harold Wald, Jeff Wald, Cardon Walker, Al Waller, Cynthia Weil, Norman Weiser, George David Weiss, Jerry Wexler, Barry White, Onna White, Andy Williams, John Williams, Paul Williams, Roger Williams, Jackie Wilson, Rich Wiseman, Stevie Wonder, Walter Yetnikoff, Thea Zavin, Lee Zhito.

Research: Bill Dochnal
        Don McGinnis

Contents

Introduction

I've known Al and Joel for over ten years. During that time, I've become familiar with their creativity and professionalism, not only as observer but as collaborator on songs for the motion picture, *The April Fools*.

Al and Joel have always cared about the development and education of new, aspiring writers. Al has taught seminars at UCLA and at universities all around the country, and he and Joel have written articles for leading musical journals.

They are uniquely qualified to write a book on songwriting. Their careers span a multitude of gold records, television themes and motion pictures. They have won two Academy Awards for Best Song, and are the composers of a new stage musical version of *Seven Brides for Seven Brothers*. All the practical and aesthetic lessons they have learned are contained in these pages.

No one can teach inspiration, but everything else composer/lyricists need to know to equip themselves for a musical career can be found in *If They Ask You, You Can Write a Song*. In my opinion, it's the definitive book on song-writing.

Marvin Hamlisch

Prologue

On March 23, 1973, when we stumbled to the stage of the Dorothy Chandler Pavilion and nervously accepted our Academy Award for the song "The Morning After" from a bare-midriffed Cher and a beaming Sonny, we both had an identical mental image—something we discovered the next morning when the excitement had died down. We were envisioning a snowy April morning in 1964 when we demonstrated what was unquestionably our Masterpiece to a stony-faced, cigar-smoking publisher. It was roughly ten verses too long, had a word on every 16th beat and featured the title only once—at the *end!* Amid fantasies of hearing our work of art performed by Elvis Presley, Frank Sinatra and every other singer of note, we were—incredibly—being ushered to the door. Undaunted, we beat a tireless path through the grim corridors of 1619 Broadway (Manhattan's publishing center), without making the slightest dent, then crossed the street to 1650 Broadway for an even worse reception.

Riding home on the IRT, we kept shaking our heads and muttering, "Can't any of them *hear?* Don't any of them have any taste?" After a thousand highly creative rationalizations, we painfully admitted to ourselves that there might be a grain of truth in some of the comments.

Objectivity is a hard thing to achieve, but it's the essential factor in achieving artistic and commercial success. These publishers were not able to articulate technically what was lacking in our song—but long experience gave them an intuitive feeling of public taste, an instinct that *something* was wrong. It started us on our analytical search to learn why we had failed, and more important, why others were succeeding—a search we still follow to this day.

First we decided, within the limits of our meager budget, to buy all the sheet music we could and play it through carefully. Our selections covered wide territory—Rodgers and Hammerstein, Sondheim (show music), Leiber and Stoller (rhythm and blues, all the early Elvis Presley hits), Carole King and Gerry Goffin (pop rock), Johnny Cash, Merle Haggard and Hank Williams (country). All of these composers had their own individual stamp of genius, while at the same time adhering to a set of basic principles.

If They Ask You, You Can Write a Song analyzes these principles, and includes *everything* we have learned in the course of a fifteen-year partnership—from the elements that make up a memorable lyric and melody, a discussion of rhyme, rhythm and subject matter, and the importance of visual titles and the contrasting characteristics of movie songs, theater songs and pop songs to practical knowledge on how to cast, demonstrate, sell and protect your material. Talent is important, but a realistic knowledge of the music industry and its requirements can help you to avoid years of needless struggle. The guidelines set forth in this book have worked for the majority of successful songwriters, and if followed, they will work for you.

A.K.
J.H.

1

How Much Musical Training Do You Need?

Formal training never hurts. If you're planning to enter any field, the more you learn about it, the better. Jimmy Webb has been quoted as saying, "There's nothing wrong with a musical background. It doesn't hurt to study orchestration, especially harmony courses—courses that deal with chord structure." It certainly didn't hurt Burt Bacharach, who studied with classical composer Darius Milhaud and had a solid background in arranging before he became an Oscar-winning film composer. His odd combination of rhythm and blues and classical music could never have been created without training. Neil Sedaka is noted as a superb classical pianist, entering and winning many worldwide competitions. Marvin Hamlisch, in addition to his writing activities, gives concerts of his work around the country.

And yet this isn't true of all famous composers. Some never took lessons of any kind. Others put themselves through a kind of self-education, which necessitates a redefinition of the word "training."

Questioned recently, writer Jeff Barry told interviewers Kent McNeel and Mark Luther, "I had no formal training." He had one piano lesson and two weeks of bass lessons. Yet Jeff Barry's string of hits is endless ("Be My Baby," "Then He Kissed Me," "Da Doo Ron Ron," "Maybe I

Know," "Tell Laura I Love Her," "I Honestly Love You") and still continuing. The answer is that he *listened*. There's no better teacher than records and the radio; Jeff's success proves the value of soaking up everything they have to offer and making that information a part of you. A feeling for rock music helped, an instinctive sense of rhythm and melody that led him to become a record producer as well as writer.

If you're from a musical family, their influence will affect you. David Gates came from a musical home. His mother was a piano teacher and his brothers played instruments. Chuck Jackson (who produces and co-writes Natalie Cole's records) says, "I used to sing in my high school choir, and my mother sang in church."

Roger Nichols claims, "When I reached grade school I decided I wanted to play the violin for some reason, and I studied violin and classical music all through grade school. In high school I took up the guitar." Houston-born Mark James (who wrote "Hooked on a Feeling" for B. J. Thomas) began studying pop and classical music at the age of 8 on the violin. By the time he was 13, he was drawn into the country-blues element and switched to guitar also.

Sometimes there is training, but not to the extensive degree of a Bacharach or a Sedaka. Kenny Rogers says, "I play guitar, bass and enough piano to get me into trouble." And there's country writer Felice Bryant, who goes Jeff Barry one better by admitting, "I don't read music and I don't play an instrument." Felice composes a melody by singing it, and then her co-writer husband, Boudleaux Bryant, writes the tune down, or she sings it into a tape recorder.

Okay, you may say, but country music is relatively uncomplicated—you don't *need* classical training the way you might in other fields. Yet Paul Williams, who writes complex, sophisticated melodies in the old Hollywood tradition, claims to have a minimum of formal background. Barry White says, "I can't read music, but I have a fantastic rhythm ability."

The emphasis on a formal education diminished in the '50s with the advent of rock and roll. Rock was musically simpler than the songs being featured in films and Broadway shows. Everybody picked up a guitar and learned a few elementary chords, then sang over them. Groups sprang up on street corners, in schoolyards and gyms, and these groups worked out their harmonies by ear. Many of them, especially those who pursued composing as a full-time occupation, felt the lack and pursued a musical background *later,* but were not formally trained in childhood.

Having training can be a practical advantage. If you're a skilled musician, you can support yourself playing in recording sessions or in clubs while you're trying to make it as a writer. The same is true of singers who can read music well enough to make a specialty of doing background voices on records and commercials.

Nothing takes precedence over a love for music and constant exposure to it. Nothing can beat going down to every possible recording session and observing what writers, producers and artists do—and quoting Jimmy Webb again, "It's very important to study the work of other songwriters if it means nothing more than sitting and listening to about ten or twelve albums everyday . . . listening to the radio all the time."

There's no substitute for native ability, and as the above examples prove, a great many untrained composers do exceedingly well. Still, as Alan O'Day commented, even after the chart triumphs of "Angie Baby," "Rock and Roll Heaven" and "Undercover Angel": "In looking back, I regret that I didn't have some more formal education in music." Talent, instinct, tenacity and a receptive musical mind will eventually lead you down the road to success, but the better equipped you are for the journey, the easier the road is likely to be.

THINGS TO REMEMBER

1. Acquire as much classical training as you can.

2. If you've had the benefit of a formal musical background, keep building on it and sharpening your skills. Constantly educate yourself by studying different instruments, learning new kinds of music.

3. Remember that training can be a practical advantage, enabling you to earn money as a session musician or background singer.

2

Hits and
the Repetition Principle

What constitutes a good lyric? Lyrics—unlike poetry—are something you hear, rather than read. They go by quickly and must make an immediate impact on the listener. When *Oklahoma* had its premiere in 1943, Rodgers and Hammerstein opened the show with "Oh, What a Beautiful Morning." This was considered a daring move, because no show had ever opened so quietly before. Not only was the song a ballad, but there were no chorus girls or male dancers in evidence, merely a woman churning butter while the hero sang alone. The composers did, however, protect themselves with the first two lines:

> There's a bright golden haze on the meadow
> There's a bright golden haze on the meadow

Rodgers and Hammerstein made sure their message was clearly conveyed. They gambled that if the words and music had a folk-song simplicity and were easily remembered, listeners wouldn't object to the unusual new treatment, and they were right. Hammerstein has compared the world to audiences in a balcony, two collective bodies of people who need repetition to clarify the lyrics and melodies they hear until the song makes a permanent impression.

Moving up to 1962, we have the Goffin and King classic "The Loco-Motion." This Number One single launched Little Eva, and shows the power of a strong, commercial song to shoot a newcomer to stardom. Little Eva's career until that time was as Goffin and King's maid. "The Loco-Motion" accomplished similar chart magic for the Grand Funk Railroad twelve years later.

> Everybody's doin' a brand new dance now
> Come on, Baby, do the Loco-Motion
> I know you'll get to like it if you give it a chance now
> Come on, Baby, do the Loco-Motion.

"Go Away, Little Girl," which employs this principle, is a Goffin and King *triple* winner (Steve Lawrence, 1963; The Happenings, 1965; Donny Osmond, 1972). Bob Dylan's "Lay, Lady, Lay" makes frequent use of the title phrase, and Jerry Leiber and Mike Stoller emphasize their key lines and melodies with artful repetition in such contrasting compositions as "Hound Dog" and the sophisticated "Is That All There Is." The R & B smash "Enjoy Yourself," by Kenny Gamble and Leon Huff, lets the radio listener know what the point is right away, hammering the title phrase "Enjoy Yourself" dozens of times.

Repetition isn't limited to lyrics. A melody line that repeats often will make the song memorable and qualify it as hit material. When melody and lyric repeat simultaneously, it's just about impossible to forget the record after a first hearing.

When a tune moves quickly, there isn't much time to digest the words. In cases like these, it's advisable to repeat as much as possible. "Stayin' Alive," by the Gibb Brothers, has a recurring verse composed of rapid-fire 16th notes, and the words don't vary much. The verse also has a "Ha, ha, ha, ha" group part glued on. "La la la" and "Sha na na" are commonly used vocal gimmicks on up-tempo material. When the melody is a ballad, you can include more lyric, because there's time to soak in the words and absorb them at a leisurely and comfortable pace.

The key lyric phrase in your song should express the overall philosophy of the material and should not be a cliché. Repeating "I love you," for example, won't startle anyone, except a few devoted relatives, nor will it enhance your status as a songwriter.

The Repetition Principle has many variations. In a song such as Randy Edelman's "Weekend in New England," a 1977 hit for Barry Manilow, there are lyric phrases repeated throughout, but the title itself is hardly heard. It doesn't matter, as long as some portion of the words and music is emphasized over and over again. In Bob Dylan's 1966 success "Rainy Day Women #12 plus 35" the title is never heard at all, but the sing-along melody is so simple and rousing that the musical repetition assured it of a high place on the charts.

It's true that some popular albums contain long, stream-of-consciousness lyrics which demand intense concentration and loosely structured, experimental tunes representing the composer's efforts to get at something new. This has happened often in Bob Dylan's career, but it's pertinent to point out that Dylan's hit *singles* are instantly memorable, such as "Blowin' in the Wind," "I Want You" and "Mr. Tambourine Man." Joni Mitchell's first major single, after several years of recording, was "Help Me," which spotlighted the title phrase from start to finish. Her other chart single, "Big Yellow Taxi," is perhaps the simplest, musically and lyrically, of all her works.

The Top 10 records, compiled weekly by *Billboard, Cash Box* and *Record World,* consistently demonstrate the Repetition Principle. Moving from AM radio to Broadway, we see this operating in Stephen Sondheim's music. Sondheim's words can be classified in many ways— clever, picturesque, conceptually strong, penetrating, fraught with social comment—but running through them, as an unobtrusive but constant strain, is repetition. "Small World" (from *Gypsy*) and "I Feel Pretty" (from *West Side Story*) are striking examples, and the best example of all is "Send In the Clowns," which repeats and develops one simple melodic phrase. "Send In the Clowns" has become the biggest hit single of Sondheim's solo career (the record, as performed by Judy Collins, hit the charts twice on separate occasions) and a Grammy Award winner.

THE WHISTLE TEST

It may sound obvious to pound away at the idea that popular music must keep repeating, but writers, especially new writers, are so eager to pour out their thoughts, to bare their feelings and complexities, that they overload a song with words and innumerable melodic sections. Some take the attitude that simplicity is square, childish and creatively beneath them. But "stone simplicity," as hit country writer Bob McDill calls it, is the hardest thing to achieve, and distinguishes an amateur from a professional.

Joel and I have fallen into the trap of writing overly complicated, unwieldy songs. The temptation is always there. To counteract that, we subject our tunes to what we call the "whistle test." Shorn of chords and orchestration, devoid of meaningful images and philosophy, can the piece be whistled, hummed, remembered? Is the melodic core strong enough to exist independently of all the icing? That's the big question. Listeners will rarely be in the mood to analyze. They tend to react emotionally, and if their interest wanders, you'll be quickly obliterated with one careless flick of the radio dial. They don't care about your intentions, about how much work you've put into the song and what conflicts you're working out through your music. It boils down to: Are they entertained? Can they sing it?

Listeners aren't the only ones who get impatient when a song doesn't capture them immediately. Another, equally crucial person must be satisfied—the program director. No matter how strong your record is, how exciting or original, if he turns thumbs down, the public will never get a chance to register their reactions. This reality is more formidable than ever, because program directors don't choose just for individual stations—they control nationwide radio chains, giving them the awesome power to assemble pop playlists for 20 to 50 stations at a time.

When your single is brought in by the record company's promotion man, the program director will listen to a few bars and make his decision (except, maybe, if you've written a new Eagles or Fleetwood Mac record, in which case you can probably skip this chapter). You need to hook him in the first verse.

A record composed by someone who has had ten smashes in a row may occasionally—though not always—pass the program director's desk without adhering strictly to convention. "Mac Arthur Park" ran over seven minutes long, was constructed in a classical vein, and climaxed with a lengthy Aaron Copland–like instrumental interlude—yet was deservedly hailed as an artistic masterpiece. A newcomer, though, is not likely to receive the kind of attention Jimmy Webb did after such national favorites as "Wichita Lineman" and "By the Time I Get to Phoenix." Keep your songs as simple as possible—at least at the beginning.

EXAMPLES OF THE REPETITION PRINCIPLE

Soul

"That's the Way I Like It"
ARTIST: *K. C. and the Sunshine Band*
WRITERS: *H. W. Casey/R. Finch*

"The Rubberband Man"
ARTIST: *The Spinners*
WRITERS: *Linda Creed/Thom Bell*

"I've Got Love on My Mind"
ARTIST: *Natalie Cole*
WRITERS: *Chuck Jackson/Marvin Yancy*

"Isn't She Lovely"
ARTIST: *Stevie Wonder*
WRITER: *Stevie Wonder*

"I Love Music"
ARTIST: *The O'Jays*
WRITERS: *Kenny Gamble/Leon Huff*

Country

"It Was Almost like a Song"
ARTIST: *Ronnie Milsap*
WRITERS: *Archie Jordan/Hal David*

"Behind Closed Doors"
ARTIST: *Charlie Rich*
WRITER: *Kenny O'Dell*

"Another Somebody Done Somebody Wrong Song"
ARTIST: *B. J. Thomas*
WRITERS: *Larry Butler/Chips Moman*

"If You Ever Get to Houston (Look Me Down)"
ARTIST: *Don Gibson*
WRITER: *Mickey Newbury*

Pop

"You Make Me Feel like Dancing"
ARTIST: *Leo Sayer*
WRITERS: *Leo Sayer/Vini Poncia*

"The Right Time of the Night"
ARTIST: *Jennifer Warnes*
WRITER: *Peter McCann*

"Gonna Fly Now" (theme from *Rocky*)
ARTIST: *Rhythm Heritage*
WRITERS: *Carol Connors/Ayn Robbins/Bill Conti*

"Slip Sliding Away"
ARTIST: *Paul Simon*
WRITER: *Paul Simon*

The above-noted songs are all different from one another, even those which are placed in the same broad categories of R & B, country and pop—yet they all have repetitive musical and lyric sections in common.

HANGING ON A HOOK

The Repetition Principle may refer to one note or a series of notes. It may also refer to a lyric phrase, full lines or an entire verse. When a complete section is repeated in popular music, this section is known as the Hook.

"Hook" is a tiny, innocuous-looking four-letter word, but it's the foundation of commercial songwriting, particularly hit-single writing.

Some examples include a rhythm and blues record by Tavares, "It Only Takes a Minute, Girl," written by Dennis Lambert and Brian Potter. The hook here is repeated four times. In David Bowie's Number One "Fame," written by Bowie, Lennon and Alomar, the title is repeated fully thirty-seven times.

This principle applies to all markets and crosses all lines. A brilliant country writer and singer, Tom T. Hall, makes sure his songs, such as "Your Man Loves You Honey," are hook-oriented. Soul writers like Kenny Gamble and Leon Huff, Smokey Robinson, Ron Miller, and Holland, Dozier and Holland do the same.

Joel and I have always built our songs around hooks. A hit country single we wrote for Marie Osmond in 1976, called "A, My Name Is Alice," illustrates the point:

A, my name is Alice
And my boyfriend's name is Andy

> We come from Alabama and we like apples
> A, my name is Alice, and I wanna play the game of love.

This section repeats throughout, and we added an extra hook ingredient by having all the key words—"Andy," "Alabama," "Apples," "Alice"—begin with the letter "A."

A hook can also be a "sound," such as "Oobla Di, Oobla Da" by Lennon and McCartney, or "Da Doo Ron Ron" which was a hit for the Crystals in the mid-'60s and a gold record again for Shaun Cassidy in the '70s.

Hooks shouldn't be repetition for repetition's sake. Ideally, they should contain one or more of the following:

    a. A driving, danceable rhythm;
    b. A melody that stays in people's minds;
    c. A lyric that furthers the dramatic action, or defines a person or place.

Suppose you choose the phrase "I went down to the grocery store" as your hook line. No matter how throbbing the orchestration, how deeply felt the performance, nothing can really make that phrase come to life. Conversely, an explosive title can be destroyed by dull, diffused melody writing.

Remember, the hook is what you're selling. It should include the strongest elements of your melody and lyric. Consider these:

> "We Are the Champions"
> *(Freddie Mercury)*
> *Recorded by Queen*
>
> "I Did It (My Way)"
> *(Anka/François/Revaux/Thibault)*
> *Recorded by Frank Sinatra*
>
> "Wastin' Away (in Margaritaville)"
> *(Jimmy Buffett)*
> *Recorded by Jimmy Buffett*

"I Would Give Everything I Own"
(David Gates)
Recorded by David Gates

"I Feel the Earth Move"
(Carole King)
Recorded by Carole King

"Nobody Does It Better"
(Marvin Hamlisch/Carole Bayer Sager)
Recorded by Carly Simon

The first one, "We Are the Champions," is aggressive, defiantly emotional. The beat of the hook section is a militant, marchlike tempo, appropriate to the firm declaration of the title. The melody has a simple and haunting force.

"My Way" is a declaration of a more personal nature, in which a man defines his overall attitude about life. The hook phrase is sweepingly dramatic, both musically and lyrically, and makes a universal statement about retaining individuality and not conforming or knuckling down under pressure.

"Margaritaville" deals with a man's dissipation, and doesn't take the clichéd route. In the words of the song, "Some people claim there's a woman to blame, But I know it's my own damn fault." The Latin rhythm is infectious, and the hook tune stays with the listener after one hearing. Even a gentle balladeer like David Gates is highly intense on the hook, claiming "I Would Give Everything I Own," and the melody has a folk-operatic quality. Carole King doesn't just feel satisfaction, she announces, "I Feel the Earth Move" to a drivingly danceable beat, and in "Nobody Does It Better" the heroine triumphantly tells us that she's spent the night with a sexual superman. The rhythm is slow but insistently seductive.

Popular music doesn't merely project emotion, it exaggerates it. Songs have three minutes or less to make an impression, and they condense a lifetime of feeling into those three minutes. This exaggeration is present from the first verse on and gathers force in the hook sections.

The above-mentioned lyrics are larger than life, and so are the melodies that accompany them. These tunes fairly shout for attention; they have a built-in cry, a need to enlist the emotional participation of all listeners around the world. And they succeed because of this raw desire to communicate.

A hook should have a strong, unifying point of view and a conflict. If the words can stand as a capsule summary of the entire lyric, so much the better. All the hooks in these songs supply enough information to exist apart from the other sections.

Hooks are the lifeblood of commercial advertising, a field that depends on selling a product quickly. Consider "You deserve a break today at McDonald's," "Fly the friendly skies of United" and "I'd like to teach the world to sing," which succeeded brilliantly on their own terms and crossed over onto the pop scene.

Many songs go through a great deal of exposition before getting to the hook. Others barely have a hook at all. They can, and do, become hits. There are times when a writer bursts forth with a highly personal statement, and the sheer power of his feeling is enough to involve listeners whether or not he follows commercial rules. In an interview with *Songwriter* magazine in November 1977, Janis Ian told columnist Paul Baratta, "On the *Miracle Row* album, everybody likes 'Maria,' and yet it's a difficult song. Musically it's difficult. There's nothing to hang on to."

Nobody can dismiss inspiration, the power of a personal story, the force of a unique or innovative idea. But speaking generally, your chances of gaining an audience are increased substantially if your songs are hook-oriented, and the odds improve even more if your hook opens the record. Some of the best and most original thoughts have been lost because the composer or lyricist made the fatal mistake of taking too long.

THINGS TO REMEMBER

1. Be objective about your work. Don't fall in love with everything you write, or you won't be able to appraise it accurately.

2. Buy and study the records and sheet music of popular songs.

3. Make sure there are lyric and musical sequences repeated throughout your songs.

4. Study the *Billboard, Cash Box* and *Record World* charts weekly, and the *Songwriter* charts monthly, and see how many hit records observe the Repetition Principle.

5. Make sure you can sing or whistle your tunes without instrumental accompaniment; make sure they can stand on their own.

6. Repeat words more frequently in up-tempo tunes. You can relax and write more nonrepetitive lyrics to slower-moving melodies.

7. In repeating, establish a pattern from verse to verse.

8. Don't indulge yourself and ramble. Remember that listeners, program directors and prospective buyers have very little patience.

9. Make sure you have a strong hook, one that contains a memorable melody, dramatic and colorful words and a pulsating rhythm.

10. Try to have a self-contained hook, one that stands as a capsule summary of the entire lyric.

3

What Comes First,
the Words or the Music?

This question is asked at the beginning of every new class I teach. There are almost as many answers to it as there are composers and lyricists.

In some partnerships the procedures are defined. One writes a melody and brings it to a lyricist, or one writes a lyric and hands it over to his tune-writing partner. Collaborators like these have established a working arrangement which is clear and comfortable, and they rarely deviate from it. But sometimes a melody writer can't just compose the tune without visual aids from the lyricist—he needs words that give him a picture, a story, an image. He needs to know if the story is set in Kentucky or Manhattan or Hong Kong, so he can work with a preconceived musical flavor. He may function best with the form neatly laid out, such as A A B A (verse, verse, bridge, verse) or A A A A (verse, verse, verse, verse).

On the other hand, there are lyricists who tend to wander aimlessly unless they have a tune which gives them borders. The way melodies move suggests rhyme patterns. The rhythm gives them a feeling of how the words should flow.

This kind of collaboration, in which each individual assumes responsibility only for his own specialty, is common in movies and the theater.

In film, a scorer generally creates the music for the whole movie, including the title tune, and then gives it to the lyricists who have been signed to work with him on it (e.g., Michel Legrand/Alan and Marilyn Bergman; Charlie Fox/Norman Gimbel). In theater pieces, words and music are almost always handled by separate people.

HAND-IN-GLOVE WRITING

When there are partners, such as Joel and I, who get involved in both the lyric and the musical ends of songwriting, a hundred things can set off creative chain reactions; there is no preplanned order of who does what first. The dialogue might go something like this:

AL: I have a great title . . . "Waking Up in Georgia Without You."

JOEL: That should be kind of *sad,* because the girl's left him.

(Joel plays a few melancholy chords.)

AL: I like that, but the beat is too fast. It should be more of a ballad.

JOEL: Okay.

(He sings a few words as he plays the suggested slower tempo.)

"Waking Up in Georgia Without You . . . having my breakfast without you . . ."

AL: "I never had reason to doubt you . . . Till now."

JOEL: I like that. And I like that rhyme pattern. That's our first verse.

AL: Why is he in Georgia?

JOEL: Because . . . because they were touring the United States.

AL: College students!

JOEL: They were on vacation, and then she left him. Say, if they're in Georgia, there should be some bluesy feelings in the chords.

AL: Try it.

JOEL: *(Plays the blues intervals and Al likes them, starts singing an extension of what Joel has played.)*

How's this for a hook?

AL: Too fancy. Do it like this.

(He hums a simpler, guitar-type tune.)

Say, who do you think this is for?

JOEL: George Benson.

AL: That's a good idea. Try this. . . .

(He sings a jazz note at the end of the bridge, because George Benson is an expert jazz singer and is capable of doing daring intervals.)

And so on.

There's tremendous freedom and excitement to this kind of hand-in-glove writing, in which one suggests a melodic strain, another extends it, and this melody suggests a lyric, or a musical hook. By coordinating efforts and letting each partner spark the other, dynamic songs get written.

There are titles that direct writers. If a lyricist comes up with "Goin' to a Go Go," the melody writer isn't likely to turn it into a dreamy ballad. The idea demands rhythmic drive. If the idea is "Cryin' Time," which announces misery and lovesick loneliness, the melody writer will automatically try to catch that hopeless mood. Similarly, "Joy to the World" leads the tune writer into a buoyant, up-tone vein. His imagination may lead him in a pop/gospel direction (as Hoyt Axton's did), or disco, country or soul, but he wouldn't write something slow and tragic.

Sometimes a melody writer accidentally touches a note and the lyricist will cry, "What's that? What's that you did?" and the melody writer, puzzled, will tap that note. The note, to him, was unimportant, a slip of the finger, but to the lyricist, it may fill his mind with a whole series of images, an entire scenario.

There are occasions when a lyricist will say, "Damn, did you read that terrible headline in the *Times* this morning, about the girl who was trapped in a coal mine?" and this will set the tune writer's hands whirling.

Or the two of you may work from a whole list of titles, compiled over a period of time. The phrases in this title book may have been suggested by movies, TV shows, current events, your mother's grievances or your girlfriend's infidelities. One partner may read them down, until the other shouts, "That's it" and starts scribbling or playing. Sometimes, too, a title that suggests nothing one day may set a whole song in motion the next.

Two verses may be written of a lyric, and they make no impact on either collaborator, until one of the writers gets the bright idea of reversing them. All of a sudden, in proper sequence, the verses sparkle, the story makes sense. A melody writer might devise a bridge (the midsection of a song, other than verse or chorus), and the lyricist, objectively, will realize that the bridge is strong enough to be the *hook* instead, that the most powerful part of the song is being tossed aside, relegated to an unimportant position.

When one person is doing both words and music, he can begin with either melody, words or rhythm, arranging them into a pattern as he pokes along, feeling his way. Then there are gloriously rare times when lyrics, music, everything comes together in a flashing, unified vision.

The mind is a capricious thing. It moves up, down, sideways, at its own pace. The only rule is to let it operate without imposing rigid controls on it. Be open to your co-writer's ideas. Don't say, for instance, *"I'm* the lyricist . . . I won't listen to any of his suggestions. His job is to write the melody," or vice versa. Don't say, "This is a ballad. I'll ignore any thoughts I get about making it up-tempo." Your mind is always trying to tell you things. Maybe that busy subconscious knows more than you do!

In other words, don't worry about what comes first, the words or the music. It doesn't follow any pattern and it doesn't matter, as long as what finally emerges is a good song, a tuneful song and a song that reaches and moves people.

THINGS TO REMEMBER

1. If you're someone who needs predefined borders in a collaboration, decide in advance with your partner which of you will write his or her part (words or music) first.

2. Try hand-in-glove writing, developing a song in bits and pieces and bouncing creatively off each other.

3. Allow room for feedback. Don't say, "I do words and you do music," locking your partner and yourself into roles that discourage free and spontaneous input.

4. If you're a lyricist writing to a melody, try to match the mood of that melody in your words, and vice versa.

5. Examine the structure of your song to see if the verses, lyrically and melodically, are in proper sequence.

6. If writing alone, don't force yourself to conceive of words or music in any particular order; let your mind function without imposing rigid controls.

7. Listen to the work of other composers to give yourself realistic commercial knowledge of the record industry and its requirements.

8. Never stop trying to broaden your horizons—learn new instruments, new modes of music. Keep acquiring as much formal education as you can.

4

Titles That Write Themselves

There are certain titles that manage to suggest a complete story and full, rounded characters. These titles are worth the effort it takes to conceive them, because they virtually write themselves.

"Calendar Girl" (Sedaka/Greenfield) is an excellent example: it commands the lyricist to describe every girl from January to December. "Calendar Girl" falls under the heading of what the late Bob Hilliard (creator of "Wee Small Hours" and "Tower of Strength") called "laundry-list songs." These are songs like "A, You're Adorable" (B, you're so beautiful, etc.) and Cole Porter's "Let's Do It" (Birds do it, bees do it, Even educated fleas do it), which tell a story in terms of listing and itemizing actions and/or events. Paul Simon's laundry-list song is "Fifty Ways to Leave Your Lover." Simon's tongue-in-cheek psychological approach may not be the way you would handle it, but the title gives you leeway to supply your own creative laundry list.

Moving to the masculine front, the R & B oldie "Playboy" (Holland/Bateman/Stevenson/Morton) suggests a specific person. Within the broad boundaries of the title, the playboy could be a neighborhood heartbreaker or a sophisticate of the Robert Redford school, but he would possess one trait that unifies the remaining verses—a need to toy with the affections of women and then discard them.

David Houston's version of "Almost Persuaded" (Sherrill/Houston) is an original way of dealing with infidelity. You know from these words that a man or woman is tempted to stray, nearly succumbs, but remembers at the eleventh hour where his true loyalty lies. "Daytime Friends (Night-Time Lovers)," by Ben Peters, also leaves no doubt about the adulterous nature of the situation, only this time it's consummated. Still a third look at adultery is provided by Mel Tillis' "Ruby, Don't Take Your Love to Town." The man singing has been, or is about to be, betrayed. Within that framework, the songwriter's genius can embellish the thought and develop a drama of a crippled war veteran and his inability to satisfy restless Ruby, making her seek satisfaction elsewhere. In any case, a title like this one sketches the main story points and acts as a powerful guideline.

"The Guitar Man" (Gates) immediately conjures up pictures of a musician, and the tone of the phrase makes you feel that this guitar player is dedicated, probably married, to his instrument. On the other hand "Rock and Roll, I Gave You the Best Years of My Life" (Davis) also dramatizes the feelings of a performer, but there's a built-in sadness and regret. It's a goodbye song, to lost dreams and ambitions unfulfilled. The title almost forces the writer to treat it that way.

Titles that write themselves are generally greeted with joy by composers, because they know their work is half done. "My Way" (Anka/François/Revaux/Thibault) *has* to be a statement of one's personal philosophies and feelings. So, even more, does "I've Gotta Be Me" (Marks). "Please, Mr. Postman" (Holland/Gorman) says it all—a love-sick person is waiting for a letter. "Seven Rooms of Gloom" (Holland/Dozier/Holland) *had* to describe a houseful of empty rooms that were once filled with love and happiness.

MOOD TITLES

Sometimes there are titles that don't actually spell out a story, but they create such a strong mood that dozens of story possibilities immediately occur to the writer who conceived them. "In the Ghetto," by Mac Davis, is an example. The actual plot centers around a ghetto boy who turns to crime and is eventually killed in a shoot-out with the police. But let your mind flow with that title, and innumerable other ghetto stories have to occur to you: the poor boy who wants to become rich and rise above his circumstances, the girl who loses her boyfriend to prison or death, the father who drinks, the mother who suffers silently. Each is a mini-movie. Ths is one of the best of the mood titles.

The Eagles hit "Life in the Fast Lane" (Walsh/Henley/Frey) doesn't tell you who the main characters are, but you certainly know from the words "Life in the Fast Lane" that they're headed for destruction—fast cars, drugs, liquor, women! You're on your way.

Sometimes self-explanatory titles are mounted on a soapbox. If, like John Lennon and Yoko Ono, you came up with the title "Woman Is the Nigger of the World," chances are you'd have little trouble developing your theme. "Only Women Bleed" (Furnier/Wagner) is another phrase which, as delivered by Alice Cooper, characterizes a whole sex. The actual content is more innocent, emotionally and politically, than the sound of the line suggests, but it was enough to raise the hackles of feminists around the world.

Certain titles project honest, real-life emotions and relationships. They get under the skin of their subject in a way that totally involves the listener before he's heard a word of the lyric. They would be soap opera if they weren't so charged with genuine feeling. One in that category is "She Never Said a Word to Daddy," by Dolly Parton, dealing with a put-down, devoted wife and mother who suddenly leaves to create her own life after years of neglect. If you wrote that title, your details would probably differ from Dolly Parton's, but the emotions would be the same.

Here is a list of titles. Would you have handled them as the authors did?

"Help Me Make It Through the Night" (*Kristofferson*)
"I'm the Only Hell Mama Ever Raised" (*Viceroy/Kemp/Borchers*)
"Heartbreak Hotel" (*Axton/Durden/Presley*)
"Wedding Bell Blues" (*Nyro*)
"Kung Fu Fighting" (*Douglas*)
"Tears of a Clown" (*Robinson/Cosby/Wonder*)

There's no rule that says a title must convey every aspect of a song in advance. If it has emotional force and intriguing imagery, it might serve the material well and become a giant hit.

There are rhythm numbers that break through, disco records whose lyrical content is secondary to the sheer, pounding energy of the production. Some examples are "Disco Inferno," by the Trammps, and "Let's Dance" by Donna Summer.

But the process of writing a song can be greatly simplified if the title is a short, capsule summary of the entire story. Not only that, but you'll feel doubly rewarded when this title lends the song a stronger identity and engraves it firmly in the public's mind.

Finding colloquialisms and utilizing them as titles often results in hit records. These expressions are familiar and trigger a spontaneous reaction from people the first time the song is played on the air. Some examples of colloquial titles: "New Kid in Town," "Stand Tall," "Hot Line," "Enjoy Yourself," "When I Need You," "Night Shift" and "Right Back Where I Started from."

Once your mind has formed the habit of thinking in titles, they start occurring to you all day. You may be in the office, on a plane, crossing a street or painting your house—they flash into your mind without warning and fade out just as quickly if you don't write them down. You should try to have a notebook and pencil handy. Many times I've hit upon a strong title and said, "I'll remember it," even repeating the words over and over to imprint it in my mind. It never works, any more than a middle-of-the-night resolution to recall a dream guarantees a memory of it the next morning. Thoughts are fleeting things, like butterflies, and they have to be caught in flight or they'll disappear and never return again in quite the same way.

A FLAIR FOR FIRST LINES

I've discussed the importance of a title in securing interest. Now that you've got it, you have to solidify your gains, hang on for dear life and not relax your hold. A good way of doing that is to write powerful first lines, lines that stir the imagination and build tension.

Look at any popular lyric and you'll find a provocative phrase, a striking or startling image or a direct thought that sums up the entire song. In "Feel Free" (Payton/Bridges/McNeil), the lyric is launched with directness: "Feel free to feel me, Baby, every mornin', noon and night." The opening of "Rambling Fever" (Haggard) sets the conflict and clearly defines what the character is singing: "My hat don't hang on the same nail too long." And "Legend in My Time" grabs the attention with irony. The hero asks: "If heartaches brought fame in love's crazy game, I'd be a legend in my time." You're involved immediately because you know the protagonist's problem, you wonder what he'll do to soothe his heartache and as a plus, you're caught up by the writer's clever and original lyric treatment of the situation.

In "Sometimes When We Touch" (Mann/Hill), the opening lines are "You ask me if I love you, and I choke on my reply." The words have a built-in sensitivity, but already the mind is logically asking: Why does he choke on his reply? Is he afraid to hurt her? Does he have trouble expressing how much he loves her? The lines tell just enough to whet the listener's appetite.

In Barry White's "Can't Get Enough of Your Love, Baby" he doesn't just say, as sex songs sometimes do, "Come on, Baby, do it." Instead the first line goes: "I've heard people say that too much of anything is not good for you, Baby." There's more sexuality in that phrase than in complete directness, because you know right away that the singer's lust is insatiable, that as far as he's concerned there can never be too much loving between him and his girl.

The Leiber/Stoller classic "I'm a Woman," which became a hit for both Peggy Lee and Maria Muldaur, sets a scene and a character through action, in a way that captures the ear: "I can wash out forty four pairs of socks, and have them hangin' out on the line." Right away you're wondering: Is this a workhorse, a housewife chained to her chores? And yet the title says, "I'm a Woman," so you instinctively prepare for the character to transcend her dreary fate and prove her womanliness in other ways. There's pleasure in watching the tongue-in-cheek unraveling of a story, as the woman makes the transition from scrubbing floors to giving her man the "shivering fits."

Sometimes the opening lines are theatrically effective because of their shock value. "It's Only Rock and Roll" (Jagger/Richard) begins with this unnerving statement: "If I could stick my hand in my heart, I would spill it all over the stage . . . Would that satisfy ya?" Hostile? Weird? Even unlikable? Maybe. But gripping.

The opening words of "I Write the Songs" (Johnston) have to elicit a reaction of some kind: "I've been alive forever, and I wrote the very first song." Is God speaking? Is this a symbolic way for a lover to speak of his feeling for someone else? There's a breadth, a sweep to those lines that carries the listener along.

There's a cliché in the music business—that the first verse must pack a punch, and then the second verse can mark time until the bridge. That's not strictly true. No line should be thrown away; each section of a song should be as dynamic as the writer can make it. But it is true that your opening sets the stage, and if it doesn't succeed dramatically, people may become so indifferent that sustained excellence later on won't offset the initial weakness. No matter how you accomplish it—through blunt sexuality, ethereal imagery, irony, humor, odd character traits or controversial ideas—the opening statement must grip your listener. If you develop that flair for first lines, you can ride along on the goodwill you've built up, secure in your audience's attention and in the knowledge that you've written a potential hit.

THINGS TO REMEMBER

1. Try to find titles that write themselves, titles that suggest a complete story and fully characterized people.

2. Look for mood titles, ones that may not actually spell out an entire story, but create a mood that brings story possibilities to mind.

3. Find colloquialisms and familiar phrases that will make intriguing titles.

4. Once you've formed a habit of thinking in titles, carry a notebook with you at all times and write them down.

5. Make sure your first lines stir the imagination and build tension, whether they be shocking, touching, sexual or provocative.

6. Don't assume that because your first verse is strong, your second verse can mark time until the bridge. Give every line the same care.

5

The Rhyming Revolution

There's been a rhyming revolution for quite some time now. Polished, theater- or movie-trained lyricists of the '30s and '40s look with horror on that increasingly prevalent phenomenon, the "false" rhyme. "Down" and "around" is enough to set them off on a tirade about the laziness and lack of talent among the new generation of writers.

Younger writers see this unbending emphasis on craft as constricting. Their byword is honesty. They settle for sound-alikes, rather than exact rhymes, as though a rhyme would compromise any sense of reality in their work. As always, the answer lies between the two extremes, and varies with the particular song being written.

As a fan of pure rhyme, and once a diehard opponent of false rhymes, I had a mind that was dogmatically closed. Recently, however, I read an article in *Songwriter* magazine by Grammy-winning lyricist Norman Gimbel in which he admitted that he had once held the same attitude, but now felt that individual cases dictated different approaches. He remarked that his early mentor, Frank Loesser, got "a little slick in his later shows," leading to a certain bloodlessness. And lyricist E. Y. (Yip) Harburg, who wrote *The Wizard of Oz* and *Finian's Rainbow* and was the recent recipient of a tribute on CBS' *60 Minutes,* said, "People who rhyme just for rhyme's sake are hacks. Above all the *thought* must be the consideration. The thought is more important than the rhyme."

No one would deny that Kris Kristofferson, a former Rhodes scholar, knows *how* to rhyme. Witness, in "Sunday Mornin' Comin' Down":

> Well, I woke up Sunday mornin'
> With no way to hold my head that didn't hurt
> And the beer I had for breakfast wasn't bad
> So I had one more for dessert.

But on the other hand:

> . . . Cause she seemed to be so proud of me
> Just walkin', holdin' hands
> And she didn't think that money
> Was the measure of a man.

As a craftsman, Kristofferson made that conscious choice. He could easily have found a perfect "pure" rhyme, but he *chose* not to. Your songwriter's instinct has to convey that to you, but you should learn your craft first, as Kristofferson did, so that your decisions are thought out, rather than the result of fumbling in the dark.

An acknowledged master like Tom T. Hall rhymes "castle fair" and "shaggy hair" in "Your Man Loves You, Honey" and then turns around and rhymes "sighed" and "cry" or "tie" and "style" in other portions of the same song. He followed his instinct about what would be more natural, more like the character talking, yet there's no doubt that, like Kristofferson, he could have found perfect rhymes if he had wanted to.

In "Blue Bayou," a smash for Linda Ronstadt, writers Orbison and Melson were determined to avoid rhyme, because they wrote three sound-alikes in a row, "mind," "time" and "dimes." Rod Stewart's touching Number One record "You're in My Heart" combines "lyrical" and "physical," and Bob Welch's "Sentimental Lady" features "again" and "wind."

A problem today is that new writers are using this license to write "as they feel," which means in many cases simply avoiding the challenge of making their rhymes work and sound like natural human speech at the same time. Barry Mann and Cynthia Weil wrote "Here You Come Again" for Dolly Parton, and every rhyme is a true one, yet the song flows believably, with no trace of strain or slickness in it. The fact that this can be done, and yet the "soul" of the story retained, is the reason many people regard false rhymes as a cop-out—writers such as Bobby Weinstein ("Goin' out of My Head," "Hurt So Bad"), who groan when they hear one.

If you ask a writer whether he turns to a rhyming dictionary or a thesaurus, the answer will often be "no," even if he does, or a mumbled "yes," which projects discomfort or embarrassment. Admitting that not everything comes from their own minds is an artistic sin to some song-writers, an admission that they aren't "true artists."

These people are suffering unnecessary guilt pangs. Our foremost craftsman, Stephen Sondheim, employs both aids, as well as synonym and antonym books. The Osmonds cheerfully admit that they use a rhyming dictionary too.

Rhyming dictionaries save time. Any lyricist knows the familiar mental process of running alternatives through his or her mind . . . "O, blow, crow, doe, flow," etc. All the dictionary does is get you to the word you're seeking a little faster. In either case you'll find it, but when dead-lines loom, those lost days of self-imposed mental strain are best avoided.

The ideal attitude would be to incorporate all the craftsmanship possible, but in a way that doesn't call attention to itself. The thing to eschew most strenuously is self-conscious cleverness. If there's no way to find a perfect rhyme without being show-offy and intruding on the mood of the song, you're better off choosing one that says your thought most honestly.

RHYME SCHEMES

Rhyme schemes used to follow certain simple patterns, such as rhyming lines 2 and 4. We used that in "The Morning After":

> There's got to be a morning after
> If we can hold on through the night
> We have a chance to find the sunshine
> Let's keep on looking for the light.

Some others that are commercially popular include the setup used in the R & B classic "Shop Around" (Berry Gordy, Jr./Bill "Smokey" Robinson):

> Just because you've become a young man now
> There's still some things that you don't understand now
> Before you ask a girl for her hand now
> Keep your freedom for as long as you can now.

The first, second, third and fourth lines all rhyme.

Or Hank Williams' country standard "I Can't Help It if I'm Still in Love with You":

> Today I passed you on the street
> And my heart fell at your feet
> I can't help it if I'm still in love with you.

Lines one and two rhyme of a three-line verse.

Or: "After the Thrill Is Gone," written by Don Henley and Glenn Frey for the Eagles:

> Same dances in the same old shoes
> Some habits that you just can't lose
> There's no telling what a man might use
> After the thrill is gone.

There are all sorts of variations. In Jim Croce's "Bad Bad Leroy Brown," verse one and verse two have different rhyming schemes altogether. In the hit record "Devil Woman," done by Cliff Richard, the first four lines are not rhymed at all, but when that section returns after the hook, the rhyme scheme is a conventional 2 and 4. Sometimes a line in one verse can be rhymed with the same line in the next verse (e.g., the fourth line in verse one rhymed with the fourth line in verse two).

"Bad Bad Leroy Brown" and "Devil Woman" are mavericks, rhymewise, but they work. Still, it's safer to establish an overall consistency, patterns that have some relationship from verse to verse.

ALLITERATION

Alliteration (the use of the same letter to begin several words in a line) can be found in every generation of songwriting. It appears in an old standard like "Love Me or Leave Me" and a new one like "Take Me to the Limit."

Alliteration can be misused, as in "Let me lie back and love you, Laura," and then it sounds pretentious and dishonest. Ideally, the conversational flavor should be retained, as it is in "Take Me to the Limit." When employed properly, the device adds grace, rhythmic flow and a feeling of polish to lyric writing.

VOWELS

Some words are easier to sing than others. Vowels provide round, strong tones. Words like "free," or "go," or "high" are frequently used to end songs and are stressed with big notes because they pour richly and easily from the lips of singers. Whenever you can use a voweled sound for important notes, do it. Your material will benefit tremendously.

"Inner rhymes are out," say a whole school of "natural" writers, who regard them as slick and phony. "People don't speak that way." They may have a point when confronted with such lines as "Nobody *knows* I *chose* a *rose* for you," but when inner rhymes are used with subtlety, they add smoothness and sparkle.

The trick, as in "false" vs. "true" rhymes, is not to let your writer's ego show, unless you're Cole Porter and your entire creative thrust is toward cleverness. The popular writing team of Nicholas Ashford and Valerie Simpson display an outstanding example of seamless inner rhyming in "Ain't Nothin' like the Real Thing":

> I got your picture on the *wall*
> But it can't *see* or come to *me* when I call your *name*
> It's just a picture in a *frame*
> I read your letters when you're not near
> But they don't *move* me and they don't *groove* me

The inner rhymes abound, but you don't count them, you're not aware of them except in a subliminal sense. They coast along, carefully incorporated into the song's overall structure.

DO YOUR LYRICS "TALK"?

The best way to check if you're on the right track is to "talk" your lyrics. Recite the lines with feeling, as though they were dialogue in a play. If they're actable and convincing, you'll know you've done the right thing, whether you used inner rhymes, false rhymes, alliterations, vowels or any other craftsmanlike device. The ultimate achievement is lyrics that are conversational pictures, like these lines in Joni Mitchell's "Just like This Train":

> I used to count lovers like railroad cars
> I counted them on my *side*
> Lately I don't count on nothing
> I just let things *slide.*

Here you have a true rhyme ("slide" and "side"), the strong sound of "I," a vowel, a colorful, poetic metaphor (counting lovers like railroad cars). And though craft is evident everywhere, Ms. Mitchell employs honest, human speech when she says "I don't count on nothing," as opposed to the "anything" your old schoolteachers would have approved of. She even uses the word "count" two times, and the repetition is natural and unforced and makes the point.

This is the biggest test. All the craft in the world doesn't amount to much if what you say lacks humanity and feeling. Learn all the principles and then apply them when needed, never forgetting that your first job is to reach people emotionally, and these tools are valuable only if they aid you in accomplishing that.

USE OF CURRENT EXPRESSIONS

In 1919, nobody would have used the rhyme "Don't fret about your tape cassette." Nobody *had* a tape cassette in 1919. A rhyme like "My heart flickers when you wear knickers" is a lot more appropriate for the period, just as "tape cassette" carries a modern '60s or '70s ring.

Words such as "psychedelic," "sit-in," "disco," "hippie," "jeepers," "happening," "Yo-Yo" all belonged to specific eras, and many songwriters used them, either dramatically or as rhymes. Keeping abreast of current expressions will give you good rhyming material to work with, and will also increase your chances of having hits. To bone up on the popular words of the day, comb all magazines and newspapers and make note of the lingo you find. Jot everything down in an organized notebook for future use. Listen to TV shows with this objective in mind, as well as daily conversations you have with people, and your storehouse of expressions will rapidly grow to impressive proportions.

There is, however, a built-in danger. Words date quickly, and although you'll have hit records by drawing on this fund of material, the likelihood of the songs' living on as standards is reduced. Film critic Pauline Kael once remarked, "Being up to date is always to be out of date," and while that may strike you as overstatement, it's true that a song using sharply representative words of an era generally winds up a curiosity piece, something that can't be revived unless dressed up as camp.

When Joel and I wrote the score for Walt Disney's *Pete's Dragon,* we were tempted to use some "now" expressions and rhyme them, but producers Ron Miller and Jerry Courtland objected. "We want this movie to have a classic quality," they explained, "so we can release it in future generations." When you do utilize current slang, use it sparingly, or if not sparingly, recognize that the particular composition it appears in will be fixed forever in a certain time frame.

Rhyming of proper names, such as "I saw a neon sign on Hollywood and Vine," or "No one can barter with President Carter," is an appealing and colorful rhyming approach. Satirical lyrics specialize in it, and writers of special material for nightclub performers turn to proper names all the time. Cole Porter used names of actual people and places in practically every song he wrote.

THE THEATUH!

The legitimate stage is much stricter on the subject of rhyme than the world of popular music is. One false rhyme, one lapse of cleverness, and the critics are on your back like a crowd of hysterical hounds. Stephen Schwartz is one of our most "commercial" Broadway composers (*Godspell,* from which emerged "Day by Day," and *Pippin,* which yielded "Corner in the Sky"), but there's still that craftsmanlike neatness to his words. Ed Kleban's lyrics for *A Chorus Line* are marked with the same care.

Motion pictures are changing, relaxing their previous standards in this respect. Movie producers have just rediscovered how important hit sound tracks can be for their film's grosses (*Saturday Night Fever, Grease, Thank God It's Friday, American Hot Wax, FM, The Rocky Horror Picture Show*), so they're sending out emergency calls to rock groups and singers. The Bee Gees songs for *Saturday Night Fever* are phenomenally successful, tuneful and exciting, but not polished in the old ASCAP tradition—false rhymes appear in all of them. Commercial writers like Linda Creed ("The Love Song" from *The Greatest*), David Gates ("The Goodbye Girl") and Carole Bayer Sager ("Nobody Does It Better") are being paged by the studios, and because of their track record and proved commercial instincts, they're going to be allowed to operate freely. As long as they come through with smashes that can promote the movie, there'll be no Arthur Freed of the old MGM days poring over every syllable.

Perhaps the answer to this lies in the fact that movies have become primarily a young person's entertainment (the major share of the audience is between 11 and 32), whereas the theater still exerts its greatest appeal to the over-30 generation.

THINGS TO REMEMBER

1. Learn how to rhyme "purely" before you use false rhymes.

2. Don't rhyme only for rhyme's sake. The thought must be the first consideration.

3. Don't write a false rhyme because you can't come up with a real one. If you do use such rhymes as "down" and "around," make them the result of conscious choice, not because you're stuck for a word.

4. Remember that the ideal rhymes are those which rhyme perfectly and still have the believable ring of human speech. The main criterion, no matter how you achieve it, is honesty.

5. Try to adhere to the same rhyme scheme from verse to verse if possible.

6. Use alliteration, as long as it sounds flowing and natural, rather than artificially contrived.

7. Use vowels whenever possible on big or key notes. They have a rich, open sound.

8. Perfect unpretentious inner rhyming.

9. Use a rhyming dictionary or thesaurus and don't be embarrassed about it. Most successful composers do.

10. Test your lyrics as though you were an actor, to make sure they "talk."

11. Try to make the words "conversational pictures."

12. Learn up-to-date expressions, but don't overuse them or your work will date quickly.

13. Develop skill in rhyming proper names.

14. Make sure you employ pure rhyme in the theater, where standards are stricter.

6

The Eyes and Ears of a Songwriter

VISUAL IMAGERY

A good lyric is made up of many things—the technical polish of structure and rhyme, an intriguing idea, emotions the whole world can identify with. However, what often separates a good, workable lyric from a great one is the imagery. A colorful, flavorful image is generally remembered after the bulk of the words have been forgotten.

In the '50s, "Misty" (Garner/Burke) contained the memorable phrase "Look at me, I'm as helpless as a kitten up a tree," which perfectly portrayed the wonder and nervous excitement of a new love. Moving ahead to the early '60s, "Moon River" (Mancini/Mercer) spoke of "my huckleberry friend." The spirit of freedom was conveyed; no other words were necessary.

These images are clear, easily defined. Sometimes word pictures are open to a variety of interpretations, such as those in "Punky's Dilemma," from the Paul Simon *Bookends* album: "Wish I was a Kellogg's cornflake, floatin' in my bowl takin' movies, relaxin' awhile, livin' in style, talkin' to a raisin who 'casionn'ly plays L.A." Everyone sees *something,* although the reactions are personal. No imagination can remain neutral and unengaged in the face of those pictures.

In the 1940s, a writer might have conveyed the need to escape pressure by saying, "Let's get away from it all." This is direct and clear, but how much more moving and vivid it is to show that emotion visually, as Goffin and King do in "Up on the Roof": "When I come home feelin' tired and beat, I go up where the air is fresh and sweet. I get away from the hustling crowds and all that rat race noise down in the street." The contrast of a quiet rooftop with the tension and hostility of everyday life is projected in a way that engages the senses of every listener.

Sometimes a new writer falls back on clichés rather than digging for more colorful expressions. In rare instances a mundane lyric can achieve hit status if joined to an exciting rhythm or a particularly strong melody, but taking the lazy way out will eventually slow a writer down in the long run. Only by stretching visually will your words make a lasting impression.

Here's a verse from "Margaritaville" (Buffett) that supplies a thousand images in six lines:

> Nibbling on sponge cake
> Watching the sun bake
> All of those tourists covered with oil
>
> Strumming my six string
> On my front porch swing
> Smell those shrimp, They're beginning to boil.

Taste, sight, smell, hearing . . . no camera could capture this scene in so much detail.

A visual sense comes naturally to certain people, but it can be acquired. Detail is the key word. Don't just wander absently through a day: really notice things around you, develop an awareness of gestures, idiosyncrasies in speech and dress. Everyone has individual traits, and you can zero in on them if you just pay attention. It's true that the sky is blue, the sun yellow, but most beautiful skies offer extraordinary color combinations, cloud formations. It's amazing how many sights and sounds most people come in contact with and never see, but you can train yourself to notice it all.

Reading constantly, both prose and poetry, is a way of stimulating your imagination. The great writers are all picturesque; they all project their visions uniquely. When you read, don't just read for the plot or the meaning: concentrate on the manner of expression, the special turns of phrase.

All this isn't an endorsement for obscure, long-winded rambling. Billy Joel, Joni Mitchell and Jackson Browne are as poetic as writers can be, yet their material is easy to understand. You can maintain simplicity while injecting imagery to heighten the effect. If you allow your mind to travel alternative routes without clamping down too tightly on it, you'll be surprised at the offbeat, multidimensional results you can achieve.

TONAL FLAVOR

Stephen Sondheim's mastery of tone is complete, from the backstage seediness of *Gypsy* to the brittle New York wit of *Company*. Yet in a lecture he delivered at the 92nd Street YMHA, he referred to "I Feel Pretty" from *West Side Story* as one of his tonal mistakes. The song, sung by Maria, an uneducated Puerto Rican girl in a Manhattan slum, contains the elegantly sophisticated line "It's alarming how charming I feel." As Sondheim later admitted, "She would not have been unwelcome in Noël Coward's drawing room."

Everyone speaks differently. A wine merchant from France doesn't use the same language a Texas Ranger does. Pampered children from Palm Beach don't sound like poor children from the Lower East Side of New York, and you, as a writer, must learn to portray the difference.

Joel and I learned about tone the hard way. The first hit we had, "Why Can't You Bring Me Home," by Jay and the Americans, was based on a real-life incident. We were still living in Manhattan at the time and Joel was dating a very poor girl from Staten Island. She allowed him to take the ferry across with her but never to bring her home because she was ashamed of her small, ramshackle house and less-than-modest living conditions. Nothing he could do or say succeeded in changing her mind about bringing him to her home, so we decided to write a song expressing his frustration:

"Why Can't You Bring Me Home"

Why do we always meet on the edge of town
Why do we have to wait till the sun goes down
Where do you live and why don't you even give me a place to phone
Come on, Baby, why can't you bring me home
Baby, Baby, why can't you bring me home

I've asked around and nobody knows for sure
But they agree that your folks are mighty poor
Are you ashamed of where you were raised, is that why it stays unknown
Come on, Baby, why can't you bring me home

You may not wear such pretty clothes
But when you're in my arms, you look like a rose

What do I care if I see a broken chair
Why do I need the best kind of silverware
All that I need to make me complete is your tender love alone
Come on, Baby, why can't you bring me
Baby, Baby, why can't you bring me
Come on, Baby, why can't you bring me home

Why did this record only go halfway up the chart? The answer lies in the last verse:

What do I care if I see a broken chair
Why do I need *the best kind of silverware?*

This would have been more appropriate on a shopping expedition at Tiffany's. At the time we were, admittedly, knocked out with the use of the word "silverware." There's no doubt that it's the cleverest rhyme in the song. It reads well; it impressed many of our peers. But it's also dishonest; it threw the listener out of the mood and the story, forcing him to consider *us* as authors and our cleverness. We indulged ourselves at the expense of the tone, and people listening to the record actually laughed out loud when that line came on. In the words of a guitar-player friend, the song became a "jive."

Just as an amusing footnote to all this: "Why Can't You Bring Me Home" was an early example of the personal-biography approach to songwriting which became the norm a few years later (this was 1966). Not only did the record fail to reach the Top 10, but Joel's girlfriend became incensed at the exposure and retaliated by playing only the "B" side when they were together.

Certain lines define character and mood. For instance, Shaun Cassidy's "Hey Deanie" opens with "Hey, Deanie, can you come out tonight?" That sounds like a teen-ager. Seems obvious, but if composer Eric Carmen had said, "Deanie, may I call for you at eight?" he would have been perilously close to Cary Grant.

"What Are You Doing the Rest of Your Life?" (Alan and Marilyn Bergman/Michel Legrand), on the other hand, had to be spoken by an experienced, worldly person. Michel Legrand's reflective, jazz-oriented melody, with its consistently minor mode, accented the quality of sophistication inherent in the title.

Joel and I wrote the English lyric to a Charles Aznavour song, "The Old Fashioned Way," and we worked conscientiously to preserve the tone of nostalgia. The lines read:

> Dance in the old fashioned way
> Won't you stay in my arms
> And melt against my skin
> So let me feel your heart
> Don't let the music win
> By dancing far apart.

These lines were meant to evoke a past era, both in the references to close dancing and in the flavor of the images. "Melt against my skin" has a yesteryear feeling. We felt we had succeeded tonally when Fred Astaire recorded the song.

Jerry Leiber and Mike Stoller are tonally impeccable in any medium they choose. As a young and aspiring composer, I turned to Jerry for guidance and he gave me that along with warmth and inspiration. Jerry and Mike are internationally known for writing the rock classics that elevated Elvis Presley to superstardom, but two songs sum up their versatility and unparalleled command of tone beyond anything else they've written. In "Charlie Brown" they begin:

> Who's always writing on the walls?
> Who's always goofing in the halls?
> Who's always throwing spitballs?

Could that be anyone but a troublemaking student?
The next two lines read:

> Who walks in the classroom, cool and slow?
> Who calls the English teacher Daddy-o?

The time is identified as the mid-1950s. A feeling of the *Blackboard Jungle* era is conjured up. But suppose the line had been altered to read:

> Who ambles into the classroom, cool and slow?
> Who refers to the teacher as Daddy-o?

The words "ambles" and "refers" are *not* Charlie Brown, and while they pass quickly, they manage to shatter the total authenticity of the piece.

"Is That All There Is," written by the same team twelve years later, is tonal perfection applied to different subject matter.

Is that all there is?
Is that all there is
If that's all there is, my friends,
Then let's keep dancing
Let's break out the booze and have a ball
If that's all there is

This masterpiece was originally written for Marlene Dietrich, and it's easy to imagine the world-weary Dietrich delivery, singing of disillusionment and raised hopes that are constantly dashed to the ground. The words and music both have a feeling of 1930s Germany. A listener can visualize the smoky cabaret, people laughing too loudly and living it up because the end may come at any time. The tune is sad, mournful, contemplative, in keeping with the mood of Existentialism. It starts in lazy half steps, then leaps a fourth, conveying for a second the urgency and subdued emotion before calming again.

Certain descriptive phrases have a tone that immediately defines the character. In the Vance/Pockriss song "Playground in My Mind," you could picture who was speaking and the kind of nursery-rhyme bubble-gum song it was with the words "My name is Michael, I got a nickel, I got a nickel shiny and new—I'm gonna buy me all kinds of candy, That's what I'm gonna do."

Maintaining tone means remembering at all times who is talking and adhering to what that person would do or say. You have to develop a third ear, listen to people, be alert to dialogue in films, television and the theater. Listen to all kinds of records—country, R & B, pop, jazz—and acquaint yourself with the different colloquialisms used, the places most often referred to, the varying attitudes defined by different life-styles.

ASSOCIATIVE ADJECTIVES

Associative adjectives are related images, such as in Johnny Mercer's "Old Black Magic," which uses such terms as "witchcraft," "spell," "icy" and "weave." The more of them you can use, the more cohesive your overall lyric will be.

In our song "Your Time Hasn't Come Yet, Baby," which Elvis Presley performed in his 1968 movie *Speedway,* the subject is a little girl who has a crush on the reckless race-driver hero played by Presley. The lyrics went:

> Your life is still a *lollipop heaven*
> With *Teddy bears* at the foot of your bed
> *The little boy next door* who only makes you sore
> Is gonna someday turn your head.

The words "lollipop," "Teddy bears" and "little boy next door" are all images that tie in with a small girl's dream.

In our tune "Showtime," recorded by Sammy Davis, Jr., there are even more associative adjectives:

> You can hear my heart beat
> The *trumpets* are ringin'
> The *bass man* is swingin'
> *Dancin'* through a new street
> The *trumpets* are blowin'
> And *crowds* keep growin'
> You've waited, hopin' and dreamin' for days
> You've waited, no more delays
> And it's showtime, showtime, showtime
>
> Happy feelings tug you
> The *drummer* beats rhythm
> You're *marchin'* right with 'im
> Yes, you've come of age now
> The pick of the litter
> In *spangles and glitter*
>
> You've waited, done your *rehearsin'* in jeans
> You've waited, learned your *routines*
> And it's showtime, showtime, showtime
> Showtime for everyone

All the images used relate to putting on a show, to the musical instruments, the costumes, the rehearsals and the emotional trials. Associative adjectives are a foolproof way of ensuring tonal consistency in your work.

THINGS TO REMEMBER

1. Use colorful imagery.
2. Don't settle for clichés. Search until you find the image you want.
3. Develop visual awareness by becoming observant of the sights around you, styles of dress, the variations of nature. Read constantly and soak in the imagery of great authors.
4. Don't use imagery to ramble and fall into obscurity. Simplicity can be maintained in combination with offbeat, imaginative word pictures.
5. Make sure your song is tonally correct. Don't put illogical ideas into the mouths of your characters.
6. Be natural and honest, rather than clever at the expense of the tone.
7. Develop a third ear for speech. Attune your ear to colloquialisms.
8. Use associative adjectives whenever possible.

7

Who, What, Where, When and Why?

It's time to go back to our cigar-smoking publisher friend. In the days following his negative reaction to our material, he became fixed in our minds as a disapproving parent, and we labored to win his approval. Our next song was designed to be clever and intriguing—a slow unfolding of hidden meanings and feelings half-expressed. We thought of ourselves as Top 40 Harold Pinters.

Our critic paced the floor, then patted my shoulder and said, "Kid, what the f———k is it all about?" I obligingly pointed to the last verse and explained, with an air of superiority, "It's *implied* here. The public will get it." He grabbed my lapel and insisted, "Kid, I'm public. If *I* don't get it, *they* won't get it."

In literature, there are novels like *War and Peace* and *Doctor Zhivago,* sprawling canvases which require a long period of reader commitment to follow the plots and counterplots, as well as shifts of time and endless streams of characters. On the other side of the scale is the short short story, where economy is everything, where each word stands alone as a vital piece of the puzzle and the conflict must be established in the opening paragraph.

THE SHORT SHORT

A song is a musical short short story. Most songs have a total of 50 to 80 words, and each word is a separate and dynamic unit. The story skeleton must be there, but so must atmosphere, emotion and multilevel motivation. Even the choice of linking words, such as "and" and "but," is of tremendous importance. Careless use of these can adversely affect the tonal flavor. There is no time to waste!

Here are some examples of the short short:

"We Kiss in a Shadow"

Words: Oscar Hammerstein
Music: Richard Rodgers

We kiss in a shadow
We hide from the moon
Our meetings are few
And over too soon

We speak in a whisper
Afraid to be heard
When people are near
We speak not a word

Alone in our secret
Together we sigh
For one smiling day to be free

To kiss in the sunlight
And say to the sky
Behold and believe what you see
Behold how my lover loves me

"We kiss in a shadow, We hide from the moon—Our meetings are few And over too soon" is one of the best examples of this art. Hammerstein's verbal camera supplies an overall view of the situation. We know instantly that the two characters are lovers. They don't stand in the shadows, they kiss, indicating the romantic element involved. "Shadow" connotes secrecy and lack of freedom. Nighttime is established with the reference to moonlight, and the urgency of the situation is dramatized by the fact that even the moon is too bright and piercing for these two haunted people. "Our meetings are few" clearly implies the feeling of deprivation, the fact that their moments of happiness are rare. "And over too soon" emphasizes the danger in these meetings, the constant threat to their safety if they remain together for too long. In four lines, Mr. Hammerstein has stated the problem.

The camera moves in for a close-up in the second verse, and we begin to see and feel the people behind the conflict. "We speak in a whisper, Afraid to be heard" shows the strained circumstances under which this romance must exist. It also points out how much sacrifice they are willing to undergo for each other. "When people are near, We speak not a word" eloquently portrays the double life these lovers lead, the necessity for caution and the ever-present possibility of exposure.

The bridge in a short short frequently pauses to evaluate the conflict and hint at possible solutions. "Alone in our secret, Together we sigh For one smiling day to be free" is a linking thought to the conclusion, or "punch line." Its wistful, speculative tone has the seeds of resolution in it.

"To kiss in the sunlight And say to the sky" is the positive side to the coin of "We kiss in a shadow, We hide from the moon." The beautiful unity, contrasting images (sunlight, moon, shadow, sky), in related yet diametrically opposing ways, is a testimony to Mr. Hammerstein's dramatic cohesion. He's completely aware at all times that he's writing a short short, and a great deal must be compressed into a small space.

"Behold and believe what you see, Behold how my lover loves me" has an upbeat ring that suggests hope and gives the listener emotional satisfaction, although no guarantee of a happy ending is offered.

In 72 meticulously chosen words, Oscar Hammerstein has told us the lovers' problem, the manner in which they must relate to each other, their aspirations and possible alternatives for the future. Two lines, "We speak not a word" and "Behold and believe what you see," evoke an Oriental atmosphere faithful to the vehicle the song appears in, *The King and I,* but the tone is suggested rather than painted too heavily, which would remove the song from a commercial idiom.

A hit song of our own, "Will You Be Staying After Sunday," done by the Peppermint Rainbow in 1970, is a fully rounded short short:

> Will you be staying after Sunday
> Or go home on Monday
> Will you be staying after Sunday
> Or go home
>
> Your lips are warm on Friday night
> The next two days you hold me tight
> But when it's done, you always run
> And I'm alone
>
> Will you be staying after Sunday
> Or go home on Monday
> I keep waiting for that one day
> You'll be mine
>
> I'd give the world to keep you here
> Why do you need to disappear
> And when I press, you do your best
> To stall for time
>
> I wouldn't try to own your soul, you can be free
> I only want you here each night, loving me
>
> Will you be staying after Sunday
> Or go home on Monday
> We've got to let this feeling grow
> Or let it end
> You say you care, well if you do
> Don't ever go, I'm begging you
> Please don't let a lonely Monday come again

With the first two lines, "Will you be staying after Sunday Or go home on Monday," you know immediately that one of the parties is anxious to keep the other from leaving. The next two lines, "Will you be staying after Sunday Or go home," repeat the thought, stressing the heroine's concern. "Your lips are warm on Friday night, The next two days you hold me tight" points out that, on one hand, the weekend has been sexually and romantically satisfying, but there's an underlying insecurity, and the following lines, "But when it's done, you always run And I'm alone," confirm the anxiety, sum up the overall conflict of the song and create an atmosphere of suspense.

We now know that the two people are lovers, that one wants a commitment the other isn't prepared to give, that they have a satisfying sex life on these terms, but that the heroine is pushing for permanence and risking a breakup in the process.

The camera moves in for a close-up on the second verse. "Will you be staying after Sunday Or go home on Monday, I keep waiting for that one day You'll be mine" suggests that the heroine has waited and suffered silently for a long time. "I'd give the world to keep you here, Why do you need to disappear?" expresses her own needs, and shows she is a caring, analytical person by asking, "Why do you *need* to disappear?" Then, despite her attempt to be adult and reasonable, the ambivalence and fear show again, when she says, "And when I press, you do your best To stall for time."

"I wouldn't try to own your soul, you can be free" is a concession, a final effort to show how broad-minded and understanding she can be. "I only want you here each night, loving me" is a further embellishment of that attitude, and suggests a solution.

"Will you be staying after Sunday Or go home on Monday, We've got to let this feeling grow Or let it end—You say you care, well if you do, Don't ever go, I'm begging you—Please don't let a lonely Monday come again" lays it on the line, but still highlights contradictions in the character. We tried to catch those contradictions, because love relationships are never simple in real life. People generally say one thing and mean two. The last verse is alternately pleading, threatening, emphatic and vulnerable, but still gives the impression of resolution, that they will live together and share all the Mondays to come.

A Short Short can be given a final check, what I call the *Who-What-Where-When-and-Why test*. In other words, who is it about, what is the character doing, where is the situation taking place, when is it happening and why is it happening? In the case of "We Kiss in a Shadow," the "Who" is the couple involved, the "What" is that they're hiding in the shadows, the "When" is evening, "Where" is the shadows and "Why" is that their love is being threatened by external forces and these secret meetings are the only way they can preserve it.

In "Will You Be Staying After Sunday," the "Who" is the heroine pressuring her lover, the "What" is their argument, the "Where" is her apartment, the "When" is the weekend—Saturday and Sunday—and the "Why" is their differing views on the way the relationship is going and her desire for permanence.

Once again the oracle of 1650 Broadway was right when he said, "Kid, what's it about?"

To sum up: A Short Short is a three-minute movie, with a first verse that establishes conflict, and a second verse that restates and develops that conflict. The bridge is generally an evaluation of the overall situation, with reflections on how to solve or cope with it. The last verse supplies a whole or partial answer.

I'd like to quote Oscar Hammerstein again, who said, "There is in all art a fine balance between the benefits of freedom. An artist who is too fond of freedom is likely to be obscure in his expression." So remember—when asked the time, don't tell the public how the watch is made. Get *to* it!

THINGS TO REMEMBER

1. A song should be the musical equivalent of a short short story. The characteristics of a short short are:
   a. Simplicity and clarity—making every word count;
   b. Defining the conflict in the opening verse;

  c. Restating and developing it in the second verse;
  d. Hinting at possible solutions in the bridge;
  e. Resolving the conflict in the final verse.
  2. Apply the Who-What-Where-When-and-Why test. In other words Who (is it about), What (are they doing), Where (is the situation taking place), When (is it happening) and Why (is it happening).

8

Basic Melodic Points

WRITING INTRODUCTIONS

Writing introductions is an element of composing that too many writers ignore or dismiss as unimportant. The tendency is to play a few bars to establish the rhythm and then get to the part that matters.

Actually, *every* part matters. If you think about your favorite records, chances are you'll remember their intros as vividly as the songs themselves.

A musical introduction can be many things. It can be a background line that recurs throughout the song (e.g., the guitar line in "Southern Nights"). This way, your intro can serve as a secondary hook, in addition to your main one.

Very often the intro will be a piece of your actual melody, and by the time the song begins, the listener feels familiar with the tune and is beginning to remember it. It can be a variation on the melody (as in the opening of Albert Hammond's "It Never Rains in Southern California"), a part of it (as in "We've Only Just Begun") or a new melody altogether.

Introductions set the mood. A hot, driving rhythm lets the listener know he's in for an exciting dance record and raises his expectations accordingly. Soft, gentle strings set him up for a mellow, romantic experience. A twangy guitar gives him the feeling that the record is country, that the subject matter is down to earth, rather than sophisticated. These things also give the program director some idea of what's in store for him.

Within the enclosed space that introductions are allotted, there can be considerable variety. On "Singing the Blues," an old Guy Mitchell record, a whistle was used to usher in the song, and on "The Way We Were," Barbra Streisand hummed! Sometimes openers can be foolers, as in the case of Ron Miller and Michael Masser's "Touch Me in the Morning"—the introductory segment began without specific rhythm, then launched a few bars later into a strong beat. An intro can be a group singing sounds, rather than words, as demonstrated by the Carpenters' version of Joe Raposo's "Sing." In that one, a group of children sang "La, la, la, la la." On rare occasions, a record can open right away without any musical preparation, which is all right too. The point is, when you do a preparatory tune or beat, don't let it be a throwaway, dead air until the song gets started.

Introductions, like a master of ceremonies announcing a performer, should set the mood up quickly, establish a tone and then move quickly offstage. One or two recordings violate this rule and get away with it (as "Year of the Cat" did, with its lengthy instrumental opener), but the practice is risky. On a practical level, intros give the disc jockey time to talk, to announce a record and give it some kind of buildup.

Many of today's radio listeners are dial turners. As they go whizzing by, sampling chunks of this song or that, a compelling introduction which identifies your song may be the factor that calms their restless dial fingers down. A record has a short time to make its point, and not even 3 to 5 seconds up front are dispensable. Every second counts.

GIVING THE SINGER A BREAK

When you're playing the piano, your range is limitless. You can leap from one octave to another and still create a melody that sounds flowing and comfortable. Remember, though, that a singer's vocal equipment isn't that flexible. Lingering on impossibly high notes will only render your soloist hoarse, and awkward, illogical jumps will sound more like a vocal exercise than a song. Try to keep the range between an octave and an octave and 2, and let the bulk of the melody remain in the middle, with highs and lows for dramatic expressiveness. Neil Diamond, for instance, has a way of dipping down to low notes for color, then coming back up. He includes a section in "Cracklin' Rosie" in which he sings a few lines in an exaggerated, almost put-on bass voice. This works effectively, but the other sections of the song are in a normal register. In "Rocket Man," Elton John generally focuses on the medium range, but returns periodically to a falsetto note. John Denver's "Calypso" features a repetitive yodeling section, with piercing high notes to add excitement to this folk-flavored waltz.

Pop composing isn't an intellectual process. Your aim is to trigger a powerful emotional reaction from the listener. The best way to do that is to feel the song intensely yourself as you're writing it, to give yourself chills. It means shedding your self-consciousness. You should be comfortable enough to raise your voice, pound on your instrument, stamp your feet—whatever is needed to turn your adrenaline on. If you take a cautious, cerebral attitude toward composing, the result may also be timid—properly constructed, neat, professional, but bloodless.

Years ago, Joel and I worked in my Central Park West apartment in New York. A female agent, now well known, lived next door, and she would knock violently on the wall every time our voices rose above a whisper. Before long we were writing soft, nondescript melodies, so intimidated were we by the constant, thunderous banging. It didn't occur to us for quite a while that her complaints were out of line—at three in the afternoon on weekdays! Once we saw what was happening, we just ignored the harassment and wrote with uninhibited emotion. If you feel hemmed in—by parents, children, relatives, neighbors—either train yourself to turn off the distracting sounds, or find another place to work. Your creativity could depend on it.

Certain songs project author intensity, and are the obvious results of the chill factor. Listening to "The Impossible Dream," you can be certain that composer Mitch Leigh didn't plot it out in a detached, mathematical style. Nor was "Somewhere Over the Rainbow," with its opening octave leap, conceived without strong personal involvement by Yip Harburg and Harold Arlen. Barry Manilow's recording of "Mandy" has a hook that soars. It would never have moved the public so much if it hadn't moved the composer first, and "You Light Up My Life," after a quiet first verse, seems to burst right through the record.

BUILDING

Finding a nice tune isn't the whole answer. You've got to build it, with little climaxes that taper off, a series of digressions that eventually lead to an emotionally satisfying resolution.

A good example of a song that builds is "We've Only Just Begun." With these four words in the first two measures, writers Paul Williams and Roger Nichols use rapid-moving eighth notes, as though to convey the breathlessness of young love. With "to live," there is a momentary relaxation, a slowing of tempo, as though in reflection on the future, after which "white lace and promises" resumes the sense of movement with quarter-note triplets. The melody reaches up a seventh, from the F above middle C to an E, emphasizing the significance of "white lace." "A kiss for luck and we're on our way" combines the eighth notes and the quarter-note triplets, propelling the tune ahead. It's worth noting that measures 4 and 5 are repeated but compounded in measures 6 and 7. This is an example of musical sequence, or what I call the ask-and-answer effect, in which a theme is introduced, then played again with chordal or rhythmic variation. By the end of the first verse, the melody (which began on middle C) has risen an octave and a fourth to a high F. Within one verse, there has been a steady and dramatic sense of build. The melody has moved forward, paused (as people pause when they speak) and moved forward again, all the time stretching to wider intervals. For this reason, "We've Only Just Begun," though gentle in nature, never becomes boring or static, never loses the ear of the listener.

RHYTHM

Today's record buyers still enjoy tuneful melodies, but they rarely get excited over a record that lacks rhythm, no matter how beautiful it is. They're conditioned to look for syncopated sections that give the song drive. Something—a bass, a piano, a guitar part—must be in constant motion, to maintain the record's pulse.

The following are a list of popularly utilized rhythms. If you familiarize yourself with all of them, you'll have a strong base to build tunes on.

Shuffle Rhythm

Consists of dotted-8th and 16th-note patterns:

Typical examples of a medium shuffle are "Kansas City" (Leiber/Stoller) and "Help Me Rhonda" (B. Wilson). The shuffle rhythm is used quite often with the 12-bar blues progression (e.g., "Kansas City"):

(Note: 6th of chord is being used. This is common in most shuffles.)
  Shuffle also works well with a walking bass line:

And of course, the "Boogie" is a great example of the shuffle with the broken octave pattern in the left hand of the piano! Example: "All Shook Up" (Blackwell/Presley):

Folk/Country 2

  The secret to folk/country 2 lies in the fact that it consists of a straight 8th-note pattern (usually from the guitar) and an emphasis on beats 1 and 3 (usually from bass and bass drum). Of course, the drum back beat on 2 and 4 is equally important.
  Examples: "Take It Easy" (D. Henley/G. Frey), "Lyin' Eyes" (D. Henley/G. Frey), "When Will I Be Loved?" (P. Everly), "Take Me Home Country Roads" (J. Denver).

Usually in a country 2 (as opposed to a folk 2) the guitar picks broken chords instead of strumming:

Waltz (3/4 Rhythm)

In a waltz the emphasis is on the downbeat (1 of each bar).

Examples: "You Light Up My Life" (J. Brooks), "Scarborough Fair" (P. Simon).

What is known as the "Jazz" waltz puts an emphasis on the upbeat of 1:

The jazz waltz is usually played in a brisk tempo:

Here is a category of the "waltz" that is rather difficult to explain, as it is actually 4 beats to the measure! *But,* it has a feeling of 3/4. This is because each beat is a triplet. This is common in R & B songs such as "When I Need You" (A. Hammond/C. Sager). Tempo is very slow, and you should feel an emphasis on 2 and 4 from the snare drum. Notated, it is in 12/8 time and looks like this:

Latin Rhythms

Latin rhythms lie mainly in the percussion section. It would be wise to purchase a drum book indicating the basic beats for the samba, conga, cha cha, etc., if you wish to learn authentic Latin beats. However, there are certain Latin "feels" used in contemporary writing that are a marriage of rock and Latin. The obvious ones are:

1. CHA CHA

2. RHUMBA

3. SAMBA

(The samba feel has been used quite successfully with rock for the "disco" sound.)

4. BAION

(The baion is a very subtle Latin beat. You can find many examples of it in contemporary songs such as "Walk On By" (Bacharach/David) and "Do You Know the Way to San Jose?" (Bacharach/David).

While we're on the subject of Latin rhythms, we may as well mention "Reggae." Its origin is Jamaica, and its forms are many. But basically, the rhythm pattern is to push the third beat of the bar.

Examples: "Mother and Child Reunion," "Me and Julio Down by the Schoolyard" (P. Simon). And how about the "Chiquita Banana" commercial?

(Note: This first example has an authentic Jamaican bass line. The second is more like what you would hear on a commercial record.)

Other Rhythm Patterns

A few rhythms stand on their own and are easily recognized.

1. STRAIGHT FOUR (Motown)

Example: "I'm Gonna Make You Love Me" (Gamble/Ross/Williams)

2. MEMPHIS BEAT

(Named after the song "Memphis"—C. Berry—it's a straight 4 beat with heavy emphasis on 2 and 4.)

3. BO DIDDLEY BEAT

4. *BOOGALOO RHYTHM*

(There are many variations on this, but it is basically a slow 4 with the rhythm section and bass playing "double time" rhythm.)

5. *"LOUIE, LOUIE"*

6. *"SOUTH SEAS"*

(Like "Bali Hai" by Rodgers and Hammerstein)

7. CHARLESTON RHYTHM

A proven method of composing rhythmically is to write tunes over tracks. Pick out the rhythmic records on the charts you'd like to emulate, or cuts from disco albums, then conceive your own melody against their movement. You can attempt this while the track is playing, or learn to reproduce it on your instrument first.

PERSONALITY SONGS

Try to decide on the personality and mood of your tune. In certain cases, you may just put your fingers on your guitar or piano and wing it, letting creative impulse guide you—but a preconceived idea helps. Jagger and Richards wrote a memorable personality song, "Honky Tonk Woman." Once they came up with the title character, it was easy to bring her to life with a tack piano, thumping out the honky-tonk beat and chords. "Say, Has Anybody Seen My Sweet Gypsy Rose" gained its personality through the logical '20s melody that sprang from it. A personality title like "Boogie Woogie Bugle Boy from Company B" had Andrews Sisters harmonies from the '40s, which Bette Midler presented successfully to a later generation. "The Stripper" was a striking instrumental, because the idea was carried out musically by wailing trumpets and trombones, and the melody moved with· enough bump-and-grind abandon to fix clear images of a burlesque house in the mind of every listener. The initial concept of a stripper made it possible for those involved to develop and dramatize this personality-packed atmosphere.

Ideas like these serve two purposes. They give a composer specific direction, and they protect him from creating a bland, characterless product. Personality songs always possess inherent color and appeal because they deal in tangible things; they never wander through hazy, unclarified emotional territory.

Sometimes you'll have lyrics or titles to work from that a collaborator has given you, or ones you've devised yourself. That makes it easier. But even if you don't, close your eyes sometime and summon up a setting or a person, and you'll find your mind functioning immediately. This approach worked for Burt Bacharach when he evoked his European atmosphere, and John Denver in bringing alive the world of Rocky Mountain peacefulness and harmony, and it will work for you.

In 1954, Judy Garland did her classic rendition of "The Man That Got Away" in the Arlen/Gershwin film version of *A Star Is Born*. Amid the general excitement and acclaim, a few music critics of the period dared to mention that the word "the" was lingered on and given a big, sustained note, as in the line *"The* writing on the wall." They couldn't decide if this was the fault of the lyric and melody, or of Miss Garland's interpretation. Whatever the case, the fact is that expansive, booming notes shouldn't be glued onto such weak words as "the," "and" and "but." These transitional terms are not inherently dramatic. A song should talk, it should be actable. If you were given this sentence to say, "My friend died *and* I'm miserable *and* so I'm going *to the* funeral," and you emphasized the words stressed here, it would sound ludicrous. Yet beginning songwriters feature irrelevant words all the time, underscoring them with aggressively misplaced climactic notes.

THINGS TO REMEMBER

1. In writing introductions, give them the same attention and thought you give to other elements of your song. They set the mood and the tempo, and are the first thing a listener hears.

2. Keep your melodies within a reasonable octave to octave-and-2 range, unless you're writing specifically for a singer with unusual vocal ability. Don't linger on high, difficult notes.

3. Don't be self-conscious when writing. Let yourself feel the creative process intensely, and your music will have the same emotional impact on others.

4. Make sure your tunes build steadily from beginning to end.

5. Write rhythmically. Even ballads should have an underlying pulse, a feeling of syncopation.

6. Write your tunes over the rhythm tracks of other records. This will teach you to write rhythmic music automatically.

7. Write "personality songs" as often as possible, building your melody around a colorful character ("Honky Tonk Woman") or setting ("Rocky Mountain High").

8. Don't place unimportant words like "and" and "but" on top of big, booming notes.

9

Musical Progressions and Sequences

I touched briefly on sequential writing in a previous analysis of the Williams/Nichols song, "We've Only Just Begun." This point is vitally important and deserves elaboration. A sequence is a form of repetition, and can mean a repetition of melody, rhythm and chords, alone or in combination. In the following example, the first measure presents a basic sequence, which is repeated in the second. The third measure repeats that sequence, doubling the speed of the rhythm. The sixth measure speeds it faster, using sixteenth notes, and in the eighth bar, the notes are elongated to twice the length of the rhythm in the first two measures. The key element is those first few notes, whether tripled, doubled or halved—they supply the basic sequence, the cluster of intervals which gives the tune its foundation.

Example #1

In this example, the sequence of *notes* is the same, but the chords alter beneath them. The Holland/Dozier/Holland hit "Baby Love" utilizes a sequence in which the notes are the same, but the chords vary:

Example #2

In measures 1 and 2, the interval relationships are the same, but in different keys:

Example #3

A very popular sequence (used in Jimmy Webb's "All My Love's Laughter") is one in which the tones keep rising a third. This constant development by thirds gives the piece a steady feeling of build and keeps it interesting:

Example #4

Composer Jule Styne once observed that writing sequences is like writing little bits of scales, but once you've got the scales going, you have to make jumps and do the unexpected. The note jumps or rhythm changes should take the listener slightly off guard, yet make perfect sense. They can't be illogical and unrelated to the sequence, or else you'll lose all cohesiveness.

In "Someone I Touched," a song written for a television drama,

Joel and I wrote sequentially. The first measure introduces the basic sequence, and the second repeats it, developing by moving up a step on the last note. This is a good example of the ask-and-answer effect:

Example #5

In a song Joel and I co-wrote with Charles Aznavour, "We Can Never Know," the rhythmic sequence is unchanging throughout, but the melodic sequence keeps changing, hitting unexpected notes, yet alternating whole and half steps in exactly the same pattern from measure to measure:

Example #6

Here the notes change, but the chord pattern (G, Em, Am, D⁷) keeps repeating:

Example #7

You can always build a sequence stepwise like this:

Example #8

You can, as in Example #2, maintain the same notes and change the chords, or keep both melody and chords the same. You can repeat your sequence for two bars—or four or five—before altering and building on it. Or you might prefer to keep notes and chords the same, but alter the rhythm. It doesn't matter what choice you make, as long as there is a sequence of some kind. Be aware of this at all times when composing, and train your ear to follow sequential patterns every time you listen to music. Even the most mysterious twists and turns of the material will eventually prove to be intelligible on a second hearing, part of the composer's consciously planned design.

PROGRESSION PRACTICE

Billy Preston (responsible for the hits "Will It Go Round in Circles" and "That's the Way God Planned It") confided to authors Kent McNeel and Mark Luther that his manner of composing was to write melodies over chord progressions.

A progression is a series of chords that recurs throughout a song, the chord pattern the melody is built on. These chords can go downward in half steps:

Or whole steps:

Or they can move in an upward pattern, in the same series of half or whole steps. They can move in thirds, fourths, fifths and octaves. All that matters is that they have a pattern which repeats throughout the entire tune.

Progressions can jump back and forth on two notes (D C D C—"Memphis"—Chuck Berry), three notes (C F G—Latin/rock a la "Cherry Cherry"—Neil Diamond) or four notes (G A⁷ D⁷ G—"Love Me Tender").

A good basis for popular composing would be to familiarize yourself with as many pop progressions as you can. Buy sheet music, not just of your favorites, but of country, soul, pop and jazz standards. Don't play only the tunes: play the chords over and over again until your ear grows accustomed to the various patterns. Before long you'll know which ones are the most often utilized in the different genres.

After this practice, write down the progressions and compose your own melodies over them. If possible, notate them without identifying the song they belong to, and come back to them a day later when that association has faded or been forgotten. You'll be literally *forced* to write in a commercial vein.

Before long, these progressions will be internalized and you'll know them automatically. With that as a foundation, you'll start elaborating on them and coming up with progressions of your own—but the initial homework will keep you realistic and commercial.

Here are a sampling of often-used progressions, alongside hit songs that were built on them.

C   Cma⁷   C⁷   F

"If"—*David Gates*	Pop
"I Honestly Love You"—*Jeff Barry/Peter Allen*	Pop
"Something"—*Harrison*	Pop
"Hooked on a Feeling"—*Mark James*	Country pop

C   Dmi⁷   G⁷

"Everybody Loves a Rain Song"—*Mark James/Chips Moman*	Country pop
"I Never Promised You a Rose Garden"—*Joe South*	Country
"Killing Me Softly with His Song"—*Charles Fox/Norman Gimbel*	Latin pop
"The Same Old Song"—*Holland/Dozier/Holland*	R & B
"By the Time I Get to Phoenix"—*Jimmy Webb*	Country pop

C   Am   F   G⁷

"Please, Mr. Postman"—*Holland/Bateman*	R & B
"All I Have to Do Is Dream"—*Everly Brothers*	Country

F   C

"You're in My Heart"—*Rod Stewart*	Pop
"Runnin' On Empty"—*Jackson Browne*	Pop
"My Girl"—*Smokey Robinson*	R & B

C   G   B♭   F

"Never My Love"—*Addrisi Brothers*	Pop
"Natural Woman"—*Goffin/King/Wexler*	R & B

C (C⁷) F (G⁷)

"Delta Dawn"—*Alex Harvey/Larry Collins*   Country
                                                           pop
"Detour"—*Mel Tillis*   Country
"Heartaches by the Number"—*Harlan Howard*   Country

C Em F G⁷

"Georgy Girl"—*Jim Dale/Tom Springfield*   Pop
"If I Had a Hammer"—*Pete Seeger*   Folk
"Jean"—*Rod McKuen*   Folk pop
"The Way We Were"—*Marvin Hamlisch/Alan and Marilyn*   Pop
Bergman

C G⁷ F

"Okie from Muskogee"—*Merle Haggard*   Country
"Hey, Jude"—*Lennon/McCartney*   Pop

OTHER PROGRESSIONS TO WRITE OVER

C F⁷ C
F F⁷ B♭⁷ F
G⁷ C
Cma⁷ Am Cma⁷ Am
F B♭ C F Bb C
B♭ Dm⁷· Cm F⁷
D Em⁷ A⁷ D
Am G F G⁷ Am G F G⁷
F G⁷ C⁷ B♭ F
Dm⁷ Am⁷ Dm⁷

Sometimes a rhythm comes first, sometimes a tune, but working with progressions is a highly effective way of producing good material.

Examine the catalogue of the brilliant Gordon Lightfoot ("If You Could Read My Mind," "Wreck of the Edmund Fitzgerald," "Early Morning Rain") and then bear in mind that he says, "The chord progression comes first . . . then decisions are made about rhythm and tempo and style."

WRITING AWAY FROM AN INSTRUMENT

There are many classically trained pianists, now writing pop music, who can construct and play any chord on the piano. They have so much chord facility at their fingertips that they run into a peculiar kind of problem . . . they become overly focused on the chord changes, to the detriment of tune and rhythm. As Irving Berlin once commented, "You can't sing chords."

First and foremost, a composer must think of the melody, and if he becomes too bogged down with chord development, he fails to give the tune proper attention. Often he wants to show how many chords he knows, as though that were a badge of genius, but it's artistically and commercially self-defeating. If there's a chord on every note, movement is restricted and becomes leaden. In the rhythm and blues standard "Dancing in the Streets," there are thirteen bars of one chord, another five of a different one. The movement sails. A whole group of extra chords could have been inserted into that space, but at the expense of the excitement. The answer: less is more, if you want rhythm.

Sometimes the answer is to liberate yourself from your instrument. The danger is less apt to occur with guitar, which is why Paul McCartney has stated that he writes up-tempo songs on guitar, rather than piano, but even so, there are benefits in conceiving melodies a cappella (without accompaniment).

For one, the tunes are certain to be less complicated, easier to sing. They'll automatically pass the whistle test. You won't be as concerned with theory and orchestration.

Some writers worry that this approach will result in simplistic, rather than simple, material. Not possible. If you have a chord sense, you don't lose it just because you're away from the piano or guitar. Those chords are still in your head; they're just not as predominant, they don't overshadow your melody writing. You're freer to concentrate on intervals. You can move around, which immediately generates its own kind of emotion. As for the fear of writing simplistically, you can consider Burt Bacharach again. Nobody would call him a simplistic composer, and yet he admits to composing melodies in his head and with his voice. He stays away from the piano in the early stages because his fingers automatically fall upon familiar chords and tunes.

Anthony Newley and Leslie Bricusse compose their shows away from an instrument, yet their scores for *Stop the World, I Want to Get Off* and *Roar of the Greasepaint* are tuneful and rich in chordal color.

Joel and I recently tried this approach when we felt we were becoming caught in the chord trap. We wrote a gospel song, "Pass a Little Love Around," for a film entitled *The North Avenue Irregulars* and a country song for another film, *Hot Lead and Cold Feet*. Both surprised us with their liveliness and authenticity. We'd been talking for years about trying to write this way, but dependence on an instrument is a strong, deeply ingrained habit, a crutch, and we had trepidations about testing this approach. Now we feel that a whole new area has opened up for us.

After you've come up with your ideas, try them out on the instrument. If there's a guitar available, and the song is powerfully rhythmic, that might be the next logical place to test what you've done. In either case, whether guitar or piano, you can add chords to the material if you feel it needs any, beyond what you've devised in your mind.

The chord trap isn't a pitfall that all composers tumble into. Some can easily achieve that delicate balance between music, rhythm and chords and never leave their instruments. But for the writer who can't seem to make his music swing, who winds up writing ballads all the time and is frustrated because he yearns to produce up-tempo material, the practice of writing away from pianos and guitars may be just the answer. Phil Spector, whom Thomas Wolfe once called "the tycoon of teen," composer and producer of countless hits, claims that every rock and roll song should be able to be reduced to four chords, and this is one surefire way of meeting the Spector requirement.

STRUCTURE

Most popular music is built on established structures. Roger Nichols stated in a *Songwriter* magazine interview, "I feel that if you escape form you lose it. My favorite form is A A B A." The following forms are guidelines, and the imaginative writer can vary them. There's more flexibility in today's music than there ever was. Music today is largely dictated by what *feels* right. The projection of power and emotion is all-important, and if form can be varied while these elements are still preserved, there are few purists who would look down at the change.

Some of the standard forms:

A	A	B	A
Verse	Verse	Bridge	Verse

This is a basic setup, and works equally well in such diverse material as the blues classic "Kansas City" or the Barbra Streisand Oscar winner "The Way We Were." Joel and I used it in our own "Morning After."

A	B	A	B	A	B
Verse	Chorus	Verse	Chorus	Verse	Chorus

This is used in the gentle "Killing Me Softly with His Song" and the pulsating "Bad Bad Leroy Brown." In this format, there is no bridge (or release, as it's also called), just an alternating of the first two sections.

A	B	A	B	C	B
Verse	Chorus	Verse	Chorus	Bridge	Chorus

Here the pattern is varied slightly. This is extremely popular, perhaps the most often employed by today's writers. It is used in the B. J. Thomas hit "Don't Worry, Baby."

The bridge used to be a must, but many hit songs now eliminate it altogether, building cumulative emotion on the sections already introduced, rather than digressing to a new theme or rhythm. Jeff Barry, when he writes a bridge nowadays, prefers to keep it short.

The Johnny Cash classic "I Walk the Line" is a simple

A	A	A	A
Verse	Verse	Verse	Verse

In other words, all the sections are musically identical, although the words change.

The structure of "Lyin' Eyes," as done by the Eagles, is comparatively odd.

A	A	A	B	
Verse	Verse	Verse	Chorus	
	A	A	B	
	Verse	Verse	Chorus	
			B	
			Chorus	(repeating till fadeout)

This format is commercially daring, because it takes much longer to get to the repetitive chorus (hook) section. Yet it's also a case in which breaking rules is valid, because the story is so compelling, the drama so vivid, that the form seems perfectly logical, the slow development appropriate.

The Elton John/Bernie Taupin "Your Song" does it still another way.

A	A	B
Verse	Verse	Chorus
A	A	B
Verse	Verse	Chorus
	C	C

New tag section, which fades the record

The "C" section is memorable enough to stand on its own, so the listener doesn't feel cheated because the record doesn't return to the "B" section.

These are just a few of the variations. It should be obvious by now that there are no rules, formwise, beyond the most sweeping generalizations. Modern hits are not just *songs*—they're record productions, often patched together in the studio, where touches are added or subtracted as the producer and performer feel them.

Singers can elongate the ends of verses if they feel it. Writers can add lines that make the structural symmetry uneven if, in their opinion, the musical or lyric message is enhanced.

The only precaution, until you gain experience and intuition, would be to choose a basic and discernible pattern before building on it, as Roger Nichols does. Just think back on how often you've read about motion pictures in which the actors and director "improvised," rather than shooting from a working script, and how rambling and unintelligible the movie turned out to be. Within a structure, a multitude of changes are possible, but operating from a solid base will prevent confusion and loss of direction later on.

PROSODY

Prosody is the correct marriage of words and music. In a previous chapter, we mentioned that a big, powerful note on a word like "and" and "but" was inappropriate. That is an example of bad prosody.

Good prosody can be seen in the Bacharach/David song "I Say a Little Prayer." On the first line, "The moment I wake *up,*" the melody moves up, escalating with the word. Good prosody should approximate human speech. Certain words, certain emotions cause inflections to alter. A tone of voice rises when there's cause for excitement, lowers with sadness or maintains an even level when the information is matter-of-fact and lacks drama.

In Elton John's "Your Song" (John/Taupin), he sings, "And you can tell *every*body this is your song." On the "every" the tune rises urgently, because the singer is trying to convey the depth and force of his feeling, and wants the whole world to know it. If it had gone down, the whole song would have been destroyed.

In "You Made Me So Very Happy" (B. Gordy, Jr./F. Wilson/B. Holloway/P. Holloway), the first two lines are melancholy, as the singer laments, "I've lost at *love* before—Got mad and closed the door." In this instance, the melody logically drops on "love." But then a surge of optimism takes over and he bursts out, "I chose you for the *one,* Now I'm having so much *fun,*" and the direction of the tune is vibrantly upward, reaching its high note on "one" and "fun."

A good example of actable prosody is the Oates/Hall hit "Rich Girl," in which the angry hero declares, "You're a *rich* girl, and you've *gone* too far, 'Cause you *know* it doesn't matter anyway." If you were speaking that line, your voice would swell with emotion on the words rich, gone and know. Just try to say it, and you'll see how accurately the writers emphasized the key words.

Children's songs have a logical prosody to them, and stand as definitive examples of this skill. Look at "London Bridge is *falling* down, *falling* down," in which the melody keeps curving downward to accentuate the title sentiment. Or "Ring Around the Rosy," in which the melody maintains a consistently circular movement. In a song of our own for the movie *Pete's Dragon,* we wrote "A *drag*on, a *drag*on, I *swear* I saw a *drag*on," and with each repetition of the title word, we shot up an additional third, to point out the panic the character in the story felt when unexpectedly witnessing a monster.

If you're writing to a lyric, try to decide what the main emotional intention of the song is, and what words you should highlight musically to give them force. If you're matching a lyric to a tune already written, the same thing applies. Don't let the most exciting parts of the melody slip by with uninteresting, impersonal words. Develop your story in the quieter sections, and really let go with your strongest, most vivid descriptions and adjectives when the notes rise.

Analyze hit songs, examining them for prosody. You'll find, in almost all cases, that the words and music complement each other when they should. A helpful exercise is to take lyrics of hits and write your own tunes to them. Learn by experience which notes, which sections deserve which colors. Maybe a reflective, descriptive section would benefit from several repetitions of the same note, to capture the monotone of reflective speech. Maybe a tearful section might come most effectively alive if you raise the melody upward suddenly, then swoop down again, to convey instability or uncontrolled desperation. Sometimes an unhappy emotional feeling is best captured by going down instead of up, because the hurt being expressed is of the resigned, lump-in-the-throat kind, rather than an outward explosion of despair. These are decisions that you, as a composer/dramatist, must make, decisions that will give dimension and shading to your overall musical portrait.

FIGURES—THE FOUNDATION OF HITS

If you were asked, "What is a song?" your answer would probably be "A melody, with lyrics that match and enhance that melody." You'd be right . . . but only partially. From a commercial standpoint, a vital element in hit records today is a "figure," or "riff"—a recurring vocal or instrumental phrase that ties the material together and in many cases provides the foundation for the song.

"But that's not my job," new writers sometimes complain, "that's the job of the producer or arranger." True, these figures are often inserted by arrangers and producers, but whatever the writer can contribute to his musical brainchild will add life and luster to the final product. It makes sense to give the producer and arranger as much creative material as you can.

Stevie Wonder, chart king and multiple Grammy Award winner, has utilized figures to maximum advantage. Take "Superstition," which opens with a rocking guitar strain that repeats after every line. It provides a dance beat and adds cumulative emotion. It's almost hard to imagine what this record would be like if that recurring figure were removed.

Lennon and McCartney based many of their early classics on figures. "I Feel Fine" features a driving guitar riff that supports the tune and is integral to its conception. "Do You Want to Know a Secret" leans on a vocal figure (". . . Ooo . . . ooo . . . ooo . . . Do you want to know a secret . . . ooo . . . ooo . . .ooo").

Figures don't function only for purposes of dance pulse or excitement. They add an extra dimension to ballads as well. It's a safe bet that listeners everywhere remember the opening guitar strain of "Never My Love," subsequently repeated throughout the song. This five-note melody set a tone that brought haunting magic to a beautiful ballad.

Naming records on which added melodic and rhythmic riffs increased commerciality and listening pleasure is an enjoyable game as well as a valuable ear-training exercise. When you think of the Diana Ross hit "You Keep Me Hangin' On," doesn't the linking SOS figure come to mind, which sounds like a lover in distress? And "Baby, I Need Your Lovin' " wouldn't have been the same without its repeated refrain. Proof of that is the fact that the figure was used in the original production by The Four Tops, and recalled for fresh service when Johnny Rivers did an updated version.

New or old, the device is, at the least, added color, and at most an indispensable factor. "Southern Nights," as performed by Glen Campbell, is light, lively and pleasing—but the guitar figure certainly contributed to its Number One chart position. "I'm So into You" and "Lonely Boy," both Top 10 recordings, employ instrumental riffs to advantage.

Here are a list of records with built-in background figures. See if you don't remember them with, and in some cases more than, the song itself:

"Baker Street"—*Gerry Rafferty*
"Day Tripper"—*The Beatles (Lennon/McCartney)*
"Gentle on My Mind"—*Glen Campbell (John Hartford)*
"Diamond Girl"—*Seals and Crofts (Seals/Crofts)*
"Bad Blood"—*Neil Sedaka (Sedaka/Cody)*
"Live and Let Die"—*Paul McCartney (McCartney/Eastman)*
"Everybody's Talkin' "—*Nillson (Fred Neil)*
"Boogie Fever"—*The Sylvers (Perrin/St. Lewis)*

Figures come in all shapes and sizes. They may be one note, stabbed home by the brass, as in "Saturday Night in the Park," or consciously cute echoes, like the group answers in "What's New, Pussycat?" They may be disco-funky, as in the 1965 version of "Expressway to Your Heart." Going back a long way, they may be sing-along, as in the early Dean Martin winner "Memories Are Made of This" ("Sweet sweet, the memories you gave to me"). They may employ Chuck Berry's "Memphis" riff, or the Bo Diddley rhythm which accounts for a huge percentage of rock and roll.

Figures are sounds, like "Ba ba ba" in "Barbara Ann," by the Beach Boys, and "Doo wa diddy diddy," in Mannfred Mann's early hit of the same name. Where would pop music be without "Sha la la," "Shooby dooby" or "Yea yea yea?"

The examples are too numerous to list, but no great rock and roll creator has omitted figures from his or her repertoire. The wailing sax in an early Leiber and Stoller composition (the Coasters recording of "Yakety Yak") was effective as rhythm and as satire. Phil Spector's "Till He Kissed Me" (done by the Crystals) and his much later "My Sweet Lord" (done by George Harrison) had the helpful glue of memorable connective notes in common. Realistic producers like Michael Lloyd, Mike Curb, Gamble and Huff, Bob Crewe, Gary Klein, Charlie Calello, Paul Leka, Richard Perry, Jack Gold, Lambert and Potter, Don Davis, Freddie Perrin, Ray Ruff, Billy Sherrill and Vinnie Poncia are always alert to any possibility of using imaginative fills in their work.

THINGS TO REMEMBER

1. Familiarize yourself with as many pop progressions as you can. Buy sheet music and play them down.

2. Write out progressions and compose your own melodies over them.

3. Try to write sequentially in the interest of creating tunes that are instantly singable, logical and memorable.

4. Train your ear to follow sequential patterns every time you listen to music.

5. Practice writing away from your instrument so you don't concentrate on chords at the expense of the melody.

6. Remember Phil Spector's comment "Every rock and roll song can be reduced to four chords."

7. Learn the basic song structures before you experiment with new ones of your own. Whatever structure you use, try to achieve an overall consistency throughout the tune.

8. Make sure you use good prosody—the smooth and comfortable marriage of words and music.

9. Whenever possible, incorporate instrumental and/or vocal figures into your writing. When listening to records, acquire a heightened consciousness of their presence, and you'll start to conceive them automatically as part of your songs.

10. Carry a tape recorder or cassette player with you wherever you go, so you can record ideas as they develop.

11. Analyze what you've done on tape a day or two later, so you can evaluate it objectively.

12. Remember that danceability is still a key factor in pop music.

10

Where Ideas Come from

A common complaint of new lyricists is "I can't get any ideas. I've run dry." The professional writer also experiences this block, and sometimes it leads to uneasiness and even panic. If you're asking yourself, "Have I lost it? Will I ever come up with a great idea again?" you're in a crowded boat. Everyone has been there.

At a time like that, you've got to focus your attention on the people and places around you. The sources of inspiration are endless, and you're probably staring right at them without recognizing their significance.

One of the richest, most fertile areas for dramatic material is human relationships. Before the 1950s, lyrics primarily dealt with love, sad or happy, in general terms, such as "You're Breaking My Heart," or "Love Walked In." Now the field has opened to encompass all problems, and the subjects are characterized in depth. Consider the characters you meet in songs—you see them around you all the time, and the trick is to become aware of them as dramatic material. Some are On Top of the World. Others are Alone Again, Naturally. But behind these generalities, definite universal types can be found. If you're at a carnival, you're likely to run into a Gypsy Woman. You've met the Rich Girl, the snob who depends on her old man's money. Or the girl portrayed in "Love Child," illegitimate, embarrassed by her background, not wanting to inflict that misery on her unborn children.

While you're wondering, "What can I write about?" you might open your mind to problems your friends are having. Take adultery, for instance, which was cautiously treated years ago in "Midnight Confessions" and far more explicitly in "Me and Mrs. Jones." The people you know—maybe even yourself—who are wrestling with this situation may be following the same patterns in broad outline, but the details which individualize their relationships will be different and possibly intriguing in song form.

"D-I-V-O-R-C-E" took a novel approach to divorce, dealing with a mother who spells out the word so her children won't understand what's taking place. You could handle the same topic in a courtroom, or write about a weekend visit during which animosity develops between the estranged couple. There are thousands of ways to handle a potentially explosive subject like this one.

The "swinger" is someone we've all met, whether The Little Town Flirt of the '50s or the more blatant Ruby Tuesday and Honky Tonk Woman. People have many facets, all of which can be dramatically utilized. Vanity is delineated with sardonic brilliance in "You're So Vain." Other characteristics, such as lying (Lyin' Eyes), uncertainty (How Can I Be Sure), alienation (The Sounds of Silence, Nowhere Man) and macho pride (You Don't Mess Around with Jim) can form the basis for an absorbing lyric.

Everything is grist for the creative mill. Titles of movies from the late show can turn your mind on, as *Along Came Jones* turned on the creators of the song with that title. Books, television shows, newscasts, even the want ads (which did actually provide the idea for a Number One record in the early '70s entitled "Want Ads") . . . all of these have the seeds of hit songs sewn into them.

History offers a wealth of material. Lady Godiva found herself on top of the charts. "The Night They Drove Old Dixie Down" painted a colorful picture of the Civil War period, and more contemporary history was touchingly drawn upon in Dion's "Abraham, Martin and John."

Analytical problems are a well that can never run dry. We've all had the experience of noncommunication, punctuated by The Sounds of Silence. We've all fought and tried to reconcile before going to bed, taking the attitude We Can Work It Out. We've all been tormented to a greater or lesser degree, feeling as though we're having our Nineteenth Nervous Breakdown. Somewhere along the way a person has said to us You've Got a Friend when we were troubled and lost.

God can be viewed in numerous ways. He can be My Sweet Lord or he can be the holder of mysterious answers to a question like Why Me, Lord? You can Put Your Hand in the Hand of Jesus, or you can turn to Him with a plea such as Lord, This Time I Need a Mountain.

Nostalgia inspired "The Way We Were" and our own "Old Fashioned Way." Time, in one guise or another, is a subject lyricists have always concentrated on. Maybe you've had a feeling you'd like to Turn Back the Hands of Time or reflected, Funny How Time Slips Away. You've probably felt that flush of excitement, the feeling that it's A Time for Us when a love affair was working out successfully. Looking back to your own past can yield memories that may add up to a meaningful song.

Think of the places you've been or thought about. You could build a love story around one of them, as Randy Edelman did in "Weekend in New England." If you've been in New York during a blizzard, you might have found yourself California Dreaming.

Social conditions provide musical platforms for the culture-conscious writers, whether it be senseless combat (War), crime (In the Ghetto), women's lib (I Am Woman) or civil rights (Blowing in the Wind).

A creative writer even makes use of inanimate objects dramatically. Think of "Wichita Lineman," "Telephone Man," "Stairway to Heaven," "Rain on the Roof" and "Heaven on the Seventh Floor," which directs its conflict around a stalled elevator.

Story songs call upon you to be a musical scriptwriter. This form of musical fiction allows you unlimited imaginative leeway. "Tie a Yellow Ribbon, Honey" and "The Night the Lights Went Out in Georgia" are fully fleshed movies as written. "Harper Valley PTA" and "Ode to Billy Joe" have already made the transition to the big screen, and "Rhinestone Cowboy" and "Hotel California" are being developed by the studios.

Philosophy may provide you with a dramatic springboard. Existentialism inspired "Is That All There Is." The Beatles turned to Indian philosophy for many of their songs.

COMMON DENOMINATORS
FROM GENERATION TO GENERATION

As you see, there is virtually no theme a writer can't tackle today, no problem, political or personal, that is considered off limits. Yet if you're still feeling confused and overwhelmed by the mass of possibilities, examine these formulas, which are always commercially viable in every decade.

Novelties

"Gilly Gilly Hossenfeffer" appeared in 1949. You might look at that title and roar with laughter, saying, "How silly, how dated," but remember that "Splish Splash," no example of deep subtlety or thought, soared to the top of the charts in 1959 with Bobby Darin. "(Itsy Bitsy Teeny Weeny) Yellow Polka Dot Bikini" was a rage in the '60s, and "Disco Duck" went to Number One in the '70s. Novelties are always in fashion, if they're funny and well written.

Classical Rock

Another genre, the "classical" pop record, had its roots back in the '40s when Chopin collaborated with Buddy Kaye and Ted Mossman on "Till the End of Time." Borodin proved a congenial collaborator in the '50s with "This Is My Beloved," and his partners were George Forrest and Robert Wright. "Lovers Concerto" was Number One in the '60s, an interpretation of Bach by the Toys, and in the '70s, Eric Carmen teamed up with Rachmaninoff for "All by Myself" and "Never Gonna Fall in Love Again."

Girls' Names

In 1945 "Laura" was an ethereal, goddesslike creature who made the Hit Parade. "Maybellene" in the '50s was a different matter, exciting and sexual, a startling rhythm and blues departure from her wistful predecessor. "Venus" (the '60s) was your girl next door in blue jeans, the apple-pie Doris Day prototype that Frankie Avalon, Paul Anka and the rest of the beach-rock heroes of that time sang to. "Maggie May," in the more liberated '70s, was the aging older woman who kept Rod Stewart from returning to school.

Travel Songs

Travel has always been a particularly seductive prospect for songwriters. Warren and Mercer wrote the joyful "Atchison, Topeka and the Santa Fe" in the mid-'40s, and it won an Oscar. Rick Nelson, with a composing assist from Jerry Fuller, was a "Traveling Man" in the '50s, and John Denver sadly contemplated "Leavin' on a Jet Plane" in the '60s. Elton John went farther afield with "Rocket Man" in the early '70s.

Inspiration

Loneliness is universal and has existed since the beginning of civilization. Songs can provide comfort and hope, and give people faith in a better tomorrow. "You'll Never Walk Alone" in the '40s offered that inspiring message, as did "I Believe" in the '50s. "Bridge over Troubled Water" is the major inspirational song of the '70s. If you can write a stirring inspirational song, it has a strong chance of becoming a standard.

From Swing to Disco

Danceability has always been a powerful factor in pop music. "Chattanooga Choo Choo" in the '40s (successfully revived in the '70s) gave way to 1955's "Rock Around the Clock," that early rock and roll classic which single-handedly ushered in a new era. "The Loco-Motion" and "Barefootin' " were more illustrations of this genre in the '60s, and in the '70s we've all had a case of "Boogie Fever."

Humor

Songs with a humorous, tongue-in-cheek approach to life are always welcome. The '40s brought "Smoke, Smoke, Smoke That Cigarette," and the '50s offered "Purple People Eater" and "The Thing" to laugh at. Ray Stevens perked up the anxious '60s with his hilarious "Gitarzan," and the '70s have been brightened by Randy Newman's "Short People" and Steve Martin's "King Tut."

Unrequited Love

Unrequited love and loneliness is a cross-generation favorite. Just a few examples: "Laughing on the Outside, Crying on the Inside" in the '40s, "Crying in the Chapel" in the '50s, and "Breaking Up Is Hard to Do," which struck with equal impact in the '60s and '70s.

No one can deny that words and music have progressed to a notable degree. The effect of rhythm and blues, with its raw, down-to-earth realism, toppled the timid and proper approach that dominated middle-of-the-road white music. But the heart of popular music is filled with common denominators, because so many basic hungers, fears and fantasies remain the same. Analyzing other songs through the years and observing their similarities is one way to acquaint yourself with the unchanging needs and passions that people have, and that knowledge can be used in your writing.

SENSING THE SOCIAL CLIMATE

There are three kinds of songwriters. There are the ones who stubbornly insist on remaining in the past, seeing life in a dated light. Nobody would be interested if the red red robin came bob bob bobbin' along today. Cupid is more than stupid—he's a serious consideration, both psychologically and sexually. The terms are obsolete, because social conditions have altered.

As a writer today you couldn't extol the virtues of acid, no matter how imaginatively you handled the topic. You couldn't romanticize the flower children in Haight-Ashbury, because Haight-Ashbury is now a deadly slum. That's where the writer's instinct comes in. He knows, he feels what the public needs, and what it will respond to.

There's a second kind of writer, one who does listen, who follows the newspapers and turns on the *Eleven O'Clock News*. He keeps himself informed and tries to reflect what he sees in his work. If he has talent and a commercial sense, he'll always make some sort of showing on the charts.

The third kind—a Dylan, a Lennon and McCartney—is much rarer. Writers of this magnitude are the trend-setters, the trailblazers. Very few of them come along, but when they do they totally transform the face of pop music. They try to analyze where the country is going, or where relationships are headed. They don't merely report and keep aware: they anticipate, they watch for signs of a changing social climate. When they peruse a newspaper, they look between the lines, never accepting what they see at face value. They get angry about what they sense is coming and issue warnings, or they voice excited approval.

There hasn't been a clear-cut leader, a new musical messiah, a spokesman for this generation. If you keep up with the times, watch the winds for signs of change and take strong positions about them, it could be you. In any case, you've got to swim with the tide even if you don't change its course. If you do that, you'll have a steady and enduring future as a songwriter.

BE ECLECTIC

Sometimes a composer finds a few ideas that work for him, and rather than reaching out for fresh ones, he reworks those ideas over and over again. Even if this brings commercial recognition, it's doing yourself a creative injustice. Don't decide, "I'm a such-and-such kind of writer" and avoid trying anything new. That's only settling for security and putting a lid over unused potential.

When Joel and I had a couple of hits with Ronnie Dove and the Peppermint Rainbow, we were told, "This is your forte. You're good middle-of-the-road writers." Not happy with the label, we wrote a rhythm and blues single for the Chambers Brothers, "Wake Up." A television producer at the time said, "Your specialty is Top 40." Resisting the limitation, we created a television show for Zero Mostel with zany special material. Somebody commented that we were really "hip" writers, that our strong suit was satire. This led us to come up with "Stay and Love Me All Summer" for Brian Hyland. Inevitably it was declared, "Their bag is bubble gum." Thinking we could lay that to rest once and for all, we entered into a collaboration with Charles Aznavour and provided lyrics for many of the songs included on his concert tours. It was artistically satisfying, but the labeling continued.

There's a tendency to typecast, to pigeonhole you once you've done something in a certain musical style or handled a certain lyrical theme. People love to categorize. They'll try to place you in a niche if you let them, but you have to fight back. Many of our moves were made with caution, and it's true there are times, if you wade in over your head, when you'll be confronted with failure. But if you play it safe the odds, unfortunately, don't improve. Some of our experiments haven't been successful, but others have, and these have given us immeasurable satisfaction. The eclectic writer never stagnates. There's always a new challenge, and in attempting that challenge, you'll surprise yourself constantly with how much you can do.

THINGS TO REMEMBER

1. Some ways of finding ideas are through
a. Studying people;
b. Dealing with personal problems like marriage, divorce, adultery;
c. Reading books, watching television shows and newscasts;
d. Writing about historical characters;
e. Thinking of analytical problems, such as loneliness and lack of communication;
f. Basing your story on God or religion;

g. Nostalgia;

h. Places you've been to or read about;

i. Social conditions;

j. Inanimate objects;

k. Story songs, musical melodramas like "Ode to Billy Joe";

l. Philosophy.

2. Certain types of material are commercially strong in every generation: novelties, classical pop, girls' names, travel songs, inspirational songs, dance records, social stances, humor and tales of unrequited love.

3. Deal with social conditions in a way that is relevant and up to date, in current terms.

4. Don't stick to a few tried-and-true ideas for security. Take chances and experiment.

5. Don't decide in advance, "I'm a such-and-such kind of writer," which puts a lid on your potential. Be eclectic.

6. Resist people who try to typecast you.

11

Sex—A Stick of Dynamite

In the early days of our partnership, Joel and I wrote two songs entitled "I Almost Loved You Last Night" and "I'll Wait till You're Ready." We took them to a publisher and he smiled approvingly, congratulating us on our careful, discreet approach. "Remember," he cautioned, "sex should always be handled with good taste. The trick is to be indirect."

We thought of him the other day while driving, as indirect lines such as "I like to do it with you" and "Move it in, move it out" thundered from the car radio. In the era of *Deep Throat,* a timid, conservative attitude toward sex is outmoded.

And yet the majority of successful sex songs today are not simply graphic descriptions of intercourse. Granted, a title like "Keep It Comin', Love, Don't Let the Well Run Dry" leaves no room for confusion, but the clever commercial writer generally dresses up his message. He'll treat it tongue in cheek, or look at it from an off-center point of view. He'll use his writer's imagination to bring more to a lyric than the raunchy facts.

CURVE THROWING

One popular method of putting across sexually explicit material is curve throwing. A perfect example of this is the chart smash "I'm So In to You," by the Atlanta Rhythm Section. Right away the title makes you visualize two people in bed, and the fact that the lead singer is male completes the physical image the listener gets. Then, just as you shake your head in amazement that material like this ever got on the air, the verse concludes with "Hopin' you'll get in to me." The meaning has been altered. Suddenly it's her *psyche* he wants to get into, and the line becomes harmless.

But not really harmless. The point has been made, and it has nothing to do with emotional communication and the durability of a relationship. Peter Frampton's "I'm in You (You're in Me)" used curve throwing the same way a month later.

"Disco Baby" assaults the ear with "Move it in, move it out, disco baby." It's a safe bet nobody hears the "disco baby" that's tacked on. Joel and I recently heard this song performed at an L.A. nightclub, and the audience cheered raucously, singing along with the lines. The artist gasped out every syllable with orgasmic intensity, and the atmosphere became more heated than that of a massage parlor. Everyone accepted the "disco baby" as a put-on and enjoyed the manner in which the writer was spoofing sex. Dance is often used as a vehicle to project animal sexuality. "I Like to Do It with You (Boogie All Night Long)" is a perfect example.

WINDOW DRESSING

Window dressing is another way of getting across explicit material in a manner that will pass by radio programmers and other voices of morality. Consider the Lennon and McCartney "Come Together." If you ask a person unfamiliar with the song what it means, you're bound to get a broad grin. If you ask those who have heard or read it, a dozen interpretations will be offered. The key phrase is surrounded by ambiguity, but again, the message has been understood perfectly by millions of people who never bother to study the implications of a lyric. They just sing along with the catchy, suggestive hook and accept that as the sum total and meaning of the record.

Ned Doheny carries the principle of poetic lyrics and pornographic titles to its ultimate with "Get It Up for Love." When the song was done at a rock concert, the mention of that title created a small riot, and the performer felt compelled to explain that it wasn't what it seemed, that it wasn't a dirty song. The lyric uses such window-dressing phrases as "love's shadow" and "the river runs cold." It talks of heaven and shooting stars. But it was no accident that these words were chosen, and the writer had to be aware that the ear of the public would pick them up in a certain way.

A similar case is "Easy Comin' Out, Hard Goin' In," which deals with an emotional problem. The hero, we're told, has slipped out to meet a girl and now has to face a guilty conscience upon arriving home. This is a definitive example of projecting one thing and meaning another.

Joel and I employed window dressing in a song of our own entitled "Sleeping Between Two People," which was recorded by Vicki Carr. A sample of the lyric:

> When he lies next to her
> Can he be cold
> Or does he hold her
>
> All I have is his word
> That he turns away
> Has he really told her?
> I'm not there in his bed
> I can only imagine what's being said
>
> Unless you're sleeping between two people
> You never know what they feel
> Sleeping between two people
> Is the only way to ever know what's real

Heard as a whole, the content is adult but relatively tame in the frank '70s. But the title "Sleeping Between Two People" automatically suggests a ménage à trois, uninhibited sexuality and orgies, and no amount of window dressing erases that automatic reaction.

ADULT THEMES

Adult themes used to be handled by implication. Now, if the treatment is sensitive, they can be spelled out. "Torn Between Two Lovers" dramatizes the plight of a woman forced to choose between two men she cares for equally. In the early '60s, the Mary Wells record "Two Lovers" dealt with the same conflict, but at the end, the men she had described turned out to be contrasting aspects of the same person! "Torn Between Two Lovers" doesn't duck its premise, nor does it pretend to be discussing a conflict of the heart. The woman is evidently sleeping with both men and enjoying it, making her decision a deeply complicated one.

Any subject is open to today's writer. Rod Stewart's "The Killing of Georgie" is a stark and honest study of a homosexual. It was a breakthrough record, the first totally direct and detailed record on this theme to be played on Top 40 radio. The uncompromising opening phrase, "Georgie was gay, I guess," leads into a grim account of three New Jersey punks who pull a knife on Georgie and kill him. The subject matter wasn't exploited or sensationalized; it was treated sensitively and sympathetically. That's why no charges were leveled against it as a "dirty song."

Jim Stafford's "My Girl Bill" goes about homosexuality a little differently. It's a spoof treatment, comically evading the issue it raises by making the listener believe that "my girl Bill" is the singer's gay lover, then introducing a twist about two friends fighting over the same woman. No doubt this twist made it possible at the time to get the record played. "The Killing of Georgie" makes future evasion of that kind unnecessary.

Rock has become an androgynous world, where sexual identities overlap. The first clear indication of this came with Jim Morrison and

Janis Joplin. Dr. Charles Winick, Ph.D., wrote at the time in *Medical Aspects of Human Sexuality:* "Both [Morrison and Joplin] convey a curiously degenderized sex. Morrison looks like a very attractive girl, and Miss Joplin looks masculine and vaguely recalls baseball player Babe Ruth. In some ways, both are like Judy Garland and Marlene Dietrich in exuding a very real but neuter and ageless sexuality."

From there it was only a short step to Mick Jagger and David Bowie, the foremost symbols of androgyny today; Bette Midler singing in an all-male cabaret; and Elton John, who has officially declared his bisexuality to the press. This state of affairs is why most of the current records can be sung by either men or women, and why you as a writer are in better commercial shape if you don't confine the lyrics of your songs to one sex.

AN "X" RATING IS NOT ENOUGH

Sometimes sex is blatantly handled. "Body Heat" never attempts to be anything other than what it is. Neither does "Finger Fever." "It's Ecstasy When You Lay Down Next to Me" hews to its main point. This kind of straightforward approach works excitingly well with a pulsating beat. The aim of a rhythmic sex record isn't to instruct or analyze or enlighten—it's the musical equivalent of a stag movie, and must turn on the dancers (or lovers) listening to it, or it has failed to accomplish its objective.

As with any other subject, a little imagination and some fresh imagery can make sex come alive more vividly than spelling out each shuddering gasp in X-rated detail. What is delineated too specifically can become boring. It's easy to settle for obvious, clinical descriptions, but actions aren't enough to get a listener involved. In bed or out, people should be individualized, or else they remain faceless bodies going through motions. Songwriting is still about people, no matter what intimate situations are being dealt with, and people have a million different reasons for making love, choosing particular partners, leaning toward certain avenues of satisfaction.

Rod Stewart's "Georgie" is a richly textured and recognizable human being. So is the woman in "Torn Between Two Lovers" or, going back, Aretha Franklin's "Natural Woman." The only difference between the '70s and earlier decades is the degree of frankness allowed in writing about their drives. Today's songwriter has been given a stick of dynamite, and the more creatively and responsibly he handles it, the more his career will benefit.

THINGS TO REMEMBER

1. Treat sexuality with imagination. Some ways of doing this are:
a. Curve throwing—implying sexually explicit things and then altering the meaning cleverly at the last minute;
b. Window dressing—choosing titles that fix sensual images firmly in the listener's mind (e.g., "Come Together") and then treating them in a safer, more conservative way;
c. Spoofing the subject, as in Jim Stafford's "My Girl Bill."
2. Feel free to deal with adult themes, such as adultery, homosexuality.
3. Bring flesh-and-blood characterization to your sexual songs, rather than just providing X-rated musical stag movies. Being too specific can become clinical and boring. Bring the people in these intimate situations alive.

12

Writing for Albums

There are few achievements as gratifying as a hit record. Calling the trades and hearing, "Yes, that's Number 10 with a bullet" creates a special shock wave of excitement impossible to explain to someone who hasn't experienced it. But chart fever shouldn't become such an obsession that it becomes the writer's only focus. It's not artistically healthy to concentrate only on the singles market. There are times when your imagination demands wide, unsupervised freedom.

On a realistic level, there are albums to be filled, and in the words of producer Tom Catalano (responsible for dozens of gold records for Neil Diamond and Helen Reddy), "Nothing would be more boring than to have twelve single-oriented tracks in an album." He's right. An album demands pace and variety. It should be a total experience, with many shadings that result in cumulative emotional impact.

A look at the songs of consistent hitmakers bears this out. Paul Williams wrote "Out in the Country" and "Rainy Days and Mondays," but his albums include the sensitive "Let Me Be the One" and "Waking Up Alone," which were not geared for Top 40 play. Paul Simon, the most eclectic composer of them all, intersperses rockers like "Koda-chrome" with the haunting "America" and the dynamic "Richard

Corey," the latter a relatively uncommercial drama of a wealthy man's discontent and suicide.

Good non–Top 40–oriented songs fall into many categories. One is the "performance" song, as exemplified by Charles Aznavour's bittersweet "Happy Anniversary" or "What Makes a Man a Man." And this title brings to mind another point. When it was written, the subject matter, a day in the life of a homosexual, was too raw for rock or middle-of-the-road (MOR) stations. Yet Aznavour didn't say to himself, "It won't get on *Billboard* or *Cash Box*—I won't bother with it—I'll pay attention to something that might mean more performance royalties from ASCAP or BMI." It was a song he obviously felt strongly about, and he allowed himself the emotional satisfaction of writing it. This song could conceivably become more important than many fleetingly popular chart hits, but even if it didn't, a writer can't always censor himself because of practical considerations. He should dive in, with the knowledge that albums can encompass a greater range of subjects than singles can.

NO TIME RESTRICTIONS

Singles have to be short. A more-than-three-minute record is almost taboo on a Top 40 playlist. Yet there are times when you, as a writer, will resent being hemmed in by such rigid time requirements. "Lover's Lullaby," written by Janis Ian for her *Between the Lines* LP, is over five minutes. So is "Gold Dust Woman," by Stevie Nicks, as performed by Fleetwood Mac.

Barry Manilow, renowned as the interpreter of "Mandy" and "I Write the Songs," stretches out creatively in his album choices. "Sandra" is overlength in singles terms (4:35), but in its crystal-clear delineation of a dissatisfied housewife who "accidentally" cuts her wrist, it adds to his stature as a performer and dramatist of human frailties.

FOR THE OVER-30s

Singles are geared for a young public, roughly between 10 and 25 years old. Therefore, a writer who wants to reach adult audiences can't concentrate only on that area.

"Tapestry," by Carole King, is just as well remembered as "It's Too Late." Helen Reddy's "West Wind Circus" lingers in the mind, possibly after "Keep On Singing" and "Leave Me Alone" have faded out. Neil Diamond's "Brooklyn Roads" is a penetrating self-portrait, much closer to the soul of the author than "Crackling Rosie." And Jimmy Webb's "Tunesmith" captured the conflict of a traveling troubadour to perfection.

An important point to remember is that artists, although they want and need their single successes, also have an aesthetic side of their nature they long to fulfill. They care about communicating universally, and try to make sure that their material says something beyond the straight-ahead sentiments of love and breaking up. Otherwise Barbra Streisand wouldn't have recorded "Have I Stayed Too Long at the Fair," or the stylized, slowed-down "Happy Days Are Here Again," which obviously aren't as market-oriented as, say, the up-tempo and driving "Stoney End."

A favorite tune of many performers is Tom Paxton's "The Last Thing on My Mind," beautifully realized by José Feliciano and Neil Diamond, among others. You know, listening to it, that it was deeply felt and not necessarily conceived with Top 40 guidelines in mind. The Elton John/Bernie Taupin "Funeral for a Friend" is a feelingful tribute to Marilyn Monroe, and a long way from "Crocodile Rock."

THE BEST OF BOTH WORLDS

Sometimes personal, unrestricted writing does result in singles popularity as well. "Masquerade," by Leon Russell, became a hit for George

Benson, but its polished, jazz-flavored edge reveals clearly that this was not the composer's prime intention. Personal works such as "My Way" and "I've Gotta Be Me" also scored with the vast buying public. These results supply a strong argument for taking a non–Top 40 approach, but their commercial impact should be regarded as a by-product, not the main objective, when you're stretching your creative muscles.

Hits are the lifeblood of most songwriters, and dismissing their importance can lead, on the other hand, to self-indulgence and discarding of technical disciplines. I'm not suggesting the substitution of one approach for another, only the integration of all sides of your writing nature. Don't program yourself one way and adhere to it forever. Letting loose —remembering that singles are only *one* road in a writer's career—will make you a more well-rounded, fully developed communicator.

WRITING STANDARDS

A standard is a song that remains relevant and appealing from one generation to the next. There are certain elements that appear in every work of lasting quality.

• Standards are *tunes.* They have a basic lyric and melodic core that exists without icing or novelty touches. They are not "records," which grow in the studio out of collaborative effort, which attain popularity through an unusual lick by the drummer, an intriguing vocal part or any other device. Not being dependent on added frills, they can be played by everyone, not just the artists who originally cut them. This includes dance bands, school bands, marching bands, nightclub trios and cocktail pianists. They are generally built on simple chord progressions, and are not overloaded with tricky rhythms and syncopations. This musical simplicity is no small matter, because a standard is a song that can be understood and performed by all age groups. A sing-along tune like Neil Diamond's "Song Sung Blue," for example, is easily learned by young piano students. "Your Cheating Heart," by Hank Williams, poses no problems for the fledgling guitarist.

• Standards are flexible. They can be done in many tempos with equally effective results. "Can't Take My Eyes off You" has been played by dance bands as a ballad, an up-tempo swing song and a cha cha. "For Once in My Life," originally popularized as a ballad by Tony Bennett, became a disco hit for Stevie Wonder years later.

• The lyrics of a standard must be universal in content. "You and Me Against the World" is eloquent proof of that. Is there anyone alive who hasn't linked arms with another human being for emotional protection against adversity? "Games People Play," Joe South's country-pop standard, zeros in on the mind-bending psychological manipulations and hypocrisies that poison relationships. "I Believe in Music" spotlights the sunny sides of our natures, reflecting our need to struggle and win out over depression.

• Standards are perennials. They deal with holidays ("White Christmas," "Easter Parade"), vacations ("Those Lazy, Hazy, Crazy Days of Summer"), seasons ("Autumn Leaves") and significant personal events ("Graduation Day").

• Standards don't need Top 40 groups to launch them. Jack Jones and Vicki Carr don't appear regularly on the Top 100, but they can give a song lasting importance. Frank Sinatra hasn't dominated the Top 10 recently, but "Bein' Green" (Joe Raposo's theme from *Sesame Street*) and "I Believe I'm Gonna Love You" gained permanent distinction when he recorded them. Don't just say, "I want the Eagles and the Bee Gees!" Ray Conniff or Ferrante and Teicher might mean just as much in the long run.

THINGS TO REMEMBER

1. Don't limit yourself to the singles market. Write for albums, where you can stretch out creatively.

2. Think in terms of lasting standards, not just of momentary hits. Remember that standards

a. are relatively simple musically;

b. should be easy for dance bands, marching bands, school bands, choirs and cocktail pianists to play;

c. have across-the-board emotional appeal;

d. should adapt to many tempos;

e. deal with perennial themes—seasons, holidays, graduations, birthdays.

3. Don't only go after the "now" artist. People like Frank Sinatra, Vicki Carr and Ray Conniff can make your copyright a standard.

13

Don't Hide Your Personality

Many writers, particularly those just starting out, are afraid to expose themselves completely. They don't want to reveal their weaknesses, their frailties and fears, and this insistence on caution and detachment keeps their writing from being as honest and strong as it could be. Worse, their efforts are useless, because the inner person, the core, cuts through in one way or another.

In our own partnership, certain striking patterns recur again and again. I'm much more decisive than Joel is. I push ahead; he holds back and questions things excessively. The following are a list of titles—some which Joel conceived, others that were my idea. They tell the story.

JOEL

Why Must There Be a Morning After?
We May Never Love like This Again
How Can It Be Another Summer?
Who Am I?
Did She Ask About Me?
If You Only Loved Me
Why Don't You Come to My Party?
If We Can Make It to Monday

AL

There's Got to Be a Morning After (I changed it.)
That's the Way I Like It
Don't Let Me Catch You in His Arms
Run to Me
I Won't Take No for an Answer
I Worship You, Baby
Don't Come Crying to Me
Let's Dance Now

There are times I say to Joel, "Be more aggressive," or he tells me the opposite, but it never works. It would probably hurt the overall balance of our team if we tried to deny our instinctive reactions when they developed.

Other writers deal with who they are. Johnny Cash isn't afraid to reveal the hardships of his background in song—working in cotton fields, hauling two five-gallon jugs for the work gangs along the Tyronza River. He doesn't gloss over his nights in jail, or his addiction to Dexedrine. His music shows those country roots too. For all his impressive ability, the guts and blood and reality of his work would be lost if he tried to cover up, keep the world away for fear of showing what was inside him.

Joni Mitchell has never attempted to conceal her emotional difficulties with men and the turbulent, often unhappy endings of those relationships. She dealt directly with her broken marriage in "I Had a King." Hank Williams used the country market as a platform to work out his personal devils with "Cold Cold Heart" and "I'm So Lonesome I Could Cry," unconcerned with whether the audience saw him clearly. Jimmy Webb wrestled in full view of the public with his ambivalent need to commit himself to love and be free of it, embodied in such titles as "Where's the Playground, Susie?" "Didn't We?" and "The Worst That Could Happen."

Musically, you shouldn't try to fight natural inclinations, your roots, or else a phoniness will intrude. When a writer falls out of public favor, it's usually because he's no longer himself. You can feel him putting on airs, striving to be something alien to him. This can be true of a worldly person who tries to "get down" and is embarrassing in the attempt, or the earthy individual who gets overly slick and violates what his fans loved him for. In both cases, the listeners don't believe what they're hearing, because they sense what the writer *should* be. They can't always pinpoint the source of their discomfort, but the results are the same—rejection. If Mick Jagger suddenly switched and became a gentle balladeer singing folky odes to nature, chances are he'd lose his following. They want his songs to be angry, rebellious, consistent with his nonconforming personality.

I'm not suggesting that *every* composer write biographies. Even if you're in the middle of a song about a circus clown who's crying, a murderer surrounded by police or a girl singer in an empty club, thoughts will occur to you that strike a personal chord, because all these people have emotions common to your own experience beyond the surface particulars. When you hit those points of identification, don't begin editing automatically for fear that *your* hang-ups, your insecurities will seep through. Let them show.

MUSICAL INFLUENCES

Now and then I run into a writer who announces proudly, "I don't listen to much music. Otherwise I'll be influenced, and I want to be completely original."

Seeking total originality is a commendable trait, but music, like all art, is an ongoing process, a chain of developments linked together. It's not possible to shut out the sounds of the past, but exposing yourself to them doesn't have to threaten your originality. It only gives you the tools to reshape what you hear into your own personal vision.

Eric Carmen, for instance, has written two hits based on Rachmaninoff compositions, "All by Myself" and "Never Gonna Fall in Love

Again." This is only one aspect of Carmen, because he also composed "Hey Deanie" for Shaun Cassidy, which is in the teenybopper mold, but classical music was obviously important to his emotions and background, and he used those feelings in his pop writing.

It's safe to say that Neil Diamond was deeply affected by Latin music, because so many of his tunes, from "Cherry Cherry," for himself, to "Sunday and Me," written for Jay and the Americans, are in the Latin/rock groove. Blood, Sweat and Tears utilized jazz feelings in their songs, and Chicago continued the tradition. Bob Dylan has admitted to being heavily influenced by Woody Guthrie, and Lennon and McCartney acknowledge their debt to Chuck Berry. So does Mick Jagger, who also speaks of the effect that the blues of Muddy Waters and Willie Dixon had on his writing.

The best example of all is Stevie Wonder. Writer John Rockwell said of him, "There was his carnivorous ability to devour diverse influences and put his own stylistic stamp on the results—from the basics of gospel, blues, rhythm and blues and soul to Dylan, the surf sound, jazz, adult white pop and finally to rock, electronic music and African ethnicity."

Burt Bacharach made a statement to me when I was just starting out as a writer in New York. Like all new composers, I was fishing for the "answer," the deep secret that would ensure quick success. His advice: "Don't listen to me. Listen to who I listen to." I came to realize, after pondering the words, that he had a good point. If you want classical feelings, don't listen only to Eric Carmen—buy Rachmaninoff or Beethoven or Stravinsky and familiarize yourself with them. Chicago is great, but your need to learn and absorb jazz might be better served by tuning in to Chuck Corea, Charlie Parker, Miles Davis or Chuck Mangione.

Listening to music is no threat—it only broadens your scope. But don't acquire your musical influences solely through the smoke screen of updated, redefined work, or you'll remain a carbon copy. Even your knowledge of the pop scene shouldn't be confined to records appearing on the Top 100. Learn each musical genre in its *pure* form. Read down the lyrics and play the chords of stone country or stone soul writers, rather than just the songs in which their elements have already been fused by other composers. When you have these genres fixed in your mind and fingers, you'll have the craft to play with them, blend them, as an experienced and professional painter mixes his colors.

THINGS TO REMEMBER

1. Don't try to hide your personality when writing, for fear that your insecurities and hang-ups will show.

2. Absorb as many different musical influences as you can.

3. Don't listen only to pop records—listen to pure country and soul music as well.

14

Writing Country Songs

In country music, certain themes keep recurring. These themes must be treated unpretentiously and honestly. Your job as a country writer will be to dramatize blue-collar problems in a vividly down-to-earth way, rather than romanticizing and falsifying them.

In looking for ideas, you might consider a song that deals with roots and background. Loretta Lynn's "Coal Miner's Daughter" is a good example. She sings about her cabin on a hill in Butcher Holler and talks about her poverty. She recalls a childhood of struggle with eight kids, and yet remembers all this fondly because of the love that was in her home. The other side of the coin is a roots-and-background song that dwells on the negative side of struggle. In Dolly Parton's "In the Good Old Days (When Times Were Bad)," the memories are of hailstorms destroying failing crops, of bleeding, overworked hands and walking miles to school. Another approach is to treat country background with nostalgia, as in "Detroit City," or with pride, as in Merle Haggard's "Okie from Muskogee." The common denominator of these songs is the part that family and upbringing have played in forming the personalities of the characters involved.

The keynote of country songs is reality. Don't make the mistake of writing starry-eyed fantasies. Ray Price's "For the Good Times" is fairly typical: the man singing asks his girl to make believe she loves him one more time—for the good times. Willie Nelson's "Funny How Time Slips Away" has the hero commenting on his girl's new love, remembering when she said the same endearments to him. More often than not, people will stay together in country songs, not out of blind, unseeing devotion, but with a clear realization of the kind of people they are, people with flaws, strengths and a willingness to compromise in the face of reality. Country music hasn't always dealt with sex explicitly, but since Kris Kristofferson's "Help Me Make It Through the Night," physical intimacy can be frankly dealt with. "Behind Closed Doors" is an even more graphic example of sexual honesty.

A popular subject in country music is rambling. Country heroes hop freight trains or hitch to different places. This restlessness invites listener identification, because most of us have had the urge to move on and seek new jobs or new loves, but have been too hemmed in, emotionally or financially, to do anything about it. Jimmie Rodgers stands around the water tank waiting for the train, and Johnny Cash hears the train a-comin' as he exists, trapped, in a prison cell. In both cases, movement and travel are their route to freedom. Roger Miller was "King of the Road" in his hit of the same name, a song that crossed from country to Number One pop because of its appeal.

Cheating is a country conflict that never goes out of style, and offers you a commercial base to build on. Hank Cochran and Glenn Martin wrote "After the Fire Is Gone," and such titles as "Midnight Oil," "Almost Persuaded" and "Slippin' Around" are self-explanatory. Another country staple is the honky-tonk song. The stories in this genre generally deal with a boozy, seedy nightlife in which wild women appear to temporarily ease the loneliness of the men. This honky-tonk type of woman is defined by Shel Silverstein, in "Queen of the Silver Dollar," as an angel whose chariot is the crosstown bus, her scepter a wineglass. Billy Joe Shaver sums it up succinctly in "Honky Tonk Angels" with "For lovable losers, no account boozers And honky tonk heroes like me."

If your mind runs that way, you might attempt a religious song, such as "Amazing Grace" or Hank Williams' "I Saw the Light." Or songs that speak of the hard, sometimes monotonous and unglamorous working-man's life, songs like "Six Days on the Road," by Earl Green and Carl Montgomery, or Tennessee Ernie Ford's "Sixteen Tons," by Merle Travis. Men in songs like these keep their noses to the grindstone. Often they have a multitude of children and a wife to support. "Sixteen Tons" eloquently refers to muscle and blood and skin and bone, the assets most sorely tried in the physically taxing existence of a workingman. Another, angrier approach to this situation is dramatized in "Take This Job and Shove It," by David Allan Coe.

Once you've familiarized yourself with general country subject matter, you should examine the opportunities for poetic expression. It's not lofty, self-conscious poetry, but street poetry, colorful and conversational, belonging to what Nashville publisher Cliffie Stone calls the "trucks, booze and broads" school. In "Five Hundred Miles away from Home," by Bobby Bare and Charlie Williams, the opening line talks of heartbreak but through an everyday analogy, "teardrops fell on Mama's note." This image also *acts out* the sentiment. In "Give My Love to Rose," by Johnny Cash, this same tendency to be visual and street-poetic is beautifully demonstrated.

> I found him by the railroad track this morning
> > *(Natural one-to-one discussion. In addition, an establishing physical setting is shown.)*
> I could see he was nearly dead
> I knelt down beside him and I listened
> > *(Conversational action.)*
> Just to hear the words the dyin' fellow said
>
> He said: They let me out of prison out of Frisco
> For ten long years I paid for what I'd done
> > *(Background filled in.)*
> I was trying to get back to Louisiana
> > *(Sense of place.)*
> To see my Rose, and get to know my son

The conflict is defined and the suspense set up, because we wonder if he'll ever get to Rose and his little boy. The song also shows that country songs are rhymed dialogue.

The majority of hit songs are mini-movies, but none more than country songs. You, as a country writer, must sketch every detail of a scene, so that the listener can *hear* the railroad whistle, *see* the cracked paint on the walls, *smell* the food cooking and *touch* the people.

Country music is sometimes dramatically overstated, and this dramatic overstatement only makes it more effective and poignant. In Merle Haggard's "Jesus Take a Hold," he opens: "Like an ancient Roman empire, The world is doomed to fall." This has life-and-death power. There's nothing timid or ambivalent about it.

If you tend to think in generalities, country lyrics can be a great education. Writing them will force you to be specific. Jesse Winchester's "Mississippi, You're on My Mind" begins: "I think I see a wagon-rutted road—With the weeds growing tall between the tracks." They can also help you to be direct and sincere, especially if you have an inclination to be glib and overly slick. A classic like "I'm So Lonesome I Could Cry" is a reproach to show-offy writing, with its haunting but concise imagery: "Hear that lonesome whippoorwill—He sounds too blue to fly—The midnight train is whining low—I'm so lonesome I could cry." These words, like all good country words, sound firsthand. They never seem as though they were created by a writer, but rather as though they had emerged from the lips of the person singing them, as though they were *his* life story. They are confessions, people opening up their souls, unburdening themselves to friends.

Country music is simple. Even though records in this field are now being "popped" up with strings and lusher productions, the melodies are easy to follow and are built on only a few chords. I IV V is still utilized frequently, and in Johnny Cash's "San Quentin" the chord progression is a simple C G⁷ C C F C F F C G⁷ C. In "Folsom Prison Blues" there are four bars of G before the chord changes—briefly—to a G-diminished chord for color and then goes right back to G and G⁷. It isn't until the ninth bar that we get a C^7 chord, and that is sustained for three more bars before a return to G.

In Joe South's "Walk a Mile in My Shoes" the chords are B (for two measures), C (for two more), $E\flat$ F^7 $B\flat$. "Stand by Your Man," by Tammy Wynette and Billy Sherrill, is also simple, adding a minor chord: A E Bm E^7 A D A B E. "Put Your Hand in the Hand," by Gene MacLellan, which was a country crossover to pop, adds a little more: G D^7 Am D^7 G Dm^7 G^7 C C#dim G D^7 G. Here we see a diminished chord because diminished chords appear frequently in religious music, and the nature of the song is gospel. "Me and Bobby McGee," by Kris Kristofferson and Fred Foster, because it moves rhythmically, is even more sparing chordwise than the songs listed above. It has six bars of C, then eight bars of G^7 and returns to seven bars of C.

To sum up, then, the basic secret of writing a good country lyric is to make it sound as though it sprang spontaneously from the tongue of the speaker. Any trace of overelaborateness will mark it phony. As country words must sound like rhymed dialogue, tunes must come across as a musical equivalent of ordinary speech. It's as if the melody were only an extension of conversation, one more way of talking.

FOLK SONGS

Folk music, a compilation of songs from all parts of the world, has always dramatized the existence of the common man, his adventures, trials and triumphs. The subjects range from workers to criminals, sailors to soldiers, farmers to politicians. The stories can be as diversified as those of "Philadelphia Lawyer," in which a cowboy murders the Philadelphia lawyer making love to his wife, and "Roll down the Line," a song about black convicts slaving away in the mines.

Folk made a huge commercial impact in the early '60s. It exploded initially in Greenwich Village coffeehouses and centered eventually around Gerde's Folk City. Folk City launched an amateur night, called a "hootenanny," and these Monday nights, as well as featuring performers like Dave Van Ronk and Jack Elliott, started Simon and Garfunkel and José Feliciano on their way. It was the era of the Limelighters and the Kingston Trio, of Joan Baez, Eric Weissberg, Peter, Paul and Mary and Bob Dylan.

As the '60s went on, folk music became almost exclusively occupied with protest. It also acquired new characteristics . . . a rock beat ("Turn, Turn, Turn" by Pete Seeger, as done by the Byrds, was one of the earliest folk-rock chart hits) and a touch of oblique poetry, which Bob Dylan contributed in such compositions as "A Hard Rain's a-Gonna Fall." Folk was commercially explosive enough to lead people to suspect it might replace rock and roll, but the arrival of the Beatles signaled an end to its dominance. It still surfaces, though, in rock trappings. "Dust in the Wind," by Kansas, is a notable example.

Folk music written before 1963 has a group of loyal followers. Writing it may not assure you of quick commercial recognition, but it can teach you to be a skilled storyteller and sharpen your facility for characterization. You can meet people like "Casey Jones, the Union Scab" in folk music, or the railroad worker "Paddy, Who Works on the Erie." You can learn the story of "John Brown's Body," which dealt with a man who sacrificed his life to abolish slavery.

As in country, folk is marked by many of the qualities I've been discussing throughout this book—visual imagery, infectious sing-along choruses, arresting first lines that set up story and conflict. The lyrics talk, as though addressing close friends. The guitar-, banjo- or ukulele-oriented melodies are simple, the chords uncomplicated. But the basic ingredient of the genre is having something to say, a strong desire to communicate. This is the quality that links folk, folk blues and folk rock, and why the music, in one way or another, will always be a vehicle in which writers can express the times they live in.

THINGS TO REMEMBER

1. Remember that the keynote of country music is unpretentiousness and honesty.

2. When writing a country song, consider some of these often-used themes:

    a. Roots and background—stories of family victory or struggle;

    b. Rambling—traveling songs;

    c. Adultery;

    d. Religion;

    e. The evils of drinking;

    f. The hardships of a workingman.

3. Remember that country music is full of imagery, but is never lofty—it's "street" poetry.

4. Think of country words as rhymed dialogue.

5. Keep in mind that country songs are mini-movies, story songs about real people.

6. Make sure country melodies are simple and not overloaded with chords. Use logical, repetitive and uncomplicated progressions.

7. Study famous folk songs as a way of sharpening your storytelling skill.

15

Writing Rhythm and Blues

If you want to write R & B (rhythm and blues) music, it's a good idea to remember that rhythm and blues is a term that explains itself. The music is intense and driving, the chords and intervals a combination of blues and gospel. Most of all, it's vital to remember that rhythm and blues is a passionate music. When the heroine and hero are in torment, they gasp with emotion, feelings burning or itching in their hearts. When they feel joy, the joy is earth-shaking. A subtle, emotionless R & B song is a contradiction in terms.

Gospel songs from the church had titles such as "Reach Out for Me, Dear Jesus." If you've heard the Four Tops' "Reach Out for Me," you'll recall that "Dear Jesus" was not part of the song. "Come See About Me" and "Can I Get a Witness" are church-derived titles, with the "Oh, Lord" changed to "Oh, Baby." You might try adapting the titles of spirituals into pop form. For example, "Open the Window, Noah" is a famous gospel song. Dropping the "Noah" and making it "Love" would give the material an altogether different connotation. This applies to music as well—"Standing in the Shadows of Love" has strong echoes of "Joshua Fit the Battle of Jericho." While translating the meanings, you should attempt to retain the vivid, deeply felt emotion of gospel material. Phrases like "Bury me down—but still my soul feels heavenly bound" have power in a religious or secular context.

Sexuality is now a common thread in all pop music, but R & B has always been sexual, and this eroticism may still be more characteristic of soul material than of any other kind. Back in the early '50s "Honey Love" introduced grunts and groans and created a furor about morality from radio programmers, and in "Work with Me, Annie" this eye-opening verse appeared: "Work with me, Annie—Let's get it while the getting is good—Annie, please don't cheat—Gimme all my meat." In other words, they didn't stare into each other's eyes over an ice cream soda. Sexual realism was always primitively, powerfully built into R & B, and you can't be timid and reticent in that area if you want your songs to pack a wallop.

Dance records are an R & B staple. One much-revived classic is "Dancing in the Streets." Other dance records include "The Hustle," "Won't Bump No More (with No Big Fat Woman)" and "Get Down Tonight." There are popular disco dances like the New York Hustle, The Bump, the Reggae and Salsa. Rockers like these are always tied together with vocal or instrumental figures. Another key element is to let the rhythm move unencumbered by a batch of words. In R & B, the singer must have room to wail freely. When writing an R & B record, think in terms of production—the background singers, instrumental solos for sax or brass. On the other hand, don't make your production conception so airtight that there's no room to do anything in the studio. R & B singers and musicians don't want every note spelled out to the last sixteenth. They'll feel things when they get together, and it's your job to give them loose guidelines they can function fluidly in.

Pure animal emotion can be expended in a song like "Do You *Love* Me" by Berry Gordy, Jr. This song amounts to a shout, in which the "love" is screamed by the singer over and over again, while the listeners and dancers follow the rising curve of his desperation and experience the release of his hysterical finish along with him. Both Dave Clark and The Contours, in separate and successful versions of this song, milked the passion inherent in the title line.

R & B, though an outgrowth of blues and gospel chords, isn't limited to them anymore. Motown featured Diana Ross doing "I Hear a Symphony" and "Baby Love," both of which were soul interpretations of classical music. Within a classical framework, the melody can utilize blues intervals, or if not, the background parts can do bluesy answers and harmonies. This is not so much an R & B record as a pop record with R & B flavoring.

You can write a soft soul ballad, of course, but even when you do, remember that the Jackson Five's "I'll Be There" used expressions like "We must bring salvation back," which are church-oriented and larger than life. R & B titles, in common with the best pop and country material, are always colorful and picturesque. In "Quicksand" the hero is sinking deeper and deeper. "Up the Ladder to the Roof" is visual, and so is "Friendship Train." Colloquialisms are often used and slightly altered: "Stop in the Name of Love," for example, or "I Second the Emotion."

Musically, a bass line will be a tremendous plus. Even if you have the most brilliant bass player in the studio, who can be relied on to improvise one on the spot, it's a smart idea to train yourself to *think bass lines* all the time. Whether they are a downward line (extremely popular and commercial) or they move upward, or jump back and forth on two or three chords, they must *move,* and they can't be too busy. The aforementioned ballad "I'll Be There" is built on a downward bass line. And once you've chosen your chord movement, repeat it. Build as much melody as you can over the bass pattern you've chosen (within reason), but keep that figure going. You can switch from the bass to the guitar or piano, giving everyone a turn up at bat.

Pop R & B lyrics are frequently clever. In "My Baby Must Be a Magician," the title provides for a stream of images, with metaphors like rabbits in a hat or pigeons up a sleeve flowing naturally from the thought. R & B subject matter is virtually limitless, as long as it has the required blues flavor and feeling. In "Love Child," the heroine was illegitimate and worrying about becoming pregnant and inflicting her childhood misery on her unborn baby. R & B songs deal with identity ("A Place in the Sun"), romantic despair ("I Wish It Would Rain"), hope ("Someday

We'll Be Together"), the instability of the home ("Daddy Was a Rolling Stone"), the solidity of the home ("Grandma's Hands"), hostility, whether social ("What's Going On?") or personal ("Don't Mess with Bill," "Don't Say Nothin' Bad About My Baby").

Writing R & B may seem deceptively easy. "After all," newcomers say, "it's just a beat and a few flatted thirds and fifths, with maybe a diminished chord here and there." If you're under that delusion, your first step would be to listen to certain artists who shaped the music, artists such as Sam Cooke (who popularized gospel nationally, after an early period of confining his singing to the church) and Chuck Berry. Berry is worth studying in detail. Not only does he demonstrate the power of rhythm, but his lyrics are among the best written in any medium, and may be the greatest R & B lyrics of all time. He's a master at characterization ("Johnny B. Goode," "Maybellene" or "Sweet Little Sixteen"). His rhymes are fresh and his imagery ("I Got the Rockin' Pneumonia, I Need a Shot of Rhythm and Blues") unique. Others: Jackie Wilson, Curtis Mayfield and the Impressions, Otis Redding, Muddy Waters, James Brown, Ray Charles, Solomon Burke, Joe Tex, Marvin Gaye, The Miracles, The Temptations, Stevie Wonder, Aretha Franklin, Gladys Knight and the Pips, Diana Ross, B. B. King, the Spinners, the O'Jays, Harold Melvin and the Blue Notes and Al Green. Then there are the blues-oriented white performers such as the Rolling Stones, Joe Cocker, Elvis Costello and Bob Seger. These artists represent a cross section of R & B, through different periods and different styles, and should attune your ear to the requirements of R & B composing.

GOSPEL

Apart from pop R & B charts, gospel music has its separate listing in *Billboard*. Many of these rousing songs sound like contemporary soul, except that the lyric content is spiritual rather than romantic.

Gospel publisher J. Aaron Brown has said in *Songwriter* magazine that a gospel song today needs a strong message and must be scripturally sound. It must also be a sincere love song for Jesus Christ, thanking him for what he has done in your life. In addition to sincerity and passion, gospel writing is blazingly dramatic. Phrases like "the light of God," "lightning flashes," "cold icy hands" and "the blood came trickling down" can be found throughout gospel material.

There is relatively little market for gospel singles, but gospel albums that succeed will sell in excess of forty thousand copies. Many sell more than that, and some have reached beyond the three-quarters-of-a-million mark.

Gospel has changed considerably in the past decade. Andrae Crouch, gospel Grammy Award winner, supplies his audiences with Motown soul. The Imperials, the Oak Ridge Boys and The Stamps work in Las Vegas nightclubs. Other opportunities for gospel records can come from secular entertainers, who perform this kind of music but don't limit themselves to it. Born-again Christian B. J. Thomas, Pat Boone, Skeeter Davis and Anita Bryant fall into this category.

A commercially viable way of approaching gospel music is to write a pop song that straddles the fence and can be read as both an interpersonal love song and a religious one. "Put Your Hand in the Hand," "You Light Up My Life" and "I Don't Know How to Love Him" are Top 10 singles that can be interpreted either way.

The religious-music field is not, however, a market for the young writer who wants to make an overnight fortune, or soar to the top of the charts. To write it, the spiritual fervor must be genuinely felt. Gospel composers don't "write for a date." Their private relationship to God and the church is strong, binding and integral to their personalities. Andrae Crouch recently visited Soledad Prison, warned in advance by an inmate that "someone might stick you." One by one, Crouch and his disciples managed to reach the hostile prisoners, and soon everyone was singing, caught in the electric message and the beat of the music. If the performers hadn't felt and believed the message they were conveying, their audience wouldn't have reacted as they did, and you, in writing gospel songs, must feel that same passion.

If you're interested in gospel, and feel artistically and emotionally equipped to be part of the field, some of the key labels to familiarize yourself with include Word, Nashboro, Jewel, Peacock, Ranwood, Light, Glori, Birthright, Savoy and the major secular labels, which have separate gospel branches as well.

THINGS TO REMEMBER

1. Remember that rhythm and blues is a passionate music, intense and driving.

2. Try taking gospel titles and rewriting them with personal romantic meanings.

3. When writing sexual R & B songs, let them be primitive, erotic.

4. Make sure they have good, strong dance beats.

5. Check to see that your titles, even on ballads, are larger than life.

6. Concentrate on finding an exciting bass line to build your tune over. Make sure your tune moves.

7. Keep in mind that R & B subject matter is limitless, ranging from illegitimacy ("Love Child") to family pride and love ("Grandma's Hands").

8. Listen to all the great blues, gospel and R & B singers and writers.

9. Gospel songs should be scripturally sound, have a strong message and convey a blazingly powerful feeling for Jesus Christ.

10. A way of having a Top 40 gospel hit is to write a lyric that can be read as both spiritual and romantic, such as "You Light Up My Life."

16

Writing for Movies

In the 1930s and '40s, songwriting was a separate and clearly defined specialty. Writers such as Sammy Cahn, Harry Warren, Johnny Mercer and Harold Arlen created the songs, and Max Steiner, Erich Korngold, Franz Waxman, Bernard Herrmann and Alex North, among many others, turned out the background scores. Occasionally these two creative functions would overlap. Alfred Newman's exquisite melodic sense resulted in such popular hits as "Anastasia" and "The Best of Everything," and David Raksin made history with his classic "Laura," but by and large there was a clear division. The beloved tunes from MGM musicals, the Astaire/Rogers series and the 20th Century–Fox Betty Grable/Alice Faye vehicles originated from the pens of Kern, Gershwin, Berlin, Harburg, Styne, Porter, Rodgers and Hammerstein, Livingston and Evans, and so on.

The division began to blur when versatile composers such as Henry Mancini, Dimitri Tiomkin and Victor Young demonstrated an ability to consistently wear two hats—to write hits and do an equally fine job with background music and orchestration. These men helped to usher in the era of the scorer/songwriter. Producers began to assume that the man who could write arrangements and conduct large orchestras could dash off something as short and seemingly simple as a tune without effort. Because of this, the free-lance film songwriter found himself replaced, far less in demand than his counterparts twenty years before.

The gate may be closed, but it's not locked. If you have the ability, a logical course to pursue would be the study of orchestration and conducting. Another is to compile a catalogue of commercial hits. Working in television and the theater offers artistic and practical training.

A composer must bring his songs to the attention of producers. Marvin Hamlisch performs at parties and exposes his material. Harry Warren is on record as saying that he felt people didn't know him because of his reluctance to attend social gatherings. As a result, almost no one connected him personally to his endless gallery of standards (e.g., "You'll Never Know," "I Only Have Eyes for You," "The More I See You"). Since scorers are generally determined to do the title songs of the movies they work on (making it a stipulation in their contracts if possible), it's evident that the producer must be a fan, so that he is willing to fight for an independent writer.

You should assemble a tape of your best material and send it around to the active producers in town. Heads of studio music departments must also be included on your mailing list, as well as the men who run the studio publishing divisions. The tape should spotlight a variety of moods to underline your versatility. Make sure a biography is enclosed.

Film music agents concentrate on scorers as a rule, but a few will add a songwriter's name to their roster. Some agents based in Los Angeles who fall into this category are Marc Newman, Al Bart and Carol Faith.

Buy the trades every day without fail. *The Hollywood Reporter* and *Daily Variety* are the bibles of the movie business. They both feature detailed pages which list the properties that have been purchased, which are going into production and which have already started their shooting schedule.

Set your sights on the young, independent moviemaker whose pictures don't have a high budget and can't accommodate the salary of a Mancini, a Jerry Goldsmith or a John Williams.

Joel and I, recognizing that our first film assignment would not be *Gone with the Wind* or *Star Wars,* aimed at something more modest as a jumping-off point: *Gidget Goes to Rome,* the last and worst episode of that series. Another early venture, *The Fat Spy,* starred Jayne Mansfield and Jack E. Leonard. Amid the chaotic mediocrity of the script and the nonexistent direction, we tried to insert songs that would advance the story. (Twelve of them—the producer tried to use us to plug the gaps!) For our efforts, we "opened" and closed at a drive-in in the Pocono Mountains, on a *triple bill.* We were surrounded by a forest, and I recall thinking that even the bears lurking around were justified in beating a fast retreat from this fiasco.

Still, we were learning, and in another of our early credits, *Who Killed Teddy Bear,* we tried to write songs that gave dimension to the characters. However, this semipornographic yarn about a psychotic sex maniac opened to uniformly terrible reviews (one critic *did* say the music was superior to the screenplay—no accomplishment), and ended its career at a 42nd Street theater with *Girls in Chains.*

In addition to gaining experience through low-budget vehicles, it's sometimes worth taking the trouble to sit down "on spec" (in other words, without pay) and write a song for a movie. Joel and I composed a tune entitled "Your Time Hasn't Come Yet, Baby" for an Elvis Presley yarn, *Speedway,* sent it out and promptly forgot it, expecting rejection. What a wonderful surprise it was, a year later, to pick up *Cash Box* while munching on a cheeseburger at Howard Johnson's and see a full-page ad featuring Elvis' picture. Underneath the photo was an announcement of his latest single, *our* song, "Your Time Hasn't Come Yet, Baby." We felt very proud, because the song worked in the movie as an integrated piece of material, yet possessed enough universal appeal to merit lifting it from the film. Joel was stunned. He hadn't even wanted to try, because

Elvis had appeared to be completely unattainable, too great an idol for ordinary human beings to reach, especially ones from the Bronx and Brooklyn. The lesson, of course, is to try for everything, whenever there's the remotest chance of succeeding. You can never know which doors will open. Often the best results stem from the least-expected sources.

Another time we gambled with even less guarantee of results, and it was the turning point of our career. A renowned professional manager and personal friend, Happy Goday, mentioned to us that 20th Century–Fox was having difficulty finding a song for one of its upcoming productions, *The Poseidon Adventure*. Every composer in Hollywood had submitted material and been turned down by producer Irwin Allen. Even I, as the more optimistic member of our team, told Happy it was pointless. We hadn't been in Hollywood very long, we hadn't read the script, they resented people who came from the record business, etc., etc. "What can you lose?" Happy said. So we met with 20th music head Lionel Newman, director Ronald Neame and Irwin Allen. They gave us a script and said, "Go home, write something and come back with it at nine tomorrow."

"They're just humoring us," Joel complained, as we sat up all night, composing and gulping down black coffee. It was like a takeoff on an old MGM musical. Next day, bleary-eyed, barely remembering what we'd written, we stumbled into Lionel Newman's office and played "The Morning After." Irwin Allen mumbled something about not being sure, and Joel was gathering up our music when Ronald Neame, in his low-key British way, made the pronouncement that changed our lives: "I believe it has something."

The next thing we knew, the song was being recorded, but not until we actually showed up on the set and watched it being integrated with the film did we believe our good fortune. Needless to say, when we won an Oscar, we were in catatonic shock. Joel's hands sweated so much that they melted the gold plating off the Oscar—an Academy first!

If you're a lyricist, try to meet scorers, since collaboration with them is a direct route to movie songwriting. Such talented lyric writers as Alan and Marilyn Bergman, Norman Gimbel and Don Black have had repeated triumphs with, respectively, Michel Legrand, Charles Fox and John Barry.

Get to know people in filmmaking beyond producers: actors, directors, screenwriters. The more members of the industry you can meet, the better chance your name has of circulating and reaching the right ears.

DON'T TELL THE WHOLE STORY

The greatest piece of advice I ever received was from Johnny Mercer. In 1958 my brother, Lawrence Kasha, was stage-managing *Li'l Abner* on Broadway. At the closing-night party I wandered around, somewhat in awe as younger brothers are apt to be. Mr. Mercer got up on stage and sang a list of his classics with a three-piece band, and when he finished, to overwhelming applause, I got up the nerve to go over and confide to him, "I want to write for movies too." He put his arm around my shoulder, and his warmth gave me confidence. "Have you written any songs?" he asked. I told him I had composed a few rock and roll hits, and he shook his head thoughtfully. "Just keep this in mind," he said. "When you *do* write a song for a movie, don't tell the story. Tell the *feelings,* the philosophy behind the action."

I never forgot his kindness or his invaluable advice. A major—perhaps *the* major—mistake of composers writing for films is their tendency to tell the entire story in detail. However, the script is already taking care of that, and if the song is placed at the beginning of the picture, you'll be revealing all the surprises and diminishing the suspense; if it's over the ending credits, you'll be reiterating what the audience already knows. The crucial thing is to embellish the mood and express the overall philosophy in general terms.

It's often possible to write a hit song for a movie without losing the flavor and meaning of the film, but you must have certain things going for you. Cumbersome titles such as "Magnificent Obsession," "The Brave Bulls," "Death of a Salesman," "Breaking the Sound Barrier" and "Mr. Hulot's Holiday" are obstacles beyond the capabilities of any mere mortal, and Top 100 chart activity must be dismissed from mind unless you have strongly masochistic tendencies. Blake Edwards was astute, as well as merciful, when he allowed Henry Mancini and Johnny Mercer to compose "Moon River" for *Breakfast at Tiffany's,* rather than insisting on the film's title. Joel and I were equally fortunate that Lionel Newman permitted us to write "The Morning After" rather than forcing us to wrestle with "The Poseidon Adventure." "We May Never Love like This Again" was much easier to solve than "The Towering Inferno" would have been.

A good way to test Johnny Mercer's "Don't tell the story" philosophy, is to analyze the Oscar-winning songs from 1969 to 1974: "The Way We Were" (from *The Way We Were*—Marvin Hamlisch/Alan and Marilyn Bergman); "The Morning After" (from *The Poseidon Adventure*—Al Kasha/Joel Hirschhorn); "Shaft" (from *Shaft*—Isaac Hayes); "For All We Know" (from *Lovers and Other Strangers*—Fred Karlin/Robb Wilson/Arthur James) and "Raindrops Keep Falling on My Head" (from *Butch Cassidy and the Sundance Kid*—Burt Bacharach/Hal David). These songs have two things in common—they served the needs of the picture, and all became Number One records.

In "The Way We Were" (1974), the music was nostalgic and bittersweet, and the words gave a feeling of lost love and youth, but never too specifically: "Memories light the corners of my mind—Misty water color memories of the way we were."

"The Morning After" (1973) dealt with an impending crisis, and the lines indicate this, but no mention is made of the S.S. *Poseidon* luxury liner or the identities of the various passengers: "There's got to be a morning after, If we can hold on through the night—We have a chance to find the sunshine—Let's keep on looking for the light." There's a mood of hope without ignoring the perils of the situation, and the lyrics can be read in broad terms or on an interpersonal basis. The music is deliberately quiet, as a contrast to the melodramatic texture of the film.

"Shaft" (1972) is a vivid, contemporary song, with a raw, ethnic feeling and rhythm that captured the pulse of New York City, and the lyrics, though minimal, dramatized the personality and essence of the title character, a reckless, hard-loving black superhero who works on his own, bypassing the police establishment.

"For All We Know" (1971) is a song about strangers trying to relate. The lyrics begin: "Love, look at the two of us, Strangers in many ways." These words sum up a mood of searching for love, which is the main conflict of all the characters: the young couple about to be married, the groom's unhappily married brother, the bride's father involved in an extramarital affair. Again, none of the specifics are mentioned, but the overall emotion is captured.

"Raindrops Keep Falling on My Head" (1970) points up many values in the film. Musically, it's buoyant, carefree, has a Western feeling and underlines the roving irresponsibility of the two main characters. The lyrics—"Raindrops keep falling on my head, Just like a guy whose feet are too big for his bed—Nothing seems to fit"—suggest the inability of these men to fit into conventional society. You know from the tone of the words that they are footloose, easygoing rebels, rather than the criminals of the Bogart/Cagney movies.

The general content of these songs is a strong factor in their becoming hit records. "The Way We Were" touched upon a universal feeling of bittersweet nostalgia about first love. If it had dealt with a politically conscious girl fighting the blacklist and a WASP playboy unable to commit himself to social issues, its appeal would have been tremendously curtailed.

"The Morning After" speaks of a common anxiety—that love affairs won't work out beyond one night of sex. In an uncertain time, it can be read also as an expression of hope, that tomorrow will be better, that national disillusionment will vanish.

"Shaft" is musically a strong dance record, with an intriguing title that contains hostile, antiauthority elements. It summed up a national mood of restless youth feeling "shafted" and exploited. Further, *Shaft* provided a long-awaited film hero for black audiences.

"For All We Know" is romantic, and dealt sensitively with a new relationship. It had an optimistic tone, but also allowed for the realistic and honest possibility that love could fade.

"Raindrops" has a contagious, happy feeling that communicated itself to everyone, along with an audacious, fun-loving quality. The approach was lighthearted rather than preachy, but it said, in essence, "Enjoy life and do your own thing."

ROCK GROUPS IN FILMS

In the past, producers have hired rock groups for their films and been disappointed in the results. Rock groups often adhere to their own sound and image, rather than blending themselves with the mood and story line of the picture. Thus, through loud, pounding tracks, they call attention to themselves and the music attempts to be the star. It's not— at most, it's an important ingredient. It can *become* the star independently of the movie, but rarely within it.

This assessment doesn't include a separate genre—the rock movie—in which records are used to bridge the story transitions, establish time, convey period flavor or represent a character's life (e.g., Alan Freed's career in *American Hot Wax,* or Buddy Holly's in *The Buddy Holly Story*).

In all fairness, there are many rock performers and/or groups who are capable of adjusting themselves to the medium. When this happens, and they can work along with the producer, subordinating their individual identities to the project, results can be memorable. Some outstanding examples are John Sebastian and the Lovin' Spoonful, who performed the song score in *You're a Big Boy Now,* an early feature by Francis Ford (*The Godfather*) Coppola. This score included Sebastian's deeply-felt and beautiful "Darling, Be Home Soon," which took the needs of the key love scene completely into account. Paul Simon's musical contributions to *The Graduate* considerably enhanced the film. Another milestone was "Live and Let Die," created for the picture by Paul and Linda McCartney and sung by McCartney and Wings. The instrumental break of "Live and Let Die" produced a sound that dramatized the mood of danger and suggested the reckless James Bond personality. The melody also stressed that droll humor which Bond exhibits through all his hair-raising escapades.

Barry Manilow wrote and performed the infectious "Copacabana" for *Foul Play,* and Neil Diamond was responsible for the soaring music behind *Jonathan Livingston Seagull.* Most significant, of course, was the rock score for *Saturday Night Fever.* "Stayin' Alive" established the inner core of the John Travolta character as completely as the script, and "How Deep Is Your Love" added a sentimental tone to the ending that projected hope, love and uncertainty all at the same time.

An important point to remember is that the scorer will frequently utilize your melody for background. If it has a flexibility which lends itself to use in a variety of tempos, he'll be more inclined to keep repeating it. Thus, the value of the song increases, to the picture and to you as a composer. The more a tune is played, the greater its chances of gripping audience attention and gaining popularity.

Whether you're a singer/writer, a writer for a group or a free lancer, you can train yourself to write material that serves the movie and lives away from it. A good deal of split-level thought is called for, but once you accustom your thinking to this requirement, it becomes surprisingly natural and automatic, as well as enjoyable.

UNDERSCORING

Learning to underscore (write music that plays under the foreground action in films and TV) is a way of gaining enough control and power to put your songs into films, but it should never be considered as a songwriting route alone. The requirements are too complex, too specialized for an aspiring composer to look upon it simply as a device to get his songs heard. Many excellent books (four of the best are by Earle Hagen, Henry Mancini, Dick Grove and John Cacavas) have been written on the technical aspects of scoring, but on a more general level, there are certain skills a scorer should have if he hopes to carve out an enduring motion picture career:

1. He must know when to build a scene and when to tactfully keep himself out of it. Sometimes, in a suspense film, the ultimate horror is silence, rather than the use of madly dramatic strings that war with the imagery rather than enhancing it. On the other hand, Bernard Herrmann's chillingly high string stabs in the shower scene of *Psycho* made a potentially frightening sequence turn into one with classically nightmarish qualities. The same applies to love scenes—often they may be heightened by a recurring romantic theme (as in *Love Story*); other times they're so sentimental by themselves that thickly romantic music will make them soapy and mawkish. Certainly the scorer must build with energy and imagination during chase sequences. Continuous, action-packed music is demanded at those moments.

2. Audiences would be shocked if they viewed most movies without the presence of a musical score. They would seem disjointed, and in cases where there are quick jumps and montages, completely chaotic. Or they might seem dead, tedious, so that the producer and director would think in alarm, "What a bomb!" The scorer's job, one that film arrangers have always done brilliantly, is to give all this a sense of cohesion and continuity. Somehow, in the hands of a master, the fragments all come together into a unified whole.

3. A scorer must spot empty moments that need help. The sight of a person crossing a street or bending down to tie his shoelace isn't inherently dramatic—but perhaps his thoughts are, and can be transmitted through music. Maybe, in the plot mechanism, he's afraid of being killed, or that his wife will leave him, or that he'll lose his job. Music can then heighten the scene and make prosaic actions meaningful.

4. If a movie is set in a foreign country, the scorer must evoke a sense of that country, of the customs and the people. If it's set back in another time, such as the Civil War, his job will be to bring the atmosphere of that period to life.

5. The scorer will have to supply "source" music—music that plays from a radio, a record player, an orchestra or any other source that appears visually on the screen.

6. The scorer must have enough innate taste to know when a huge, thundering orchestra is called for and when an intimate four-piece combo might be more appropriate, or even a single piano or guitar. Producers often want a "big" sound, for fear that the tension or excitement of the film will collapse if it goes quiet even for a second, but if the scorer has a valid argument about his choice of instruments, chances are the producer will listen to him.

7. A good scorer won't give the scene away by telegraphing comic or dramatic moments in advance, except when the effect is deliberate and repetitive (e.g., John Williams' horror theme for *Jaws*).

8. The scorer can supply what actors call "subtext" . . . true or deeper attitudes than appear on the surface. For example, a character may be laughing, but behind his frivolous facade is hatred or panic. The music can suggest those smoldering passions and alert the audience to their existence.

9. Music can do more than dramatize what viewers see—it can add extra dimension by playing against it. Bizarrely happy music during a murder scene might, paradoxically, add a greater sense of tragedy if properly used.

10. A composer can devise a specific theme for each character, a theme which defines that character's personality and emotional needs. He can also come up with a thematic score—one which features the same melody played over and over. This can be effective, as well as commercially potent, but many inventive scorers feel that reliance on a single tune is superficial and ignores the complexities which should be highlighted in the movie.

As I mentioned earlier regarding title songs for films, the theme should be integrated seamlessly and not distract from the total framework. This is true of scores too. In the words of a master, Alfred Newman: "Good film music must always be inspired by the picture of which it is a part, not by the desire of a composer to express himself. The effect of music in films is largely one of association, the important thing being to evoke the proper mood and spirit." Henry Mancini agrees: "I feel sorry for the young composers coming into the business now because they are expected to be good immediately. They're also expected to come up with hit songs, which tends to persuade them the picture is secondary. In my own case, the successful songs have been secondary considerations—they were all written specifically to *serve* the picture."

A few practical tips:

1. Take orchestration lessons, privately or in a good school like Juilliard. Read every arranging book you can get your hands on.

2. Learn about every instrument. Read scores while playing the records and memorize all the sounds, colors, ranges. Copy the scores until your hands automatically know every instrument's capabilities. Work for a copyist, and become one if you can.

3. If you play an instrument well, join an orchestra or band and familiarize yourself with its arrangements and the individual parts played by the different men.

4. If you're orchestrating for a scorer, sit with him while he "spots" the film (decides where music should go).

5. Work along with film editors at the moviola machine and watch how they adjust their timings in synchronization with the film.

6. Study conducting.

7. Don't think only of big-budget motion pictures or a TV series as areas in which to build up your scoring credits and skill: there are public television, Army and Navy films, university films, cartoons, commercials.

8. Take all kinds of odd assignments. Henry Mancini's apprentice-

ship prepared him for a wide variety of projects. Early in his career he supplied background to *Francis (the Talking Mule)* and *Bonzo the Chimp*, then moved on to *The Glenn Miller Story, The Benny Goodman Story*, the sprightly jazz theme of *Peter Gunn* and the dark dissonance of *White Dawn*.

SCORER AND SONGWRITER—CAN YOU BE BOTH?

There's a sharp division made between background scorers and songwriters. The assumption (widely held by various publishers and producers) is (a) if you can score, you can't write songs and (b) if you write songs, you can't score. This discourages songwriters from stretching their creative muscles and moving into the scoring arena, and scorers feel they're not taken seriously enough as pop composers.

In truth, many background scorers have written fine songs—hit songs—and are continuing to do so. Another group—a smaller one, but growing—broke through initially as songwriters and are now composing notable movie scores.

Consider these scorers, who wound up writing hit songs for films: Fred Karlin ("For All We Know," "Come Saturday Morning"), Henry Mancini ("Moon River," "Days of Wine and Roses"), Elmer Bernstein ("Walk on the Wild Side," "True Grit"), Maurice Jarre ("Somewhere My Love"), André Previn ("You're Gonna Hear from Me," "Valley of the Dolls"), Michel Legrand ("The Windmills of Your Mind," "I Will Wait for You"), Walter Scharf ("Ben"), John Green ("Body and Soul," "I Cover the Waterfront"), Alex North ("Unchained Melody") and John Williams ("Star Wars").

Looking at the situation from a reverse angle, we can mention Burt Bacharach, who had a string of hits with Hal David before arriving in Hollywood to score *Butch Cassidy and the Sundance Kid* and other films. David Shire wrote material for Barbra Streisand ("What About Today") before his movie scoring career took wing.

Marvin Hamlisch is another person who made the transition from songwriting to movie scoring. He gained national recognition originally with Lesley Gore hits such as "California Nights" and "Sunshine, Lollipops and Roses." Curtis Mayfield's concentration on background music for films such as *Superfly* was preceded by years of writing Top 10 records for the Impressions, Major Lance and Jerry Butler. Cy Coleman, Perry Botkin, Jr., Quincy Jones, Isaac Hayes, Barry De Vorzon and Charles Fox wrote commercial hits before attaining fame in the movies.

The examples listed above are not intended to convey that every background scorer is a hit songwriter, or vice versa. Songwriters often lack the ability to subordinate themselves to the needs of a movie, or simply don't possess the range and taste required. They may also lack proper formal training. Scorers, on the other hand, are effective mood writers, but can't always pare down their rich variety of knowledge into the tightly economical framework of song structure. They tend to overload a tune with themes, and not repeat as often as a pop song must. They resist being hook-oriented.

The only point is this, and it is one that I made earlier: don't be discouraged by the pressure of rigid pigeonholing. Ignore remarks you may hear to the effect that one gift renders you incapable of mastering the other. Test yourself and employ your musical capacities to the fullest, exploring and studying the very different fundamentals and craft requirements of both fields. In the end, the only one who can truly know what versatility lies inside your heart and brain is you.

THINGS TO REMEMBER

1. Don't be retiring—perform your material wherever you can.
2. Assemble a tape of your best work and send it around to producers, heads of studio music departments and agents.

3. Buy *The Hollywood Reporter* and *Daily Variety* every day.

4. Try for assignments that are seemingly beyond your grasp, and you'll surprise yourself.

5. Get to know actors, directors, screenwriters.

6. If you're a lyricist, try writing with scorers.

7. Don't tell the whole story when writing a movie song—tell the philosophy, the meaning behind the action.

8. Don't try to overshadow the film by calling attention to your song. The music isn't the star, just one important ingredient.

9. Write a song that can be played in many different tempos, so the scorer can utilize it more frequently in the film.

10. When writing a background score, you must

a. Give the action an overall sense of cohesion and continuity;

b. Heighten dead spots that need help;

c. Evoke a sense of place, customs and people;

d. Know when to use a big orchestra and when to use only a few musicians;

e. Be careful not to telegraph important plot points in advance;

f. Supply "subtext" . . . suggest character complexities that may not appear on the surface.

11. Don't feel you must be either a songwriter or a scorer if you feel you have the ability to be both. Don't let yourself be pigeonholed into one category.

17

Writing a Movie Musical

All our lives Joel and I envisioned writing a movie musical someday, with a main character like Gene Kelly dancing along the streets of Paris, Fred Astaire whirling on the ceiling . . . or maybe Judy Garland in black tights, belting out a number in a renovated farmhouse. Even John Travolta in a disco would have been more logical than the hero we finally wrote for: an animated singing dragon.

Although building a vehicle around such an unlikely song-and-dance man wasn't what we had expected, the experience was invaluable, and gave us a chance to participate in the making of a musical from inception to release. We were called in by publishing head Bob Jackman before the script was written, and had an opportunity to work side by side with producers Jerome Courtland and Ron Miller, director Don Chaffey and choreographer Onna White.

Often a script is completely written before songwriters are ever contacted, but in the case of *Pete's Dragon* there was only an outline—an extended seventy-five-page treatment—by author Malcolm Marmorstein. We were given the treatment by story editor Frank Paris and asked to suggest where we thought songs belonged. Song placement is vitally important in a film or stage musical. The numbers should advance the story and not simply be thrown in at random. In the '30s, audiences didn't mind when Fred Astaire and Ginger Rogers broke into song and dance at the drop of a Top Hat, but since Rodgers and Hammerstein's *Oklahoma!* the numbers have to be organic to the plot and push it dramatically forward.

At this point there must be agreement between scriptwriter and composers about what can be conveyed in dialogue and what can more effectively be presented through music. In the case of Malcolm, Joel and me, there was mutual agreement, but this isn't always true. Musicals can suffer when songwriters clutter up the continuity with tunes and a script-writer pours on the dialogue. The overall project becomes top-heavy, repetitious and slow-moving. Sometimes these errors are made because the people see them as artistically valid, but the important thing is for the creators to work together and not compete for the most footage.

Fortunately, the ego clashes on *Pete's Dragon* were minimal. At Disney Studios, an atmosphere of democratic participation is encour-aged. There's a pervading team spirit on every corner of the lot. (Work-ing on Dopey Drive, across the street from Mickey Avenue, promotes this kind of camaraderie.)

CHARACTER SONGS

The next step is deciding what kind of numbers should be written for the different characters. Most of the songs will be "book" songs— songs that work in the context of a show, but not outside it. These songs are characterizations, defining the people, their motivations and goals.

In the plot of *Pete's Dragon,* young Pete is victimized and abused by his monstrous foster family, a group of illiterate backwoods tyrants led by Shelley Winters. The rural setting and general nature of the people inspired us to write a country and western tune, "Happiest Home in the Hills." The song was up-tempo, underscoring their aggressiveness. A ballad would have been inappropriate, not just from the standpoint of mood, but also because this was the opening number, and it's generally wise to start a musical with a lively, rousing piece of material.

A character song defines the people lyrically, as well as melodically and rhythmically. In *Pete's Dragon,* Jim Dale plays a medical charlatan, and we wrote a song for him in which he announces his questionable achievements to a skeptical crowd:

> I've been bringing cures from Pilgrim Heights to Provincetown
> Treated rabbit fever down on Queen Anne Road
> Gout or gastritis
> Mumps or bronchitis
> Bites and burns and blue abrasions
> Got a pill for all occasions

We made his credentials so overblown that his phony, con-man qualities came through to the listener. In addition to defining character, this is also a comedy song. Comedy material is always welcome, as long as it's related to the plot and not carelessly inserted at the expense of the conception.

Another kind of song is what Lehman Engel calls the "charm song." This name applies to pleasant, frequently medium-tempo melodies which provide a change of pace from the out-and-out ballad and the show-stopping production number. Numbers like these are lilting and low-key in nature, not meant to elicit howls of laughter or a passionate emotional response. In our film, "It's Not Easy" is a charm song, in which the boy tries to explain why he loves his invisible dragon. A more famous example is "Getting to Know You" from *The King and I.*

STEP-OUT SONGS

A step-out song is one that is integrated into the plot, yet can live away from it. In *Pete's Dragon,* Helen Reddy plays Mickey Rooney's daughter, a lonely girl whose sailor boyfriend has been lost at sea. Our main step-out number for her was called "Candle on the Water," which began like this:

> I'll be your candle on the water
> My love for you will always burn
> I know you're lost and drifting
> But the clouds are lifting
> Don't give up—you have somewhere to turn

As you can see, the words are double-edged. The candle is symbolic of her love, yet describes the physical flame from the lighthouse that will direct her lover to safety. "I know you're lost and drifting, But the clouds are lifting" is an emotional feeling, an expression of her secret hopes, but it's also a specific reference to the rough ocean and stormy weather. "You have somewhere to turn" means the warmth of her arms, but also the flame that will rescue him.

We did a *semi*–step-out song in another number, "There's Room for Everyone." In the first verse we wrote:

> Even a dragon deserves a place
> A wide open space with no reins
> No chains
> He wants to play games, dance with you
> Give him a chance to sing his song
> He only wants to belong

This verse is integral to the picture and couldn't be removed. But our second verse was more general, more universal:

> Just think how far out the ocean goes
> The whirling wind blows shore to shore
> Door to door
> Think of the valleys and mountain tops
> The earth never stops
> So deep, so high, with miles of sky
> We all have part of the pie

We're proud to say that we succeeded with this material to the extent that the United Nations adopted it as its song of the year for 1977. The U.N. used only the general portion, which could apply to people the world over, and eliminated specific references to the dragon.

Rodgers and Hammerstein used to approach the problem of step-out versus character songs in a different way. They wrote short opening verses to depict story action, then launched into a more general lyric. An example of this is "Hello, Young Lovers," in which the heroine recalls her own past love affair, after which the body of the tune is advice that can apply to lovers everywhere.

Casting helps to direct a composer. When Mickey Rooney was hired to play the lazy, inebriated lighthouse keeper, we immediately thought of something frenetic, to capture the energy Rooney has as a musical-comedy performer. We carried that thought to completion with his big number, "I Saw a Dragon," in which he sees the huge, green apparition of the title when no one else does. The beat is frantic, in keeping with the character's accelerating hysteria.

RANGES

The vocal range of each performer has to be carefully considered, and when two people are singing together, the choice of a compatible key may depend on which of them has the lion's share of the song. In "I Saw a Dragon," Helen Reddy enters the scene after Rooney has done a few verses. When the two actors were rehearsed, we found that there was *no* key they could comfortably share. Helen would have to talk her lines if Rooney sang, or vice versa. It was tempting to try to arrange things so that Helen would be singing, because she had the best pop voice in the movie, but we had to forgo that impulse because this was Rooney's big scene. For purposes of the story, he had to be spotlighted to maximum advantage. Therefore, Helen talked her lines and Mickey handled the melody.

TEMPO

In a musical, nothing is more boring than sameness. Three ballads in a row and you have a sleeping audience. It's not just a question of slow or fast but of varying the tempos. In *Pete's Dragon,* we included a country and western rocker, two pop/rock songs, a ballad, a hillbilly duet and a waltz.

As with all rules, there are exceptions when a composer is able to handle an innovative technique. In *A Little Night Music* Stephen Sondheim utilized a succession of waltzes, and these were appropriate for the mood of the story. But in general, rhythmic and melodic variety should be your aim.

CHOREOGRAPHY

An imaginative choreographer is vital, but you can make his or her job easier if you write animated lyrics and tunes. We were fortunate to have Onna White, who won an Oscar for her work in the film version of *Oliver.* In one of our numbers, "Bill of Sale," Onna arranged for the Shelley Winters character to hold up a piece of paper and sing, "I Got a Bill of Sale Right Here." That gesture became a key physical movement in the scene. Our words gave the choreographer clear direction, and as a result the intention of the song was captured and the dance bore a strong relationship to the plot.

ORCHESTRATION

The experienced and gifted Irwin Kostal was our arranger on *Pete's Dragon*. Not only were his accomplishments legendary (*Mary Poppins, West Side Story, The Sound of Music*), but there was a strong personal rapport between us. No matter how dynamic a score you write, all can be lost if you don't have an arranger who speaks your language. No music is powerful enough to withstand poor instrumentation, so when you have the power to voice your preference of orchestrator, do it.

Try to meet with the arranger beforehand and establish an open dialogue, letting him know how you see the song done. You may feel that four instruments will convey your thought on a particular song, then be upset at the session when the tune is arranged for fifty violins. The orchestrator, on the other hand, may have ideas you never thought of, and between the two of you, a fresh concept can surface that might never have developed if you hadn't exchanged points of view.

LAST-MINUTE CHANGES

Composers have to be fast on their feet. Characters can be changed, rewritten or removed. Along the way, "I Saw a Dragon" was reconceived because the producers decided to include more townspeople in the song. A comic-opera number for a character named Ferdinand was dropped because Ferdinand was deleted from the story. A sing-along, old-fashioned tune about cleaning brass on a lighthouse was also dropped and replaced with one that had more of a rock beat.

An even more major change occurred when the title character, Elliott the Dragon, was given added footage. In the original script, he was supposed to be real to the boy Pete but invisible to the audience. However, veteran Disney animator Ken Anderson (responsible for the witch in *Snow White,* among a gallery of other Disney cartoon stars) drew pictures of him for a dream sequence, and when he showed the sketches, everyone became so enamored with the dragon that he was inserted into a dozen other scenes. Extensive rewriting and shifting of songs took place to make the continuity smooth after Elliott began to dominate the action.

Writing a musical can provide you with a lifelong annuity because of the many benefits that accrue from it. There's likely to be a sound track containing all of your own original material. Songs in a musical (and this applies equally to musicals on the stage or screen) are often "covered" (recorded over and over again) by other artists and become standards. In addition, there are sheet-music folios, choral arrangements and band arrangements that provide enduring income.

CHANGING STYLES

The form of the musical has undergone certain changes. Some people consider it dated to let a character burst into song unless there is a justification for it, as in *Cabaret,* where the major characters sang in a nightclub. In *Saturday Night Fever* and the more traditional *Lassie, My Lassie,* the songs move the story ahead, but are done entirely as voice-overs, rather than sung visually by the stars. *Grease* is a rock musical, but only in the type of music does it vary from the middle-of-the-road musicals of the past. Otherwise the characters express themselves through song, whether in romantic love duets like "Summer Nights," which define the leads and their attitudes, solo ballads like "Hopelessly Devoted to You" or character songs like "Sandra Dee."

Every popular form of entertainment adopts new looks, new styles, but learning the basic elements of the craft will serve you in good stead no matter what type of musical is currently popular. Armed with this information, you'll never be tempted to just "throw" songs in when doing a musical project. Whether working on a traditional musical, a rock opera or a musical based on voice-overs, remember that the emphasis on character is the key to a rounded, three-dimensional work.

THINGS TO REMEMBER

1. Make sure the songs you write aren't gratuitous, that they advance the plot.

2. Don't squeeze a song in where the dialogue makes the point, and urge the scriptwriter to allow you equal space.

3. As a general rule, open your musical with a lively, up-tempo number.

4. Write "character" songs that describe and illuminate the people. Write a step-out song only if it can be done naturally and comfortably, without upsetting the balance of the piece. Audiences shouldn't be aware of your "forcing" a number into a particular spot because you want to have a commercial hit.

5. Vary the tempos. Not too many ballads, not too many up-tempo numbers.

6. Write animated lyrics, filled with action and visual imagery, so the choreographer and arranger can dramatize them.

7. Consider the ranges of your singers. Don't write operatic melodies for people who haven't got the vocal ability.

8. Let the opening song establish your main conflict.

18

Writing a Stage Musical

Although the points covered in the previous chapter on film musicals—character songs, step-out songs, charm songs, alterations of tempo, visualizing choreography in your initial conception of the material, proper keys—relate equally to stage productions, there are a few important differences to remember when you're writing for each medium.

On film, there is total freedom of movement, thanks to the availability of outdoor locations and a camera that can follow the action everywhere. On stage, a limited number of sets have to create an illusion of space and movement. It's not reality, but a stylization of it. You can open up in a film musical, but conceiving a theater piece as a series of short scenes, each with elaborate set changes, will prove awkward and unworkable, as well as financially impractical. A stage musical must also be more outgoing. The actors are tiny figures and must project powerfully to the last row. Film offers the luxury of close-ups, capturing subtle changes of expression on the faces of the cast. For this reason, there can be more ballads in a movie musical (though still not too many), whereas one or two go a long way in the theater.

Audiences watching a movie are impatient today with too many songs in a row. The brutally realistic camera makes it harder to suspend belief, and film viewers want more story than the old musicals used to provide. That's why such euphemisms as "a story with songs" and "a drama with music" have come into being. On stage, though, it's not unusual to have seventeen numbers, and if these are enjoyable, excitingly mounted and fast-paced, no one will complain.

To develop as a writer of musicals, you've got to acquaint yourself with other well-regarded, popular shows. Go to the library and read every libretto and score you can find. Observe how the numbers fit into the action. Try to see every musical play in your city, and don't attend only the big prestige productions. Visit college theater, dinner theater, high school and community theater. If you've never, for example, seen a classic like *West Side Story* and a local performance is being done at a school or church, don't miss it. The bare bones of play and music that were originally great will be visible, even if box-office names and opulent trappings aren't also in evidence.

Make sure you get your musical mounted. It doesn't matter if the first booking is in a garage behind your father's store. The point is to unravel it in front of people so you can gauge from audience response what works and what doesn't. A modest local production will teach you about lighting, scenery, costumes and choreography. You'll learn about variety and pacing, and you'll be able to rewrite at your leisure without the pressure of heavy budgets and temperamental stars to distract you.

When deciding what kind of musical you want to write, you should consider the following popular forms:

1. The Cinderella Story
2. The Revue
3. The Historical Musical
4. The Musical Fantasy
5. The Musical Biography

THE CINDERELLA STORY

Some memorable examples of this musical genre include:

a. *My Fair Lady* (Lerner/Loewe), which describes the unlikely pairing of an illiterate flower girl and a professor of speech. Where the original *Pygmalion* separated the hero and heroine at the end, adaptor Alan Jay Lerner rewrote it to unite them.

b. *The Sound of Music* (Rodgers/Hammerstein). This offbeat, romantic story pairs a would-be nun and a baron.

c. *Guys and Dolls* (Frank Loesser). Here we have a prim and proper Salvation Army girl and a gambler. Where but in a Cinderella musical comedy would these two incongruously matched people get together?

d. *The King and I* (Rodgers/Hammerstein). Again, a clash of cultures and values. This classic delineates the growing love between an English schoolmistress and a Siamese king.

An important thread that ties all these Cinderella musicals together is *conversion*. One of the principals is changed, through love, into a different person. In *My Fair Lady* the flower girl becomes an educated lady, in *Guys and Dolls* the prim and religious heroine bursts out of her shell of respectability, and in *The King and I* the narrow-thinking Siamese ruler opens his mind to cultural change.

THE REVUE

This musical form is generally a compilation of skits and vignettes with one overall theme, whether it be political, sexual or social. Revues analyze and/or break down traditions and explode long-held mores, such as

a. *Hair* (Rado/Ragni/MacDermot), in its explicit treatment of sex and contemporary attitudes toward war and the society of the '60s.

b. *Mother Earth* dealt with matters of ecology at a time when this issue was emblazoned on the front pages. (It's not generally known, but Toni Tennille of *The Captain and Tennille* composed this rock score, as well as starring in the production.)

c. *Don't Bother Me, I Can't Cope* (Micki Grant) spoke and sang of the black experience, as did *Inner City*.

Other revues include the irreverent *Oh! Calcutta!*, with its then-shocking sexual episodes, and current examples that have a documentary flavor, *Runaways, A Chorus Line* and *Working*.

THE HISTORICAL MUSICAL

a. *Fiddler on the Roof* (Bock/Harnick) musically dramatizes the plight of the Jews in Russian pogroms.

b. *1776* (Edwards) deals with the American Revolution and the signing of the Declaration of Independence.

c. *Shenandoah* (Geld/Udell) centers around victims of the Civil War, and

d. *Cabaret* (Kander/Ebb) memorably paints a portrait of Nazism growing.

The historical musical gives the composer/lyricist a chance to put the past into perspective and express his or her interpretation in the light of modern knowledge. The past is also an inspiring subject since it shows the struggles and victories of former generations and groups, many of them minorities.

THE MUSICAL FANTASY

Peter Pan (Styne/Charlap/Leigh) is an excellent example of this genre. Others include *The Wiz* (Charles Smalls), *Finian's Rainbow* (Harburg/Lane), *Damn Yankees* (Adler/Ross) and *Rainbow Jones* (Jill Williams). Musical fantasy allows the composers to trip out—to let their imaginations run loose. Thanks to its free-flowing nature, the composer can stretch farther here, musically and lyrically, than in any other form.

THE MUSICAL BIOGRAPHY

Actual characters are always a creative stimulus and challenge to writers. In films we've had biographies of Ruth Etting, Billie Holiday, Lillian Roth and Al Jolson. On stage a classic example is *Gypsy,* the Sondheim/Styne exposé of a particularly driving stage mother. Others are *Funny Girl* (Fanny Brice), *George M* (George M. Cohan) and *Minnie's Boys* (the Marx Brothers). Composing a musical biography gives the writer an opportunity to fashion a star vehicle such as *Hello, Dolly!* or *The Act.* These can be glitteringly effective and popular if the writer is fortunate and finds actresses charismatic enough for the roles.

It's not enough to write a musical—you have to get financial backing so it can be brought to life on the stage. As a first step, prepare at least five or six songs and make a personal presentation to prospective producers, directors or actors. This is called a backers' audition. Explain how the numbers fit into the plot. You can sing them yourself, but unless you're a mesmerizing performer, you'd be better off calling a group of actors and actresses in. They have the advantage of doing different parts and giving listeners distinct impressions of each character.

Another approach is inviting potential backers to see the play. Don't worry if the scenery and staging are simple. An experienced professional eye will spot the possibilities.

If you're submitting your work through the mail, send a script with typed lyrics included, as well as a tape or cassette demo of the material.

HITS CAN COME FROM SHOWS

One of the best vehicles for hit songs is the theater. I can almost hear the voices of skepticism rise when I say that: "Oh, no, the theater's old-fashioned, the shows are all geared to an older audience. You can't write pop material for it."

Wrong. The theater is changing radically. There's more to it than the traditional musical like *Mame* and *Hello, Dolly!* Many of the biggest Broadway smashes of recent seasons were written by songwriters under 35. The influence of commercial music is strongly felt in these productions, and hits are pouring from them.

Stephen Schwartz composed the rock score to *Godspell* when he was 24. The huge hit "Day by Day" came from this show. Steve's long-running *Pippin* gave birth to a Top 10 single by the Jackson Five, "A Corner in the Sky."

The number of hits from *Hair* (written by Rado, Ragni and Mac-Dermot) is staggering: the title song (a gold record for the Cowsills); "Let the Sunshine In" (Number One for the Fifth Dimension); "Easy to Be Hard" (a million seller for Three Dog Night); and "Good Morning Starshine" (Gold for Oliver).

Marvin Hamlisch, one of the key composing talents of the '70s, wrote the music for the extraordinary *A Chorus Line.* His haunting standard "What I Did for Love" is from this Pulitzer Prize winner. Charles Small's *The Wiz* has yielded "Ease On down the Road," and the Lloyd Webber *Jesus Christ Superstar* has produced "I Don't Know How to Love Him."

Remember this: a show packages not one but twelve to fifteen of your songs, which is unbeatable exposure. And the theater has now come to include college theater, dinner theater, summer stock. A show can originate from any city, any locale. Broadway is one aspect of the total theater scene, but not the be-all–end-all it was in the past. Producers don't race to Manhattan now; they keep a show running, sometimes as long as a year, all over the United States and abroad. This makes economic sense, because they want to recoup their investments before facing the firing line of New York critics. A happy by-product of their practical thinking has been to increase the importance of other places around the nation. Areas like Los Angeles, Philadelphia, San Francisco, Chicago, Washington are not just testing grounds for a production—they've become theater towns on their own.

Different media have joined each other in the past. Movies became TV shows or stage productions. Songs like "Ode to Billy Joe" and "Harper Valley PTA" became the basis of film adaptations. The latest vehicle crossover is the album-to-theater phenomenon. *Jesus Christ Superstar* and *Tommy* began as recorded rock operas and both translated vividly to the stage. Hal Prince's new production of *Evita* (which is a smash hit in London) was a record to begin with. Maybe your thinking and temperament would flourish best if you wrote a "show" for a record album, conceiving it with enough dramatic and visual forethought to qualify it eventually for the stage. In any case, it's just one of the many approaches you can take to a new, innovative and hit-oriented theater.

SPECIAL MATERIAL

Writing special material is excellent preparation for the theater. Theater writing is generally well crafted and slick, with clever rhymes. The music is tuneful and rhythmic, and must have enough personality and action to give the choreographer strong raw material. All these ingredients are required when you write for a nightclub personality or a television variety show.

If you watch an Ann-Margret or Raquel Welch in Las Vegas, you'll notice that they do more than a series of popular songs. Their acts consist of skits, with specially written words that define or spoof their performing images. These vignettes can parody political figures or poke fun at movies, shows, other actors, themselves. Sometimes the lyrics are married to an already-popular tune; other times both words and music are original. Special material is the lifeblood of any effective in-person act.

The Carol Burnett series flourished for eleven years on TV and is now doing superbly in syndication. The reason, of course, is the camaraderie and troupelike feeling established by regulars Tim Conway, Vicki Lawrence, Harvey Korman and the star herself, but it's more than that— it's the witty special material that gives the actors something to sink their comic teeth into. Watch any Bob Hope hour, or any variety program at all, for that matter, and you'll see examples of tailored musical skits. Observe how these numbers are structured to fit the stars. Make note of the subject matter. Try to write some of your own, if you think you have the requisite flair for humor. Take popular songs and rewrite them, making fun of the ideas. Think of a star like Raquel Welch and let your mind go. You could kid her sex image, putting personalized words to "Nobody Does It Better." You could present Jerry Lewis crooning "I've Gotta Be Me" and then make humorous reference to all the movies in which he portrayed ten people.

If you know any acts locally, submit things to them. It's fine to write for Mitzi Gaynor in Vegas, and Mary Tyler Moore would obviously do your work justice, but these people aren't necessarily available . . . at least until you've gained a reputation. Maybe you've heard an up-and-coming comedienne in your neighborhood, testing her repertoire at a local club. Try your routines out at parties. Is there a singer, just beginning or on the threshold of success, who needs more to work with? If you get in on the ground floor with funny patter, and his star begins to rise, you'll go along with him.

In the meantime, too, you can try contacting the large agencies— William Morris, International Creative Management (ICM) and Agency for the Performing Artist (APA). Together, they represent most performers in show business.

Get work that puts you close to entertainers if you can. A rehearsal pianist is constantly at the star's side. Arranging and conducting also establish physical ties that enable you to present your work when the time is right.

Some well-known special-material writers are Billy Barnes, Ken and Mitzie Welch, Lynn Duddy, Jerry Bressler, Larry Hovis, Ann Elder, Earle Brown, Bruce Livanche, Larry Grossman, Kenny Solms and Gail Parent. Our own prelude to show writing was through special material, composing for Zero Mostel, Liz Torres, Liza Minnelli and Charles Aznavour. When these experiences gave us confidence, we wrote the score for a new stage version of *Seven Brides for Seven Brothers,* with original stars Jane Powell and Howard Keel again playing the leads.

THINGS TO REMEMBER

1. Read as many librettos and scores as you can. Attend every musical in your town, including ones performed at college theaters, dinner theaters and community theaters.

2. Try to get your musical mounted, no matter how modest the production. Only when a play is on its feet will you be able to observe what works and what doesn't.

3. Arrange backers' auditions and perform your score for potential investors. Anytime you have a musical done at a local theater or workshop, invite possible producers and directors to see it.

4. Keep in mind that the theater is open to young composers, and can be a source of commercial hits.

5. Think of album concepts as mini-shows that can be translated eventually to the stage—e.g., *Jesus Christ Superstar, Tommy* and *Evita.*

6. Write special material for nightclub or TV performers. This is lucrative on its own terms and excellent preparation for the theater.

19

Writing Commercials

The commercial field is not an easy one to break into, but it is highly lucrative if you do succeed. It offers solid preparation for pop writing, and chances are always good that a prolific jingle composer will find his work crossing over to the Top 100.

Joe Brooks is the most recent and striking example of someone who switched from the commercial to the record area. He composed the Oscar-winning "You Light Up My Life" for Debby Boone as well as Roberta Flack's "If Ever I See You Again." Yet also high on his list of credits are the jingles for Dr. Pepper ("It Tastes Too Good to Be True") and Pepsi-Cola ("Pepsi's Got a Lot to Give").

Other pop writers who have made important contributions to the commercial field are Randy ("Short People") Newman ("Most Original Soft Drink Ever—Dr. Pepper"), Leon Carr of "Hello, Lonely Girl" ("See the USA in Your Chevrolet") and Barry Manilow ("Like a Good Neighbor"). Mitch Leigh, who composed *Man of La Mancha,* supported himself with commercials.

Pop hits have resulted from "I'd Like to Teach the World to Sing" (Coke), "Music to Watch Girls by" (Pepsi), "No Matter What Shape You're in" (Alka-Seltzer), "Little Honda" (Honda) and "You Deserve a Break Today" (McDonald's).

This link between commercial and hit suggests that the two areas have similar requirements. A commercial (as well as a pop song) must make its point quickly. It must open with an ear-catching, provocative lyric statement that grabs the attention, as a pop record does. It must have a strong hook.

The tune of any jingle must be singable and easy to remember. It must pass the whistle test. Producers prefer their jingles to be up-tempo. Above all, the message must be clear, not convoluted or ambiguous. "We *Think* You'll Like Pepsi" would never get by the sponsor.

Most crucial, the words must have a pyschological weight. Directly or subliminally, they must touch a nerve, a basic human chord, and propel you to the supermarket to buy the product. For example, "I'd Like to Teach the World to Sing" didn't just say, "You'll enjoy the flavor of Coke." Instead, by creating a commercial that related to brotherhood around the world, it made Coke synonymous with universal love! How could any upstanding citizen turn down a drink with that much social impact?

"You Deserve a Break Today" plays on the feeling we all have that we're working too hard, that we need freedom, and it tells the listener that this longed-for liberation from job and kitchen and family responsibility is at the local McDonald's stand.

A former Greyhound commercial tells us, "Greyhound's in Touch with America." This not only satisfies the yen for travel, it also implies that love and friendship await you at every turn of a Greyhound. "The Times of Your Life," Roger Nichols' Kodak commercial, which became a hit for Paul Anka, doesn't merely refer to the fine pictures you took recently. No, it's a treasury of your whole past, moments you'll long remember. What this adds up to is that a commercial must answer people's *needs*. You must be an amateur psychologist, projecting into the minds of other people. But that, after all, is what art is all about, whether it be that of a casting director of songs, a scriptwriter, a playwright or novelist . . . an anticipation of collective hopes and needs. The only difference is that the commercial must be a little more blatant, more straightforward and single-minded. It has salesmanship on its mind above all other considerations.

Jingles used to be sweet and middle-of-the-road, but now the music is right in the pop mainstream. The productions, vocal harmonies and lead singing, as well as the content of the copy itself, all sound as though they were slanted for Top 40 playlists.

Charles Stern of the Charles Stern Agency, who represents musical talent such as Artie Butler, Mark Lindsay, Jimmy Webb and Perry Botkin, recently explained to *Songwriter* magazine the way jingle writers are hired:

> "The advertising firm either contacts an agency such as the Charles Stern Agency or they contact a 'jingle' house who employs jingle writers. There are jingle houses in both New York and Chicago who will employ songwriters. In Chicago there's Dick Marx and Associates and also Com Track. In New York there are places like Music Makers and Herman Edel.
> "Jingle houses get the songwriters to work on spec and then pay the songwriter a fee for their services," Stern continues, "generally on a buyout basis. The songwriter's fee can vary from $500.00 to $50,000.00, depending on the status of the writer and how badly the ad agency wants him. The highest volume generally occurs in the $3,000.00 to $10,000.00 range."

For a commercial demo tape, Stern suggests that the writer vary the material and include different products such as a car, a supermarket or a potato chip, to give the idea of versatility. More than pop demos, demos of commercials should stress production values as much as possible. Most clients don't have the imagination to visualize the final product unless it's spelled out, and for that reason, the most complete presentation tends to outshine its simpler competitors.

Writing arrangements is one way to break into the field. Background singing is another, as witness Barry Manilow. If you know the producer, it would be beneficial to co-write with him. He has the power to get the commercial on.

Some of the top names in the commercial world are Dale Menten,

Stanley Applebaum, Doris and Don Elliott, Ken Gavin, Sid Woloshin, Jack Palmer, Ben Allen, Robert Forshaw, Ben Ludlow, Mike and Dan Navarro, Steve Carmen—all recipients of hidden gold, although you may never see them on a record chart.

THE EDUCATIONAL MARKET

If you're ever browsing in a music shop, chances are you'll notice arrangements for school symphonic stage bands, marching bands and orchestras. Out of the corner of your eye you may also notice bins containing choral arrangements, which are utilized by school and church choirs. Beyond that, in bookstores, are the inspirational books and story-and-song books.

These, as we learned while working at Disney Studios, are just a tip of the educational iceberg. There are also filmstrips, cassettes or records prepared for schoolteachers on all subjects. They teach mathematics or history or science, and can deal with such varied educational material as the history of transportation, the life-styles of the Eskimo and other peoples around the world, or the problem of overpopulation. Many of these booklets, tapes and films need musical material written for them.

Companies such as the Children's Television Workshop in New York, where staff writers are employed, turn out an endless stream of educational material. Disneyland develops young authors who write for its parks and its live shows. There are educational periodicals on newsstands where people are listed who put on local theater productions for children. These productions often travel around the country.

Firms like Belwin-Mills, Carl Fischer, Theodore Presser, Boosey and Hawkes, Chappell and Hal Leonard are famous for developing and working with writers who create children's vehicles, and these are sent around and produced in schools.

Songwriter Joe Raposo launched his career in the educational field, writing for TV's *Sesame Street*. Such tunes as "Sing" (a hit by the

Carpenters) and "Bein' Green" (recorded by Frank Sinatra) emerged from Raposo's *Sesame Street* catalogue.

On a more adult level, there are industrial films for the composer to consider. These mini-movies are produced to teach employees of large companies more about the industry they're part of. For example, a large chain of hotels might shoot an industrial demonstrating to its workers the best ways of providing efficient service; a bank might do one explaining to its employees about different currencies around the world. These films need music and are willing to pay for it. Army, Navy and Air Force films can also be financially rewarding.

There is a tendency for writers to think only of the obvious, flamboyant areas—film, theater, records; but the educational market, like special material and commercials, offers a rewarding and challenging career. The possibilities for personal glory may be less, but this can be ideal for the individual who prefers consistency to the constant ups and downs caused by worrying, "Is it a hit or a miss?"

THINGS TO REMEMBER

1. Commercials must be singable and easy to remember after a first hearing.

2. They must be geared psychologically to associate the product with the buyer's deepest needs.

3. In submitting a commercial demo tape, vary the material and include different products to give an idea of your versatility.

4. Commercial demo tapes should stress production values as much as possible.

5. Remember that there is a vast educational market, which includes children's material, industrial films, and Army, Navy and Air Force films.

20

Rewriting—
the Trademark of a Professional

Suppose you've just finished a song. You're a little bit tired of it, and you're anxious to make a demo and submit it to publishers and producers. Yet there's that quiet, buzzing voice in your brain that keeps whispering, "Maybe the third line isn't right yet. Maybe the melody could stand a little revision."

The amateur says, "It's good enough as it is" and books the musicians and the studio. The professional listens to the warning voice and plays the song over and over again, until he can identify exactly what's wrong, until that vague but persistent feeling in the pit of his stomach disappears.

POPULAR COP-OUTS

One very popular cop-out is "I don't care if the rhymes are inconsistent . . . it's the feeling that counts." When you say that to yourself, pose another silent question: "Am I defending these rhymes because I *believe* they're the best [in which case you're justified in your attitude], or only because I think they'll get by, that no one will notice them?" If it's the latter, rewrite them. There's always some sharp-eared observer around to zero in on the flaws. If they escape the attention of the publisher or producer, the artist will catch them.

Melodically you may feel that a tune projects excitement, but that nagging inner ear is repeating: "Yes, but it sounds an awful lot like X, which was a hit last month." Again, commercial songs sometimes echo the feeling of former hits; certain chord progressions, as we've seen, move well and are much utilized, especially in rock and roll. But saying, "That's good, that means it's a hit" is dangerous. Sometimes it's *too* close, sometimes an outright plagiarism. It's not worth a lawsuit because you're too lazy to double-check and rewrite some of the intervals.

Very often both melody and words are there, but the rhythm doesn't catch fire. If you're an amateur, you might say, "So what? When I get in the studio, the musicians will fix it up." There's no question that super session musicians will add a great deal, maybe even save the day. But should you depend on them to bail you out? Isn't it smarter to go in there with your rhythm as spelled out as you can possibly make it? Aside from saving studio time, it gives the players more to build on and add their creative touches to. It would seem practical to experiment at home until you feel satisfied that you've done the most you can.

DON'T LET THE BRIDGE COLLAPSE

Bridges are the one place where all nonrewriters flourish. It's tempting to use that spot of the song as filler, but you may be overlooking an opportunity to make your song stronger. A bridge, musically, can give the material added personality and appeal.

You can alter the rhythm (In "We Can Work It Out," by Lennon and McCartney, the rock beat switched to a waltz), or add different chord flavorings. You can create a whole instrumental section with a life of its own (as Jimmy Webb did in "Mac Arthur Park"). You can write highly dramatic notes for the singer, heightening the listener's anticipation of the story's climax.

After you've completed the song, you might suspect that a tonal mistake has been made. The majority of the words may be down-home country, but you've given in to an urge to inject a polished, cosmopolitan phrase in there. Yes, it's clever, but is it honest? And again, are you hoping you can "get by" with it? A famous novelist once remarked, "A good writer must murder his darlings," and this same cold-blooded observation can be applied to songwriting. If it doesn't fit, if it's 'at all contrived, remove it.

What about the ending? Your tune might just trail off when it should soar. The rationalizations pour out: "It's more sensitive that way." Or: "The Number One record last week ended like that." If all these excuses don't eliminate your uncertainty, try different alternatives. You'll be glad you did.

MENTAL BLOCKS

Rewriting can be difficult, when you finally decide to do it. You might stare at the lines and get so locked in that your mind freezes. If you've gotten used to the song in its original form and played it that way a great deal, you may find yourself resenting the necessity for change. Or it may be impossible for you to yank those original intervals out of your head. When that happens, put away lead-sheet paper and pencil and go about doing something else. Your mind will be chugging away on the puzzle even while you sleep, if you've motivated your thoughts toward changing the song. When you wake up the next morning, the solution will probably present itself.

If you want to help your subconscious along, repeat just before dropping off to sleep, "I'll have the changes when I wake up." This form of self-hypnosis can be astonishingly effective. When Joel and I are in a tight corner, we always practice it, and our minds race to the rescue.

The ingredients of a song may all be fine, taken by themselves, yet the song doesn't come to life. Possibly the hook should open it, rather than the expository verse. Or it may be long, prompting a producer or artist to request some trims. Don't reject his ideas in a huff as creative destruction. It's time to do that after you've combed over his comments with an open mind. If, on honest reflection, you agree with him, you'll have to do the rewrites.

Publishers who encourage you at the outset may grow cool and unavailable if they notice you rebelling against suggestions for change. They have to see that you're flexible and capable of alterations when they're needed.

There is always the possibility that a song will burst out, perfectly formed in every lyric and musical detail, but those happy occasions are rare. The professional knows that careful rewriting is the difference between songs your family and friends applaud and those which earn the applause of the whole world.

THINGS TO REMEMBER

1. When you're vaguely uncomfortable with a rhyme, don't push that feeling aside. Rewrite the line.

2. Let yourself be influenced by current hits, but don't plagiarize whole sections.

3. Don't rely totally on musicians in the studio to fix up the rhythm. Do as much preparation as you can beforehand.

4. Give the same care and attention to the bridge that you give to the rest of the song.

5. If you're blocked, give yourself positive suggestions before you go to sleep, and you'll find your mind flowing freely again in the morning.

6. Don't resist constructive criticism from publishers and producers.

21

Casting, Presenting
and Selling Your Songs

Have you ever heard the term "professional student"? Its definition applies equally to thousands of songwriters who polish their craft, learn to compose commercially and then stash their material in a desk drawer or piano trunk. For whatever reason—insecurity about the songs themselves, nervousness about presenting them, desire to avoid rejection—these writers keep working prolifically but never show anybody what they've done. If you're one of the vast army of professional students, you should force yourself to break through the shell of fear, or you'll regret it later on. No matter how you rationalize that "It's all politics" or "It's a world of degenerates," you'll know inside that you failed yourself. Here are steps you can take toward casting,* presenting and selling your songs.

BE A CASTING DIRECTOR

There was an article published recently in the *Los Angeles Times* quoting Dan Hill, the artist and co-writer of "Sometimes When We Touch." His collaborator on this song was Barry Mann, and Hill told the

Casting—knowing what artists are available and what kind of music they favor, so that the material can be slanted accordingly.

interviewer that he writes from emotional feeling and Mann "writes like a chemist filling a prescription." There was a hint of derision in that phrase, which ignores the fact that this drugstore approach to songwriting has made Mann, along with his wife and partner Cynthia Weil, one of the biggest writers in rock history.

Mann and Weil, Carole King, Gerry Goffin, Neil Sedaka and Howard Greenfield were taught the art of casting by Don Kirshner. They were signed as writers by Kirshner's publishing firm in the '60s, and their casting skill enabled them to dominate the charts for a full decade.

Joel and I observed their methods. The first thing everyone did—after being told who was coming up for a date—was listen to the artist's previous singles and albums, or play down his or her sheet music. The overall niche was soon apparent—country, soul, middle of the road, pop. After that, the type of chord progressions would be studied and evaluated. Say the hit song of the moment was built on the chords C Am F G. A melody would be superimposed on that progression, or one close to it. It was useful to consider the artist's range, since Fabian and Steve Lawrence, for example, were very different in terms of their vocal capabilities, and both were having smash hits at that time.

We made Monday morning our "casting director" day. Our first step was to analyze the charts and learn who needed material. One indicator was to make note of the records that had peaked and were beginning their downward slide. In addition to that, we called every producer and publisher we knew to see who was cutting in the near future. Then we asked ourselves, "Would it be a good idea to write an 'answer' record to one of the current hits, or to conceive an entirely new song?" We examined our book of titles and circled those which seemed appropriate for the artists we had chosen to try for. If there were none, we went to work inventing new ones. This pre-work completed, we began to write the actual song.

As a general principle, most artists lean toward certain beats. Some like to "sing" more and prefer ballads. Others turn out up-tempo dance records and only occasionally experiment with unusual album material, where the steely eye of a program director can be ignored. Then there's the image an artist wants to project. Elvis Presley was always virile, macho, invariably aggressive, as the titles "Hound Dog," "Don't Step on My Blue Suede Shoes," "Jailhouse Rock" and "Treat Me Nice" demonstrated. Johnny Mathis, on the other hand, favored shy, self-effacing tunes like "Chances Are," "It's Not for Me to Say" and "What Will My Mary Say."

Uncreative? Not at all, only realistic. You can't impose your tastes and prejudices on performers unless you include the basic things they want. Also, it's wise to soak in the required information and let your subconscious begin to work after the facts have been assimilated. Your own individuality will reshape the elements into a different whole from any of the work you've been analyzing. Assimilating is not copying.

Charlie Chaplin, after being honored by the movie industry in 1971, made a statement that has implications far beyond the film industry alone. He said: "I have to admit I went into this business for the money, and the art grew out of it. If people are disillusioned by that remark, I can't help it. It's the truth." In other words, he approached filmmaking as a business. Paradoxically, if you take yourself too seriously and say, "I will now sit down to create a work of art," what you often end up with is rambling pretentiousness. You never know what will be art and what won't, because a peculiar fusion of brain and heart sometimes combines to produce greatness when you're just doing your job. Songwriting is a profession, and has to be treated that way if you're to succeed. You need to put in regular hours (we work from 9 to 6, and other writers choose their own hours, but the prolific ones have a schedule of some kind). Regularity gets music and words written. You can't survive on the occasional "masterpiece." And being a casting director is one organized way of working if you're a free-lance composer. Even the singer/songwriter or the composer for a group has to keep his eye trained on the market, on fluctuating commercial considerations, on image, on the popular beats of the day.

Howard Greenfield, who wrote the lyrics for many of Connie Francis' early hits, recognized immediately that people saw her as a victim of love because of the natural tear in her voice. In writing for her, he cast every song in a tearful, melodramatic mold, with titles such as "Breaking In a Brand New Broken Heart" and "Everybody's Somebody's Fool." Carole King and Gerry Goffin took Bobby Vee's image as an understanding, altruistic and protective lover into account when they wrote "Take Good Care of My Baby" and "Sharing You." "After the Loving," by Alan Bernstein and Richie Adams, is a fine recent example of musical casting. The big notes and sing-along melody were ideally suited to Engelbert Humperdinck's expansive, nightclub-oriented style.

CLOSED AND OPEN SCENES

It's not enough to cast correctly; you also have to keep availability in mind. People like Kansas, Queen, The Electric Light Orchestra, Jimmy Buffett or Steely Dan rarely, if ever, do "outside" songs (ones they haven't published or composed themselves), and your material is likely to be discarded promptly if it reaches their offices. A weekly check of the charts and a monthly examination of *Songwriter* will prevent this time-wasting and discouraging rejection from occurring.

Among the many open scenes today are Rita Coolidge, Samantha Sang, Odyssey, Meco, Eric Clapton, Donna Summer, Helen Reddy, Linda Ronstadt, Barbra Streisand, Diana Ross, Olivia Newton-John and Frankie Valli. Some country outlets include Emmylou Harris, Mel Tillis, Margo Smith, Barbara Mandrell, Mary Kay Place, Loretta Lynn and Donna Fargo. As for R & B, you can set your sights on Barry White, Dorothy Moore, Deniece Williams, Johnny Mathis, Stargard and Natalie Cole, to name just a few.

There's one important psychological point to ponder when slanting or casting your work. If an artist is totally alien to you, if you feel uncomfortable with his musical direction or lyrical approach, it's probably best not to pressure yourself to write for him. Don't be a computer and distort your nature. If you're at all versatile, there will be many artists you can create for without anxiety.

In casting, remember that long-maintained images and musical directions of certain singers can change. After a decade of one identity, an entertainer may adopt new postures that relate to the changing times. It's pointless to gear your tunes for an artist's teenybopper image when he has grown more outspoken and sophisticated (e.g., writing "Diana" for Paul Anka, when he's turning out "You're Having My Baby" and "I Don't Like to Sleep Alone").

The trades offer all the knowledge you need to become an expert casting director, but only if you read them properly. It's not enough to comb the Hot 100 and feel you've done thorough research. There are country charts and R & B charts, and beyond those, jazz, gospel and Latin charts. *Billboard* features a Top 50 Easy Listening section, and *Record World* points out the prime movers on FM stations.

Don't stare only at the Top 10 or the selections that have bullets. The Looking Ahead listings, which print names of records that are bubbling under the Hot 100, may be indicative of a new trend, or call attention to an artist who is on the verge of breaking through. Maybe you can write for him and climb on his bandwagon before he explodes nationally, at which time access to him will be much harder.

Billboard, Cash Box and *Record World* publish foreign charts, which are good indicators of what may come shortly to America. Remember, Elton John, the Beatles, Fleetwood Mac, Abba, Queen and The Who came from Europe. If you can cast your material for artists overseas and succeed in having hits there, the records are likely to cross over to American shores. Any kind of acceptance and exposure gives a promotion man something to emphasize and plug when he brings the record around to stations; it gives him that extra hook he needs to differentiate the product from hundreds of others that haven't been heard anywhere.

CASTING FOR RECORD COMPANIES

When someone says, "Motown," what clicks in your mind? Pop rhythm and blues. If someone says, "Warner/Curb," the knowledgeable music person will immediately think, "Mid-America clean-cut rock" or

"Recycled rock." All companies vary their style now and then, but most of them have an overall image, and knowing what those images are will serve as a shortcut for the casting director.

For example, the two biggest record labels are CBS and Warner Brothers. Over the many years, they have set up different custom labels distributed through CBS and Warners. The reason for that is twofold: (1) when a promotion man goes to a radio station, the program director sees differently named labels and doesn't feel he's playing a surplus of CBS or Warner Brothers product, and (2) each of these custom labels has a specific musical or artist identity. CBS distributes a label called Philadelphia International, which is run by Kenny Gamble and Leon Huff, and basically centers around rhythm and blues pop material. Monument Records, another custom label, is based in Nashville and Memphis, and specializes in the country market. Epic, a third subsidiary of Columbia, is a straight pop affiliate.

Warner Brothers distributes Capricorn Records, which has a southern blues image (The Allman Brothers, Joe South). Asylum, a different division of Warners, is folk-oriented, and has produced Joni Mitchell, Judy Collins and the Eagles.

When you're reading the charts and analyzing hits, start making associations with the companies that release them. If you call the A & R director of each company, you'll be able to get hold of the company's entire roster. That way you won't make a mistake that a co-writer of ours did in the early '60s (we won't mention his name). He took a demo of a new song he had cast for Lesley Gore to Atlantic Records!

The most direct way of getting your songs recorded is to sing them yourself. Or you can join a group and write for them (as Bob Gaudio did for The Four Seasons in the '60s, and Glenn Frey and Don Henley do for the Eagles today).

Writing for yourself if you're a single artist allows you more personal expression. The free-lance writer must consider a number of artists. He has to tailor his songs to their needs and their images. You, on the other hand, have a preset image, which you understand thoroughly.

You may be producing the album as well as performing on it, but even if someone else is handling the production chores, your supervision over the way your material is recorded is much greater than that of the free-lance writer. You have tremendous say over arrangements, background vocals and the final mix of the record.

The free lancer is always a little insecure, worrying, "Will I get in on a scene?" or "Will I ever get this tune recorded?" These fears don't exist for the singer/songwriter or the writer for a group. He knows (at least while signed to a company) that he has a consistent outlet for his work.

Casting material for a group gives the composer clear guidelines— he knows what image to consider, what kind of music the members play, what type of material they prefer. There's a casting trap, though, for the singer/songwriter: self-indulgence. "I've Gotta Be Me" and "My Way" are dangerous attitudes if a writer doesn't maintain perspective. It's important to remember that your songs must relate to millions of listeners, that you can write about personal things only if you invite identification from others as well. Not only that, but some of the songs in your album should have wide enough appeal so that they can be covered by other artists, so that they have enough casting potency beyond yourself to last and become standards.

In preparing an album, writers often forget to consider singles. Artist/composers like Billy Joel, Jackson Browne and Paul Simon know that a single is important as a tool to promote the album. Enjoy the luxury of personal writing, but at the same time don't forget to include one or two commercially geared cuts so that you can get the AM-radio airplay you need.

THINGS TO REMEMBER

1. In casting, analyze the charts and find out who needs material, as well as the kind of music, lyrics and beat each artist favors.

2. Call producers and publishers every week to see who's coming up for a recording date.

3. Figure out the overall image of the performer you want to try for.

4. Organize your writing time. Treat composing as a profession, rather than waiting for "the mood."

5. Read *Songwriter's* monthly chart and find out which artists are open to outside material, and which ones write for themselves or have an exclusive composer they depend on.

6. Don't pressure yourself to write for artists whose work is alien to you.

7. Study foreign charts, which are reliable indicators of what trends are coming to America.

8. Study the Bubbling Under or Looking Ahead sections of the trades, to see what records and artists are about to break through.

9. Get to know the specific images of each record company.

10. Read Executive Turntable in *Billboard, Cash Box* and *Record World,* to find out the new people in power at record labels.

22

Demo Power!

Now that you've completed your song, you'll want to do a demo that clearly points up the shadings, the background harmonies, the slight but significant shifts of rhythm you have in mind.

Very often a publisher and/or producer will listen to your song and respond with enough enthusiasm to say, "Great, let's go out and do the demo." This generally means he'll foot the bill for full studio costs.

In other instances (fairly often, I'm afraid), the writer has to dig into his jeans and invest in the demo himself, then submit it upon completion to different acts and record companies. If he can't easily afford it, he'll have to achieve all his effects with minimum expense and maximum imagination.

Since it's far preferable for the publisher to assume expenses, your initial presentation must project as many values as possible in order to induce him to make this offer; the mood, the rhythm, the vocal interpretation will suggest what kind of artist and style you have in mind.

If you're one half of a team, your partner can sing a background line while you belt out the lead, or vice versa. Short explanations, without apologies for a sore throat or laryngitis, can also clarify your intentions. An air of self-belief (without arrogance) helps tremendously.

You should be well rehearsed when you perform the material. Lyrics should be neatly typed, and it's wise to have an extra copy for the publisher to read. It goes without saying that cross-outs, smudges or coffee stains won't give your audience much confidence in what you're doing.

Okay—you've passed the first hurdle. That magic phrase, "Let's do the demo" has been uttered. The publisher can now contribute his expertise—he has had considerable experience in the organization and execution of demonstration records. He also has access to the best musicians and the finest studios. It's unlikely that you'll be thrown without a life jacket into stormy waters. You'll have to gain studio experience gradually, making mistakes while you feel your way. If you're producing a demo for a publisher, either he or his general professional manager (the publisher's right-hand man, who listens to material, brings it around and generally supervises all creative activities) will be at the session. As a rule, he will welcome your ideas.

The simplest, most basic kind of demo is the piano/voice. This approach works well with ballads, particularly of the Easy Listening (or MOR—middle-of-the-road) variety, or the "straight" song which relies purely on its melody and lyric line rather than production values. The pianist in this case will have to be the entire orchestra, and he should play with as much fullness and dimension as possible.

A variation on this is the guitar/voice. The guitar/voice will often give you more scope and movement than a piano demo. You can achieve strong rhythm and blues and country effects without adding further instrumentation.

A simple word of caution: use experts in the "bag" you're working with. A legit singer who holds notes (such as Robert Goulet) will not give you a good, funky Nashville sound. An R & B singer will do more for your blues song than a middle-of-the-road singer. There are many musicians who are specialists in certain areas and will do more for your tunes than others. Finally, *don't* ask a friend to sing or play out of misguided loyalty if you don't feel he or she is absolutely up to the artistic demands of the material. Even if you do have a friend with talent, it might be safer and more practical to hire a person with professional background for your early efforts.

Early in our partnership, Joel (who was relatively new to the record business at that point) insisted that he had found a new star. He urged me not to be influenced against her because she was an ex-girlfriend of his from the Bronx. I panicked immediately but, swallowing hard and suppressing my anxiety, reminded myself I had to be fair. I rationalized: "Joel has good ears." As a result, a song named "Gettin' Down to It, Baby" was rendered by a young Beverly Sills. It was a blood-curdling experience, and I'll never forget the startled and horrified faces of the musicians. In view of the commercial sense Joel has picked up over the years, I'll charitably assume he was too emotionally involved to notice her artistic shortcomings. But this is what can happen when you choose friends instead of qualified personnel.

Another—fuller—demo is one that utilizes piano, guitar, bass and drums. This quartet, backing a strong vocal lead, can project almost anything you need. Background singers will fill the production in further. They can sustain harmonies that will approximate a string line, or do quick answers that propel the rhythmic pulse forward. The important thing is to use them carefully and sparingly, and not be so eager for a full sound that you allow them to blanket the lead and the main melody line.

This can't be emphasized too strongly—an overproduced demo can be more negative than one that is underproduced. Even if you're a Rockefeller and have the money to indulge all your whims, a large orchestra of strings, brass and woodwinds may cause confusion. You have to tantalize an artist with possibilities, not do all his work for him. Publishers today are unanimous on that point. A few hundred dollars and meticulous planning will give you the resources you need, provided the song is there. Many potential hits have been lost in clumsy, inappropriate demonstrations. The devices for presentation are endless—from your home cassette to a 16-track recording—but whatever your method, think of the *song*, not the icing. You're not spotlighting the instruments or even the vocal; they matter only as parts of an effective whole, showing off your material to its best advantage.

When a publisher lays out money for a demo, he usually subtracts 50 percent from your future royalties for the cost! That's one good reason not to run up huge studio expenses. Joel and I wrote several songs for Elvis Presley in the late '60s and made demos of them. We didn't stint on production values and overdubs. Later, "Your Time Hasn't Come Yet, Baby" was recorded by Presley and became an international hit, and we were looking forward to our first statement. The figures were disheartening: thousands of dollars had been lopped off by the publisher for these demo sessions; and after absorbing this grim reality, we vowed not to go overboard in the future (this vow was broken many times, despite good intentions—there's something seductive and hypnotic about studios, and you may find it impossible to tear yourself away).

Knowing the exact rates of demos and masters (actual recordings by artists for national release) may help you to maintain perspective. Here they are.

Demos (1 hour)

> $25.00 for first hour, up to two songs
> 50.00 for leader
> 15.00 every half hour following—one song
> 30.00 for leader in overtime

Master (3-hour session—15 minutes of music)

> $121.00 per sideman
> 242.00 for leader
> 40.34 per musician overtime (½ hour)
> 80.68 leader overtime

As you gain skill, you'll be allowed more control of your demos. Preparation is all-important, so that you don't waste hours of time and money, and you should keep some considerations in constant view. First, get together with the singers and work out a key, rather than guessing or trying to figure one out on the basis of a performer's previous recordings. Each tune is different, and if the session begins and the key is "close enough," rather than "right on the beam," the material might come off a shade too dull or too shrill, just enough to produce that uncomfortable, "*something* is bothering me" feeling. Frustration then sets in, as well as a faint mood of discouragement that may cloud the entire date.

Don't assume that if the key is wrong, the musicians can transpose it effortlessly at the session. Some musicians are only passable readers, but their brilliant inventiveness compensates. They will labor over the job of transposing, and you may be required to rewrite all the chords in the new key. Even if the transpositions are accomplished without strain, this process eats into studio time.

Try to hear your singers on record or on tape. In-person performances are notoriously deceiving. The live electricity of a performance can be largely due to a singer's personal magnetism, good looks, emotional gestures. These factors have a curious way (until the date) of distracting from shaky pitch or a vibrato that would prove maddening and commercially unacceptable. If the singer doesn't have any records or tapes for you to evaluate, bring a cassette machine with you and record him, then play his vocal back when you get home. Only one element matters—the sound.

Don't choose a singer who thinks he or she must show off "big notes." Remember that Frank Sinatra, and later on, Elvis Presley, have more presence and power on a mike than Robert Merrill does. Excessive volume tends to have a diminishing effect. Listen to the records of opera stars. Onstage they can shatter glass. Yet on wax, the sound is often thin and tinny. Imagine how odd and abrasive it would be if a motion-picture camera were right on top of an actor and he were howling away and hamming it up. But think how effective it is when a master underplayer like record-turned-movie star Kris Kristofferson conveys emotion with a slight hand movement or a shift of the eyes or lips.

Keep a sharp watch on the tempo. Musicians tend to slow down, or more frequently, speed up unless carefully observed. Quietly sing the lyrics along with the track and see if they feel comfortable at that pace. It's a mistake to think that faster is necessarily more exciting. Past a certain point, speed has a dampening effect—it reduces excitement and danceability, as well as making the words unintelligible.

When making a demo, you can increase its chances of acceptance by cutting both a male and a female version. Or you might want to do one version with a solo vocalist and one with a group. Sometimes the lyric content doesn't allow for these alternatives, but surprisingly often it does. There are other ways to enhance the across-the-board appeal of a demo—adding a dobro guitar to the rhythm section, to countrify it, for example, or switching background singers in different takes to change the flavor.

As a creative coordinator, you have to keep your cool and not blow up over the innumerable problems that may arise in the studio. An engineer may accidentally erase a guitar solo you've been perfecting for hours. Worse, Joel and I had an experience recently which is, fortunately, uncommon. We had everyone run through our tune, and the result was perfect—just what we'd been searching for all day. The singer had managed—after three hours—to conquer a "blind spot" which had resulted in 35 takes (a conservative estimate). The rhythm had a wonderful unity, the strings were rich. I sighed blissfully and turned to the engineer, grinning and wiping my brow. "What a great take!" Long pause. "Oh . . . was that a take? I didn't record it. I thought it was a rehearsal." Times like this try men's souls, but finding an axe and smashing up his board won't solve anything. (The above is not meant to put engineers in an unfavorable light. Most of them are hardworking, dedicated and imaginative, copilots and allies in discovering the best ways of enhancing the material—but these irritating setbacks do occur.)

Occasionally a musician you've booked won't show up. Panic! The absence of a pianist or guitar does cause a gaping hole, especially if you've hired only a quartet, but if another player isn't available in time, you have to do some fast reorganizing. Maybe the piano can contribute a rhythm that will compensate for the guitar's absence. Maybe a more moving bass line can do the drummer's work for it. You'll be astounded how fluidly your mind functions under these crisis circumstances after a while.

In films or on the stage, the best actors often learn everyone else's lines. Beyond your attention to obvious details like vocals and musicians, try to find out everything you can about engineering. (Some composers, like Jim Loggins, were engineers first.) Acquire a knowledge of mixing (taking all the individual tracks and blending them properly, featuring what you want to, be it a guitar lick, a cymbal crash, a piano figure or an inventive bass pattern). When you listen back to the final mix, test it out on a small speaker, which is the way the publisher and producer will finally hear it. Drowning yourself in waves of sound is a marvelous ego trip, but it's a false turn-on, and you'll be disappointed when you re-evaluate the demo on your home set.

THE RIGHT MUSICIANS

Years ago, when I was producing Steve Lawrence and Eydie Gormé, the arranger I worked with was a man named Marion Evans. I noticed, when it came time for him to book the musicians, that he chose different brass and woodwind players on the ballads than he did on the up-tempo and swing songs. They were all proficient, skillful players, so I wondered what determined his choices. He explained: "A classically oriented musician (such as musicians who play in symphony orchestras) won't slide or slur notes. He'll play them cleanly, as written, while jazz musicians, because of the inherent nature of their style, have a tendency of sliding and improvising."

It all comes down to your particular needs as a composer and record or demo producer. Musicians are all individuals, with varying abilities, preferences and personality traits.

If you're the kind of composer who demands that every note be played as written, you should gravitate toward those musicians who are known to be superb readers. For example, one writer will hand out chord sheets and say, "Feel it." Another will spell out every nuance, every rhythm, every dynamic, and become agitated if these qualities aren't reproduced exactly as he hears them.

The stickler is a rare bird in rock circles, although he does exist. Much more prevalent is the writer who permits his players to have a creative say. Rock and roll is a free and flowing art, a collaborative enterprise. No matter how much you write down, the printed page can't capture everything. If you trust your men, it's wise to let them stretch out, within the borders of your basic concept.

The super musician who isn't a top-notch reader will occasionally stumble on a complicated part. Yet if this same man is asked to let go on a solo, his contribution may be the difference between a passable record and a hit.

Generalizing about age in terms of rock is wrong. An older person is just as capable of giving the producer what he wants. It's a matter of motivation. You have to decide if the musician in question is fixed in his viewpoints, if he has tastes based on a bygone era that he can't put aside. Youthful players can be more open to today's music, and many producers automatically assess prospective musicians in terms of their age. But it's much wiser to get to know all the musicians possible and evaluate them strictly on the basis of what comes out of their instrument. Letting age determine your decision may cost you some of the best creative talent available.

In selecting your personnel, studio experience is vital. A much-employed studio man has acquired an instinctive understanding of the microphone. He knows how to shade his playing to that sensitive electronic ear. Those players who only have in-person background are liable to pound away and get too noisy, lost in a self-indulgent frenzy. As a result, you'll be wasting valuable hours balancing the orchestra. This is typical of the in-person drummer, who may become too cymbal-oriented, causing an overly splashy sound in recording. The result is leakage into the other mikes.

It's an excellent idea, if possible, to pick musicians who have played together in the past. Their personalities mesh, their styles integrate easily. They don't have to explain their feelings for each other, because a kind of silent shorthand exists that makes communication automatic.

SOURCES

If you're new in the music business and want to make contact with musicians, here are a few avenues to take:

1. Call the musicians' union. It will be glad to suggest people. Go down to the union hall and mix with the members, until you become familiar with their names and specialties.

2. Call recording studios around town for recommendations. As you get to know studio owners, engineers or producers, ask them if you can sit in on sessions. Over a period of time you can build up relationships, as well as learning a great deal of recording procedure.

3. Go down to clubs and make cassette copies of groups playing. That will give you some idea of how they sound on records.

4. Study the backs of albums and make note of the personnel used. Maybe there's a guitarist or a bass player who would be perfect for the song you want to produce.

Don't, on the other hand, let yourself be intimidated into accepting musical ideas that don't seem right to you. The fact that you're new doesn't mean you lack sound musical instincts. Don't assume that your musicians have all the answers when they volunteer suggestions. Analyze them and accept or reject them according to your own feelings and objectives. Resist any pressure that contradicts your own intuition, or you won't grow as an artist.

THE RIGHT STUDIO

Sly Stone said, "Different strokes for different folks," and this is an apt phrase when you're choosing a studio to record in. It's not enough to find a place that has good equipment and an engineer trained to manipulate the dials. There are a number of emotional, as well as practical, factors to consider, such as size, setup, distracting noise and number of tracks required.

What kind of demo do you want to make? It's easier to get a good, tight rhythm sound in a smaller studio. The major problem with a large room is one of leakage, which means instruments leaking from one microphone into another. This results in an overall lack of definition; too many overtones obscure the clarity and cleanness of each instrument.

Setup is a vital step in recording, and when you're working in a large studio (where huge brass or string sections must be accommodated) it becomes even more important. It involves the placement of instruments and mikes, reducing leakage between instruments and listening to each one through the control-room speakers. Unlike the situation in rehearsals or in-person performances, players will be scattered around the room, each assigned to his or her own area (while still being able to see the others). Sound "baffles" (portable sound barriers used to isolate instruments during recording) will guarantee good separation, and the leakage will be minimized or prevented. The drummer is generally placed behind low baffles and has as many as seven mikes on his set. Guitar players are likely to find their amps wrapped in packing blankets. Very often separate rooms are utilized for vocals and comparatively quiet instruments such as the acoustic guitar.

Equipment should be checked for intrusive, distracting noises. Any rattling or buzzing must be eliminated before the date begins.

A lesson I learned from two outstanding engineers, Bob Fein, of Fein Sound in New York, and Roy Halee, producers of such artists as Simon and Garfunkel, is to use microphones that aren't too live. The rhythm musicians play so hard, are so unrestrained in their attack, that they provide the power and dynamics needed. A high-frequency mike on these instruments can give too much of an edge, sounding mechanical and unnatural.

The first decision you want to make in a studio is the number of tracks needed. That will vary according to your artistic concept and the amount of money you're willing or able to spend. In a simple two-track recording, instruments and vocals are recorded at the same time. The sound is then mixed onto a master, rather than placed on separate tracks for future mixing. Because so many of today's records are the result of imaginative studio experimentation, on the blending of different instrumental and vocal parts, two-track recordings are considered limiting and old-fashioned by most young songwriters and producers.

The advantage of multitracking is that singers and musicians can listen to previously recorded tracks and add extra parts. They can also delete mistakes and punch in the corrections. Four-, 8-, 16- and 24-track sessions are available. For full masters (or demo masters) 16 and 24 tracks are standard. Four and 8 tracks are common for demos.

When you begin to make friends in the music business, or spend time with other writers, chances are they'll be eager to play you demos they've done. You're bound to have an opinion, and if it's favorable, you can ask them where they did their recording. Before long you'll find common denominators in all conversations about studios. A few names will pop up again and again because of their reputations for speed and reliability, because of their "good rhythm sound" or their "big string sound" or some other feature they've become associated with.

Have you ever had the experience of walking into a new home, or an office you've never entered before, and feeling immediately relaxed and comfortable? Studios can affect you that way too. There's a warmth, a sense of security that certain ones radiate which will contribute to better work.

An engineer you're in harmony with is a tremendous plus. In addition to being skillful, he should be helpful if you're a newcomer, intuitive in anticipating your needs and knowledgeable enough to guess what you want when you can't quite verbalize it. This kind of communication is possible between engineer and producer or engineer and writer when the vibes are right. But beyond professional rapport, there should be empathy, a sense of humor and an ability to maintain equilibrium under pressure. These are all vital factors, and you, as a songwriter/producer, shouldn't settle for less.

Some studios are first-rate in every way. They may have a superlative reputation and a dazzling track record. But they may also be prohibitively expensive and totally booked until the year 2000. If you're a beginner, you have to come up with second and third choices. Maybe there's a good place that's up and coming, still new enough to be reasonably priced and easy to reserve. A little searching will justify the effort. Don't get fixated on one studio and throw up your hands in despair when that studio proves impractical for one reason or another.

You might have to compromise in certain respects. If you've heard of a terrific place to cut demos that is way out in the woods or in a far-off county that requires an hour or more of driving, it's worth the trip.

DEMO CASTING

As a composer does a certain amount of casting while he writes, a demo producer should keep in mind the ingredients he wishes to highlight, ingredients that will capture the attention of the artist he's going after.

Two approaches can be taken: (a) flavor the demo with characteristics that are likely to appeal to one specific performer (the right genre— be it country, R & B or pop; the right beat, chord progression, lyric theme) while retaining general characteristics that appeal to many; or (b) take the full gamble and do everything to slant your demo for one artist alone.

As an impressionist, I'm able to do accurate impersonations of Elvis Presley and Anthony Newley, and when Joel and I wrote songs for them years ago and sent along demos with virtual reproductions of their singing, they recorded the material. These demos used arrangements similar to those of many of their current hits. Some artists resent imitation which attempts to pin them down artistically, but the majority will respond favorably to demos which capture the qualities that have made them successful.

Producing demos to display a song can be the first step toward a record-producing career. In my case, a series of demos I produced were eventually heard by CBS executives, with the happy result that I was hired as a staff producer for that company.

Many platters that have started life as demos grow up to be demo masters, hit records on their own rather than just vehicles for presentation. Some classic examples: "Young Blood" (The Coasters), "Splish Splash" (Bobby Darin), "It Might as Well Rain Until September" (Carole King), "The Twist" (Chubby Checker) and "The Loco-Motion" (Little Eva).

If you harbor secret plans to launch your own singing career, demos are a perfect place to practice. Melissa Manchester began that way, and the result was her collaboration with Carole Bayer Sager. Going back a bit, Bobby Darin's demo singing turned him into an international star. He utilized demo power to notable advantage by recording two songs (on the same date): "Early in the Morning" and "Splish Splash." He gave his multitracked performance on "Early in the Morning" a group name—the Rinky Dinks. The record made the Top 20. He promoted "Splish Splash" under his own name for Atco/Atlantic, and that turned out to be Number One in the country.

Ronnie Dante, who appeared on almost everyone's demos (his voice on a song of Joel's and mine, "Let's Start All Over Again," was heard by Ronnie Dove, who recorded it and sent it to the Top 10), burst out of the cocoon as lead singer for the Archies. The result, "Sugar Sugar," was a phenomenal success around the world. What Ronnie learned in the demo studio presumably added to the producing skills that shine on every Barry Manilow record. "Candida," by Tony Orlando and Dawn, was originally cut as a demonstration recording until purchased by a label and released as a master.

You can discover a star while writing and producing for demos. No better illustration exists than the careers of Burt Bacharach, Hal David and Dionne Warwicke. Dionne was a background singer and part of a group when Bacharach and David found her, and within a year she was turning out her legendary series of Bacharach/David compositions, such as "I Say a Little Prayer," "Alfie" and "Don't Make Me Over."

PRESENTING YOUR DEMOS

When showing your demo to a publisher, producer or artist, here are some tips on what and what not to do:

- Have A Professional Lead Sheet
Lead sheets vary. They can be meticulously sketched out, or a crinkled, scribbled mess of hieroglyphics, so carelessly notated that no one could read them. A sloppy lead sheet identifies you as an amateur and immediately sets a bad tone for your meeting. Your lead sheet should contain the following things:

a. Melody, lyric, chord symbols, as well as an indication of the desired rhythmic feel;

b. A logical choice of key. It's foolish to place the song in a range that requires a dozen ledger lines. A comfortable, middle-range key makes the song easier to sing, play and read;

c. Chord symbols above the melody;

d. Words under the notes they correspond with. This involves some preplanning. Don't write your melody out spontaneously, crowding notes together, jamming 16ths into tiny spaces. If you do, you won't be able to squeeze the lyrics underneath in their proper places. After an hour of work, you'll have to rip the lead sheet up in frustration and start again;

e. Use a pen if you can, or a dark pencil. If you tend to make mistakes, it's better to stick to pencil;

f. Don't forget the key signature. When you've finished, play the sheet over and check to see if any accidentals have been left out.

If you don't feel qualified to write the lead sheet yourself, there are specialists who can do it for you. Sing or perform your song for a copyist, arranger, musician or friend and he'll take it down. Professionals are listed in the Yellow Pages under Music Copyists, Music Arrangers or Music Teachers.

● Don't oversell—songwriters have a tendency, especially when anxious, to hype producers and artists to the sky. Give them a chance to listen and digest your work. Don't blabber on while the demo is playing. You've already provided enough background accompaniment on your demo record or tape.

● Don't apologize—"I had a cold when I sang on it" . . . "The mix isn't that good" . . . "The bass player's father died that day" . . . Excuses speak of insecurity, and are sometimes so distracting that the listener automatically turns off to the merits of your material.

● Don't discuss your emotional problems—the producer or artist doesn't care if you had a fight with your family or if you're going through analysis. He just wants to know if the song is good, and if it fits his needs.

- Don't bring a dozen songs—two is fine, and three is acceptable, but never more. After a while, songs tend to all sound alike and blur in the listener's mind if he has to absorb too many at once.

- Don't pressure the listener for an answer—if he likes it, he'll give you some indication. Maybe he'll say, "Get back to me in a couple of days," and you should accept that, not push ahead, "But what did you think?" If he says it's not for him, don't pin him to the wall for explanations, or try to change his mind by pointing out how good the material is, how commercial, how right for such and such an artist. The only result of that behavior will be a secretary telling you, the next time you call, "Mr. So-and-So is in a meeting."

Sometimes you'll want your tune presented live, rather than on a demo. If you're a good singer or musician, your tendency will be to present the material yourself, and that's fine if you can do it justice. But there are occasions when your style is wrong for the tune and your demonstration can hinder its effectiveness. Joel and I frequently perform our work and have had good results over the years, but we recently composed a movie theme entitled "Hot Lead and Cold Feet" for a Disney comedy western of the same name. The song was very twangy and country in feeling, so we contacted a group of musicians who worked at the Palomino Club in Los Angeles, a club that features only country entertainers. They played it for the Disney producers and the song was accepted. It might have gotten by with our presentation, but it would never have elicited such enthusiasm from the audience if we had sung it.

One last, uncreative but critical point: don't submit the only tape you have. Music-business history is filled with cases of new writers who work on demos for weeks and then fail to make copies! People often misplace and lose tapes, without worrying too much about it because they assume you have duplicates of your work. Don't subject yourself to that feeling of frustrated helplessness which comes when you have to return to the studio and start everything over. All it takes is a self-addressed, stamped envelope to protect you from discouraging, sometimes irreparable losses.

THINGS TO REMEMBER

1. The basic types of demos are:
a. Piano/voice;
b. Guitar/voice;
c. Rhythm section—piano, guitar, bass and drums;
d. Rhythm section plus strings and/or brass. This combination is generally too elaborate for publishers, who prefer simple demos.
2. Don't run up exorbitant bills in the studio. Chances are likely that 50 percent of the costs will be deducted from your royalties by the publisher of the song.
3. Don't guess about keys. Figure them out with the singer before the session.
4. Judge a singer as a result of hearing him on tape, rather than in person. Live performances are misleading.
5. Keep a sharp watch on the tempo. Don't let it race ahead or slow down in the middle.
6. Do male and female versions of the song. That will increase the number of recordings possible.
7. Make sure your musicians have studio experience.
8. To contact musicians:
a. Call the musicians' union;
b. Contact studios around town for recommendations;
c. Go down to clubs and make cassette copies of the groups playing;

d. Study the back covers of albums and make note of the personnel used.

9. Give thought to the casting of your demo beforehand. Decide whether the song should be presented in a general way that will appeal to many artists, or slanted in a specific manner to appeal to just one.

10. In presenting the demo to producers, publishers or artists, make sure you have a professional lead sheet.

11. Don't oversell or go to the other extreme of apologizing for your work.

12. Don't bring a dozen songs. Two or three is all a listener can absorb in one sitting.

13. Don't submit the only tape you have, and risk the possibility of losing it.

23

Record Production

Record producing as we know it today was virtually nonexistent at the beginning of the 1950s. A decade later it had blossomed into an art, marked by imagination, freshness and versatility. As often happens, this phenomenon arose out of necessity.

Writers of rock and roll in the early days of this new music found themselves in a dilemma. Their songs were looser, freer in structure, not bound by rigid, formal rules of construction. Their material didn't adapt easily to traditional recording approaches. In the 1940s, a staff producer working for a major record company, such as Columbia, Capitol or RCA Victor, would hire an arranger to come in and teach the artist the song he was to sing. A few days later, presto! the performer got up and cut the number with the orchestra in a few takes.

Closed off by prejudice and restricted by old-fashioned attitudes, the writer and record-producer-to-be went into studios and began to experiment. Frequently he was aided by publishers whose minds were not set against rock, who saw the trend and decided to move with it. First the concept of doing the vocal and band separately (revolutionary at the time, customary now) came into popular use. From there overdubbing was refined. With the addition of tracks, it became natural to separate everything—lead voices, background vocals, brass, strings, rhythm—giving the producer a chance to polish and perfect each individual element. Young musicians who were willing to pay their dues and work for minimum wages to gain experience were used, rather than solidly entrenched studio players. When these modestly budgeted, experimental records were released, millions of youthful buyers swarmed to the stores and bought them.

Writers quickly realized the exciting possibilities of working in the studio and shaping songs to their particular vision, rather than automatically handing the material to publishers and artists. They turned to up-and-coming independent record labels that were sympathetic to their aims, such as Chess and Checker, Swan, Atlantic/Atco, Scepter, Oldtown and Jubilee.

These early productions had crude energy, but strings and brass didn't appear on any of them. The Drifters' recording of "There Goes My Baby" changed that. Carole King's string parts for her "Will You Love Me Tomorrow" by The Shirelles also furthered the development. Records like "Venus in Blue Jeans" ushered in the use of brass, as well as other platters by Fats Domino and the Coasters. Blood, Sweat and Tears, many years afterward, introduced jazzlike brass, which led to further embellishment in this vein by Chicago.

Many of these songs, containing unusual syncopations and tricky note jumps, were not likely to generate interest from such middle-of-the-roaders as Vic Damone, Eddie Fisher, Doris Day or Jo Stafford. Therefore, writers were greeted by an additional challenge—to find artists of their own, cut them and place them with companies.

Burt Bacharach and Hal David were confronted with this problem. Bacharach's music was rejected by some, inaccurately done by others. The arrangements were "squared," the rhythms sawed off at the edges. Bacharach and David finally solved the problem with Dionne Warwicke, who had the ear to reproduce their songs correctly. This is one reason so many writers have become producers—to protect their songs, and make sure they're executed as originally conceived.

Record labels accepted the inevitable, and now there are several kinds of producers. One is the staff producer, a man hired exclusively by a company to produce artists signed to that company. There's the independent record producer, a free lance who may sign a production agreement with a label to produce one or more of the label's artists, but is still free to work with as many other companies as he chooses to. There's the artist/producer, who cuts himself, or a group member who produces his group. The latter may be affiliated with the label he is signed to as an *artist,* but be privileged to do outside performers in his production work for other labels, or he may be tied up in all aspects to one company. Finally there's the individual who produces an independent master with the goal of selling it to a company.

RECORD CHILDREN

The growth of record production influenced composers to think in terms of "entertainments," mini–theatrical pieces, rather than simply in words and music. We've seen how writers today give strong attention to introductions; they usually plot out background answers and instrumental figures from the beginning. A record producer must do the same. If he's also the writer of the song, he has a chance to further develop the ideas he devised in composing it. Today's writers are what we call "record children." "Records," as opposed to "songs," can't be demonstrated effectively to a publisher on a piano or guitar. The tune depends on its trappings—e.g., guitars being recorded backward, or tape delays on different instruments. It might need the seasoning of a synthesizer to make it complete. Records sell an experience, a sexual sound, a beat, a mood, in addition to a tune.

Writer/producers should ideally be adept at both the straight song ("By the Time I Get to Phoenix"), which doesn't require added instrumental embellishment, and the record, which is a studio-born, studio-dependent product. Records aren't necessarily meant to be covered by other artists, nor are they tunes that can travel—they're total, self-contained entities. A qualified professional can produce "songs" and "records" with equal ease, and find stimulation and challenge in each one.

CAPTAIN OF THE SHIP

The writer/producer must develop the ability to view things in an overall perspective. Singers, musicians, engineers are all indispensable contributors to the success of a session, but there is one person—the record producer—who must be captain of the ship, blend the parts into a whole and coordinate every facet. He must have the strength, for example, to tone down a superb trumpet solo if that solo intrudes on the general mood of the record. If a singer knocks everyone for a loop with a big note when the lyric demands sensitivity and subtlety, that note must be toned down, no matter how powerful it is. The producer keeps everything in balance. He must know the merits of the basic material and also its weaknesses, so he can decide what to highlight and what to compensate for with imaginative fills.

A very real danger presents itself when a songwriter begins to produce. Sometimes, in the desire to get his material cut, he'll load the entire date (if the artist doesn't object) with his own songs. These songs aren't always appropriate, and tunes from other writers, or perhaps a standard or two, might benefit the singer more. The producer's objectivity has to come into play again. He doesn't want to jeopardize his artist's career; he must be willing to stand aside and consider outside material. A narrow, self-serving attitude won't yield any hits, and both producer and performer will lose out.

Production choices are a highly individual matter, but make sure that your records build steadily and end with excitement and power. Whether making a demo or a master, the personnel should be as professional and creative as possible. With these elements, plus a clear idea of your artistic aims, you'll be able to do your material full justice in the studio.

To produce an independent master with the idea of selling it to a record label, you have to get initial financing. If you happen to be well heeled, there's no problem, but many aspiring writer/producers are short on funds.

It's convenient to have a friend, relative or proud parent who believes in you and wants to back your session. Another alternative is a bank loan if you're a reliable risk.

If you form a friendship with the head of an up-and-coming studio, he might be willing to gamble on you to the extent of giving you free time, off-hours when nobody is using the facilities. An attorney may back you, for a percentage or a portion of the profits when the master is sold.

Several music publishers in recent years have gone into partnership with writer/producers. An example of this is the Warner Brothers–backed "Undercover Angel," which brought Alan O'Day such popularity. Having committed himself monetarily, the publisher will be eager to recoup his investment, and will use his record contacts to get the release sold and promoted.

A manager who believes in you can be a strong business and psychological asset. If you're an artist as well as songwriter, he'll advise and direct you in such career decisions as what record company and publishing company to choose. After contracts have been signed, he'll see that label and publisher live up to their parts of the bargain in matters like merchandising, advertising and promotion. A manager should anticipate your needs, help you plan ahead and set aside reasonable time for both your performing and writing responsibilities. He should be able to advise about personnel—producers, engineers, musicians—and listen to material with an objective ear, rather than offering false and ultimately harmful flattery.

One crucial aspect of a manager's job is to pick the right booking agency, attorney and road manager. Typical percentages run between 15 and 20 percent, and a standard contract ranges between 3 and 7 years.

SELLING YOUR MASTER

Before you take your record to any of the heads of A & R (Artists and Repertoire men, who choose product for the various record companies), be certain it's in the best possible shape. This doesn't just mean the songs or the performances . . . it means the tape itself. Make sure there's no distortion, and that the sound is cut as high as you want it to be. Small things count heavily when you want to sell a master. If you're showing a tape, insert enough "leader" (blank tape) at the beginning to allow the listener to thread it without jumping in at the middle of the tune. On the other hand, if there's too much leader, he'll be clicking his heels impatiently, waiting for the music to begin. Put leader between each number and the next if there are several. It simplifies matters if the listener wants to return to Selection 2 or 3 without searching endlessly for the right place.

If you've played a disc for many people, have new copies cut. It doesn't give an A & R man confidence when he hears scratchy sounds. He likes to be one of the first to hear the record, and he won't be too enthusiastic if it's been turned down by everyone else in the business.

Have pictures and biographies ready for everyone you see.

A & R = ANXIETY AND REJECTION

The same thing applies whether you're selling a song alone or an artist along with it—don't expect an immediate decision, and don't press hard for one. There's no point getting defensive and hurt if negative criticism is offered. It would be nice if comments were accompanied by a little tact, but you can't depend on it. Some of the remarks will be crushing; some critiques will go right for the jugular. Ask any successful person in show business, and he or she will tell you of someone who said, "Get out, you'll never make it, you're nothing"; and the language is sometimes much cruder and more devastating than that. Assimilate it all, analyze it, and try to see if there are any useful points embedded in the attacks. You'll discard the rest when you see someone else and find that he has exactly the opposite opinion!

Learn the heads of A & R at each record company; but keep checking periodically, because people in that position change with dizzying speed. Find out the kind of artists that appear on each label, through the trades or a copy of the company's artist roster, and decide from that which company is likely to be interested in your kind of material. After you've familiarized yourself with the names of the A & R heads, try to meet with them. Sometimes they won't see you, and you'll be forced to send a tape, along with your bio and pictures. If you have a manager, he might be able to persuade them to come down to a club where you're playing, and that first exposure, hopefully, will whet his appetite.

In addition to your being the right *type* for the label, the A & R head will want to know if you have a unique quality, if there's something about your voice or musicianship or writing that sets you apart from other people. It's no good to be "another Streisand" or another "Kiss" or, in fact, another anything. It's amazing how often new performers or their managers claim the distinction of being another someone, but *better*. You may be better, but it doesn't matter, you weren't first. Make sure you project a vivid, individual identity.

When record executives survey the bulk of a singer/songwriter's material, they need to see many things. First, they'll examine the writer's scope—is he or she limited or capable of continued growth? They'll listen to determine if the lyrics have relevance for a wide audience, and if the melodies have staying power. Most of all, they'll examine the compilation of work to decide if there's a proper balance between album selections and the hit singles needed to sell the overall package to the public.

A & R people will want to know if the artist is a good performer, because dynamic performing has a great influence on sales. Companies have been hung with artists who sound impressive in the studio but die in front of audiences. On rare occasions the material is so meaningful and deep that it communicates emotionally and transcends unexceptional singing, but generally the in-person factor is a key one, as important as superior writing and performance on record.

THINGS TO REMEMBER

1. A record producer must view his production from an overall perspective. Individual contributions matter only as they affect the total product.

2. Songwriters who produce must think of the artist first and what material is most appropriate, rather than overloading the session with their own songs and ignoring the work of other writers.

3. Make sure your record productions build steadily and end with power.

4. To raise money for an independent master:

a. Approach friends, parents, relatives who believe in you;

b. Make a deal with a studio to use its facilities during unbooked hours;

c. Take out a bank loan;

d. Go into partnership with a publisher.

5. Try to find a manager who is 100 percent behind you, one who offers business acumen and psychological support.

6. In presenting a master:

a. Make sure there's sufficient leader (blank tape) at the beginning of the tape and in between each selection and the next;

b. Don't show old, scratchy discs. A & R men don't like to feel that the material has been widely exposed;

c. Have pictures and biographies for everyone you see.

7. Be philosophical about criticism; learn what you can from constructive suggestions and ignore the rest.

8. Make sure the selections on your master tape have variety. Check to see that there's a proper balance between singles and album cuts.

24

Choosing the Right Publisher

Every writer, in addition to his composer's royalties, would like to obtain whole or partial ownership of his copyrights. His mechanical (record sales) and performing (ASCAP, BMI, SESAC *) income is tremendously increased, and this is especially true under the revised new copyright law, which does the following:

1. Increases the term of copyright ownership to the life of the author plus 50 years. The old law, abolished at the end of 1977, provided for a 28-year term, renewable for another 28 years. The new one doesn't require any renewals. All the author's works enter the public domain at the same time—50 years after his death.

2. Increases the mechanical royalty rate from 2 to 2¾ cents per tune, or ½ of one cent per minute, whichever is larger. Everytime a song is sold (on record or tape), the income to the publisher is 2¾ cents (or ½ of one cent per minute). The publisher and writer split this income.

So a writer may well ask himself, "Why should I give my publishing up? I can do what a publisher does." If you feel that you are, by temperament, capable of pushing and placing your own material, as well as

*ASCAP—American Society of Composers, Authors, and Publishers; BMI—Broadcast Music, Inc.; SESAC—Society of European Stage Authors and Composers

bearing the financial burden of demos, lead sheets, office overhead and promotion, keeping 100 percent of your copyrights might be a wise idea.

Another alternative is to form a partnership with one of the established firms, such as a Chappell or an April Blackwood. This way someone will be sharing the responsibility of promoting your catalogue. A publisher may not want to split copyrights with you, however, unless you've made some headway in the industry or have a record contract that can supply him with a certain number of guaranteed recordings.

If you decide to entrust complete copyright ownership to a publisher, here are some things you have a right to expect from him:

1. He should make good demos of the songs he favors. It's not a promising sign if he wants all demos to be cheaply made (piano/voice) or tries to bypass the whole demo question by urging the composer to present his material in person. This is sometimes the correct approach, depending on the songs involved, but if he likes and believes in a song, he should be willing to make an investment in it.

2. He should be interested in overseeing the making of the demo, coming to the studio and giving his suggestions.

3. He should have a clear concept of where to place songs. He should be aware of what artists are coming up for dates, what their preferences are, what appeals most to their record producers.

4. He should be willing to hire independent promotion men (those free lancers who work for many companies) to push the record of a song he has gotten recorded. Record labels do this, and artists frequently hire promotion men of their own too, but it's a case of The More the Merrier. Promotion men are a key factor today, as witness the brilliant effectiveness of the Scotti Brothers in launching "Evergreen," "Here You Come Again," "You Light Up My Life."

The publisher also secures foreign representation for the song, making sure foreign lyrics are written and records are released in territories all over the world. He supervises the collection of foreign royalties and sees that sheet music is made available for sale.

In addition to that, he takes steps to secure and maintain copyright protection, and collects fees and royalties from dramatic, musical, filmed and other uses of the material. Payments are then made to the writer.

The questions thus far are: Can you afford to make your own demos? Do you have artist and producer contacts, and the time and knowledge to properly place your songs? Can you afford to hire promotion men? Do you know copyright laws? Do you have the experience and inclination to handle the question of European royalties?

Many publishers have worldwide contacts—e.g., Screen Gems, EMI, United Artists Music, April Blackwood (CBS) are international companies. Perhaps a song of yours that they publish may not be placed locally, but might secure a record in far-off places like Paris or South Africa. A song that Joel and I wrote, "Two Kinds of Lovers," which never saw the light of day in the United States, turned up on charts in Holland, Denmark and Singapore.

Publishers like the ones mentioned above have big print organizations, and can service your sheet music all over the world. Your songs will appear individually, and beyond that, in songbooks and folios that can prove lucrative.

Some publishing companies are large, independent operations (Chappell, Peer/Southern). Others are publishing arms of record companies (MCA Music—MCA records; Jobete/Stone Diamond—Motown; Almo—A&M). Still others are companies of writers, artists and producers who are actively involved in publishing (e.g., Dawnbreaker/Jasmine—Seals and Crofts; Talleyrand—Neil Diamond).

There's an advantage in placing material with a firm that has a record-company affiliation—the increased chance of getting recordings done by the artists on that label. When the general professional manager of April Blackwood goes to see CBS producers, he can be assured of strong consideration because of the relationship between them. This doesn't mean, of course, that poor or unsuitable work will be used, but if the songs are good, they may have an edge over material from other sources.

If you take a song to a record producer, and he offers a record in exchange for publishing rights, it's best not to make a snap decision before considering the following facts: How big is the artist under discussion? How vital is this particular record in your career at this time? Is the song, in your estimation, a hit of the moment only, or does it have standard value that can be mined more effectively by someone other than the producer/publisher? Keep in mind that record producers and artists, if they keep publishing, will not generally "work" a song beyond its first exposure. They aren't set up for that purpose the way a conventional publishing office is, and they don't have the same personal dedication to the material that you do. This record will most likely be the last one the song will receive unless, by some happy streak of fate, it becomes a smash and is picked up by other performers.

Motion-picture companies almost always retain publishing rights. They feel they've financed the film and they want to realize any subsidiary benefits that accrue from it. The Composers and Lyricists Guild of America (CLGA) has been engaged for years in a legal struggle to gain full ownership of songs for its members. This is because it feels (often rightly) that the copyrights are not actively promoted by the studio publishing divisions once the picture has passed from sight. At the very least, it feels that material should be returned after a certain interval if it's neglected.

There are numerous instances in which this view is justified. Many fine songs do languish and get permanently lost in an unused pile, and publishing rights should certainly be returned if no attention has been paid to the material. But the outcome of the CLGA struggle has not been determined as of this writing, and most composers still have only a slim chance of gaining copyright ownership on a film.

When a composer becomes established, his bargaining power increases. Many big studios have unalterable policies (Disney, for one, never splits publishing), but free-lance producers doing independent films are more flexible. Division of copyrights occurs frequently under these circumstances, especially if a writer can bring in a recording artist as part of a package, or is an artist himself and can supply a record.

Even the majors will occasionally yield if the writer is sufficiently in demand.

Publishing offers impressive financial rewards and security on many levels. Owning your copyrights gives you the power to sell them later on at sometimes tremendous profit. But if you're a new writer and you want to have hit records and get a large volume of product on the market, it may be necessary, beneficial and even shrewd to forgo ownership at the beginning. Later on, armed with success and experience, you can always revise your approach.

TO SIGN OR NOT TO SIGN

Let's suppose a publisher listens to some of your work and becomes excited enough to offer you an exclusive writing contract. For one glorious moment, you can envision an organized existence, free of all financial pressures. Being signed does have creative and psychological advantages, but before you scribble on the dotted line, ask yourself the following questions:

1. Do you have a personal rapport with the publisher? Remember, you're considering a possible 3- to 5-year commitment, and it's not easy to walk out if a serious personality clash develops. Ideally, your new employer should offer encouragement and support, as well as solid, sensible guidance.

2. Is he in the mainstream? Does he keep up with new developments, new artists, new trends?

3. Does he have many contacts with record companies and producers?

4. Is he well liked, and more important, well respected? Some old, established firms are extremely rich and can offer tempting financial terms, but you have to evaluate if they're in a position to get your songs recorded. Too many composers and lyricists collect their paychecks and die inside because their material receives no exposure. It's far preferable

to ally yourself with a small, up-and-coming outfit that needs to prove itself and aggressively pursues its goals.

5. Are his specialties in tune with yours? It's no use signing with a firm that concentrates on theater scores if your strong point is country music.

BEING UNDER ONE ROOF

If you sign, you'll discover that working under one roof answers many practical needs. You'll have an office of your own and a phone. Your being based in one spot enables people to reach you easily. A piano is only two steps away. Pens, pencils, manuscript paper and even the use of a secretary are available.

Once settled, you'll be in a position to know which record dates are coming up. If the publisher is active, producers and artists will call, requesting material. If they don't, he and his general professional manager will make an effort to learn about pending sessions. If you're fortunate you may be in on a "scene," with constant access to one best-selling performer. This was the case with Paul Williams and Roger Nichols (The Carpenters) when they were signed to Irving Music. Early in my career I had seven hits with Jackie Wilson while under exclusive contract to Regent Music.

If there are other staff writers in your office, a competitive spirit may spring up which will cause you some anxiety, but exert a beneficial influence on your work. This sort of competition existed and was encouraged among the staff writers of Aldon Music in the 1960s, when such people as Carole King, Gerry Goffin, Neil Sedaka, Howard Greenfield, Barry Mann, Cynthia Weil and Jack Keller were signed. You'll find yourself striving that much harder to be the one who gets the record in question. Being under contract often puts you in close proximity with possible collaborators as well.

After you begin to have a measure of success, the publisher might decide to promote you in the trade magazines, focusing the attention of the industry on your achievements.

Ironically, success can be the very thing that undermines your contentment with an exclusive arrangement. You may be offered a movie, but with a catch: the picture company wants full publishing rights, and of course you're not free to grant that request, so you're forced to turn down the film. Opportunities on TV are likely to carry the same stifling restriction. Several artists (as one look at the Top 100 will verify) have their own firms and never split their copyrights. These are realities you should face and accept before signing.

Free lancers are generally uncomfortable unless they have complete flexibility, even though their road is a precarious, unsheltered one. They can try to support themselves through publisher advances. Joel and I did this when we were first writing in New York; we would turn out songs at top speed and take them around, hoping to gather a sufficient number of $100 checks to meet our weekly bills. There is a kind of challenge in writing under the gun that way. The combination of excitement and insecurity keeps a writer on his toes and encourages versatility and resilience, but you have to examine your own temperament and determine the circumstances under which it can best flourish.

If you're free-lancing and a publisher listens to your song and says, "Give me time to think about it," you should grant him about two weeks. Don't be paranoid and start suspecting that he plans to steal the material. Only a novice thinks of publishers as enemies, out to snatch tunes they overhear in lobbies and elevators. It wouldn't make business sense for them to steal isolated songs, either, because publishers are interested in developing talented writers and acquiring an entire catalogue of their work to exploit.

A producer should be given more time to hold on to a song than a publisher—at least four to eight weeks—because he has to get with the artist and play it for him. That's not as easy as it sounds; the artist may be traveling or otherwise occupied. While you're waiting, don't shop the song to a dozen other people, and don't suspend all activity, as though this tune were the only treasure in your trunk. The hit songwriter is industrious and prolific.

Many inexperienced songwriters maintain a prima donna "show me" attitude where publishers are concerned. They sign over their songs and wait, arms folded, for results. I've had students say, "It's *his* job to get me records," and it is, but that doesn't mean you can't help. Even if the publisher is efficient and knowledgeable, you might be able to make connections he can't, or isn't aware of. Never depend totally on anyone. You, after all, have a greater stake in the placement of your songs than anyone else. To other people it's good business, but to you it's your life, your ego and identity. The publisher won't resent your assistance; he'll welcome it as long as you check with him first to make sure you're not servicing the same artists he is and causing confusion.

Being signed to a powerful publisher will help your career, but don't expect all the songs you write to get recorded. Some of them will live and die as demos, never making the master stage. Don't let that discourage you. A few hits a year will make all the investment of time and effort worthwhile. Remember, if you have a million seller and are paid at the rate of 2¾ cents a record (split between you and the publisher), your share will be $13,700. Performances will eventually double or triple that figure (especially if the tune becomes a standard). Taking sheet music and TV performances into account, as well as an album cut, you could make up to $75,000 on that one piece of material.

If a song doesn't become a hit, don't fret because "it only got in an album." Mechanical sales on an album are the same as on a 45. If the album sells a million copies, you get paid on a million records, just as if the song had been a single release. Some writers make a fortune every year via album inclusions, without one hit on the charts.

COPYRIGHT QUESTIONS

Students have often asked me, "Should I have my song copyrighted before I go to see a publisher or producer?" Copyrighting every song you write can become expensive. Try to pick the ones you believe in most and safeguard those. On the other hand, if you're a performer publicly showcasing material, make sure all of it is legally protected, since the danger increases with wider exposure that your ideas will be stolen.

Your initial step is to write to the Copyright Office, Library of Congress, Washington, D.C. 20559, for the proper forms. Form E is the one to fill out for published or unpublished compositions by writers who are U.S. citizens. A Form E foreign is for musical compositions by writers who are not citizens of the United States, or any musical composition not first published in the United States. When you've filled out the necessary papers, send along a complete copy of each work you want protected, along with a registration fee of $10. The 1976 copyright act guarantees a period of protection which is the life of the author plus 50 years.

You've probably heard the cliché "You can't copyright a title." That's true, although there are grounds for suit when the title is linked with a highly well known and successful product. "Valley of the Dolls," for example, or "Doctor Zhivago."

If you decide to start your own publishing company, your first step should be to choose a name for the company and reserve that name with BMI, ASCAP or SESAC. Affiliate with one of them and get a form from its membership department. Publisher membership in ASCAP involves an annual fee of $50. There's no fee required by BMI or SESAC.

You'll need E forms (again, from the Register of Copyrights in Washington, D.C.) to copyright your company's songs, contracts for writers you may want to sign to the firm, and contracts between your company as composer and your company as publisher. Alpheus Music, at 1433 North Cole Place, Hollywood, Calif. 90028, will give you standard forms.

When a record company contacts you, the publisher, for the right to use your song, it will need a mechanical license. If you don't have a mechanical-license form, you can request that the company send you one of its standard licenses. The standard rate is now 2¾ cents per copy, and if you have both sides of a record, that's 5½ cents. Ten songs in an album adds up to 27½ cents. When your record begins to sell, affiliate with the Harry Fox Agency, which, for a fee of 3 percent, will keep track of your sales and collect your mechanicals for you.

THINGS TO REMEMBER

1. When choosing a publisher, check to see if he has strong artist and producer contacts, as well as a substantial track record in placing songs.

2. Make sure he's willing to make good demos.

3. Try to sign your song with someone who will promote it through the years and develop it into an enduring copyright.

4. In signing an exclusive contract, make sure you have a personal rapport with your publisher/employer.

5. Make sure your publisher specializes in the *kind* of music you write. Don't sign with a firm that emphasizes country and western when your interest is theater scores.

6. Signing with a publisher will give you access to a phone, an office and a secretary. You'll be in a position to know who's coming up for a recording date.

7. If you deal with publishers, trust them. They're not out to steal your work.

8. Don't wait around while a publisher pushes one song. The successful composer is industrious and prolific.

9. Copyright your songs by writing to the Copyright Office, Library

of Congress, Washington, D.C. 20559, for the proper forms. Sign and return them.

10. If you start your own publishing company, choose a name and affiliate with BMI, ASCAP or SESAC. (Publishers generally have a firm in each society.)

25

Finding the Right Collaborator

How many times have you picked up a paper and read an announcement like this: "Composers Paul McCartney and John Lennon have decided to go their separate ways"? You can fill in Bob Crewe and Bob Gaudio (who co-wrote a series of million sellers for The Four Seasons), or Burt Bacharach and Hal David, or any number of others. Most probably your reaction is to gasp, "How can they break up such a winning combination? If it was me, I'd find a solution." But sometimes, in the light of clashing creative and emotional needs, there is no solution. A partnership is like a marriage. It involves much more than the ability to turn out good songs. There are questions of temperament, philosophy, and long-range goals, and disagreement on any of these issues is enough to shatter the team beyond repair.

The issue of similar goals and philosophies is a vital one. Before I met Joel, I was writing with many people and enjoying chart success, yet I felt confused, disoriented. I didn't want to write only for the pop market, I wanted to try my hand at movies and the theater. One co-writer didn't care about things like that—his world was framed on both sides by red bullets. Still another cared only for rhythm and blues, and a third favored the early-'60s clean-cut California sound, and kept injecting Beach Boys harmony into everything we wrote.

It was only when Joel and I got together that we recognized overall similarities of attitude. We wanted to conquer every medium of composing. We enjoyed the challenge of stretching out, testing ourselves and taking risks.

Work habits are a crucial consideration. Some writers think more clearly in the morning, others at night. If you're punctual, you'll go mad if your partner always shows up late. If your tendency is to call it quits after five o'clock in favor of a social life, and your partner is a driven workaholic who can't turn his juices off, unbelievable friction can develop. There was a case of one writing team in which all the work got done, but one of the partners frequently disappeared in the middle of the afternoon with different women. He'd return toward evening, refreshed and raring to go, while his co-writer seethed and fumed, and the latter finally ended the relationship.

Some writers have a need to let work slide, then rush hysterically to complete songs at the edge of a deadline. Others plod along, day by day, piecing the material together, leaving nothing to chance. Which one are you, and can you live with your opposite?

In many teams there's a partner whose ego demands center stage. That's the reason you generally hear about one member of a duo and have no idea the other exists. The more retiring member has to decide if artistic rewards are worth subordinating his personality. This can work out well if the retiring partner prefers anonymity, if social pressures are a burden to him. He might be happy to stay in the shadows if it means he can be left alone to create.

Maybe you're the kind of person who requires that his collaborator be a friend, a father confessor, a guide or an analyst. On the other hand, you may function comfortably with someone who is all business, efficient and creative but detached. You may even—although this isn't generally recommended—come up with good work in a situation in which friction and hostility are the norm. Some outstandingly famous men (Gilbert and Sullivan among them) turned out great scores although they disliked each other. Rodgers and Hart reportedly had their ups and downs too.

Married couples have produced enduring work. The team efforts of Gerry Goffin and Carole King made pop-music history; Barry Mann and Cynthia Weil have contributed classics. The joint efforts of Ellie Greenwich and Jeff Barry dominated the charts during the '60s, and Nicholas Ashford and Valęrie Simpson are responsible for dozens of hits. But again, Goffin and King are divorced and write separately now, as do Greenwich and Barry, although Mann and Weil and Ashford and Simpson continue to maintain domestic and creative solidarity. Only you can tell if your marriage has the basic stamina to operate under the stresses of creation, daily togetherness and the inevitable competition.

Some collaborations are total; others have more flexibility. Carole Bayer Sager has composed uniformly fine material with a string of people, including Peter Allen, Albert Hammond and Melissa Manchester. Johnny Mercer wrote brilliantly with Harry Warren, Henry Mancini and Marvin Hamlisch, and Marvin himself composed A Chorus Line with Ed Kleban, and "Nobody Does It Better" with Carole Bayer Sager. Yet Jerry Leiber and Mike Stoller found more satisfaction in a steady, 20-year partnership. You might prefer to write rock with one person, a motion-picture song with another, and that's fine, as long as the other person agrees and has the same need. These policies should be stated early in the game, or else the partner who wants total commitment may feel abandoned and resentful when you choose to try your wings with someone else.

There are hundreds of fine lyricists and melody writers wandering aimlessly around, bemoaning the fact that they don't have a co-writer to supply the missing words or music to their songs. The search for this elusive collaborator, especially with beginning composers, is generally done without organization, the attitude being that the "right" person will magically appear, as in a love affair. It's possible, but unlikely. Locating a collaborator should be approached systematically for the fastest, most fruitful results.

Potential co-writers are everywhere. If you live outside the main music centers (New York, Los Angeles, San Francisco, Chicago, Nashville, London), think of people in your own immediate circle. You probably know musicians, members of a local band, and chances are that some of them have songwriting ambitions. Dropping down to clubs in your area and forming friendships with performers there will get your name around. If they don't write, they might be able to put you in touch with people who do. The musicians' union is another rich source of possible partners.

Consider running an ad in your school newspaper if you're a student. State your desire to team up with someone, and spell out your specific requirements. On a broader level, *Songwriter* magazine prints letters of this kind, and many rewarding collaborations have resulted. Mention what you specialize in (e.g., pop, country, soul), whether you're interested in a lyricist or melody writer, and where the party reading the magazine can reach you. Here are some sample letters:

> Young composer looking for lyricist partner in the Chicago area. Jim Blake, 135 Chestnut Hill Ave., Chicago, Illinois.

> Lyricist seeks composer of popular music for collaboration. Billy Joel style. Al Parker, 2825 Claflin Ave., Bronx, New York.

Look up the addresses and phone numbers of locally based publishers and producers, and try to meet them personally. You can mail in the material, but unsolicited work is generally disregarded and returned. Nothing substitutes for face-to-face contact.

"Wait," you ask, "how do I meet these publishers and producers?" It's a cliché, but the phrase "It's who you know" still carries cold reality. You can't necessarily begin by walking into the offices of the most powerful industry people. One introduction leads to another. Meet a secretary who works for someone in a position of importance. Try to go to recording sessions and demo dates. Talk to background singers. You may know an arranger, or a copyist, or someone in advertising. Everyone you meet is a potential contact, a potential lead, a potential partner.

One day in 1964, when I was still living in Manhattan, I mentioned my desire to find a new partner to Harriet Wasser, a publicist well known for her dynamic promotion of Bobby Darin and record producer Bob Crewe. Harriet lived in the Bronx, across the street from a court stenographer who pursued songwriting part time. She thought we'd get along, and brought Joel to meet me. This unexpected development would never have happened if I hadn't sent feelers around to various people in the music business.

The performance societies (ASCAP, BMI, SESAC) can introduce you to writers engaged in the same quest you are. It helps if you've had something published. If you haven't, compile a tape of your music or a folio of your lyrics for those in charge to evaluate. BMI has workshops for new writers, such as the Alternative Chorus (run by Len Chandler and John Braheny), which it supports with time and money, and Lehman Engel's Theater Workshop. ASCAP has formed the ASCAP Writers' Workshop West, led by Annette Tucker and Arthur Hamilton.

Cash Box, Billboard and *Record World* list the national hits every week, along with the names of their writers. Make a note of these names. You might not be able to reach them immediately, but it's useful to know the styles they compose in. If you do meet them eventually, you'll have enough information to judge if you're on the same artistic wavelength and a collaboration is possible. It's a long shot, getting in touch with a famous composer or lyricist if you're still completely unknown, but "I Wanna Be Around" found its way to standard status because an unpublished writer took a chance and sent her words to Johnny Mercer. He liked what he read and completed the song, with worldwide success resulting.

Entertainment attorneys can offer you direct access to their illustrious clients, if they feel you have ability. Agents might also be persuaded to arrange valuable introductions.

Tad Danz's American Song Festival is an avenue worth investigating for the aspiring writer. Song festivals in general are becoming a major outlet for composers, with categories in the amateur and professional divisions. Impressive recordings have materialized through the American Song Festival competition by Barbra Streisand and Barry Manilow.

On a practical level, writing with producers and artists increases your chances of getting records, because these people have full control, and unlike publishers, they can automatically supply the recordings. Working with an artist (such as Bernie Taupin's partnership with Elton John) can guarantee full albums of your music.

If you're planning a trip to one of the major music centers, write to every publisher you can (publishers' names are listed in the back of this book) and set up appointments well in advance of your arrival. Find out who reviews new material in each firm, and try to establish a running dialogue with him so you won't be a total stranger when you appear. Be prepared with demos and lead sheets when you walk in.

BUSINESS DECISIONS

No partnership can operate comfortably if there are serious disagreements on a business level. Here are some points to consider and discuss when you're contemplating entering into an exclusive, or binding, collaboration:

1. Will you each get 50 percent of the royalties, or will one get a larger share? Will the partner who accepts the smaller share feel resentful later on if the record is a hit?

2. Will you both co-own the song's publishing? Again, there's fuel for bitterness if one owns the entire copyright and has the power to sell it later on and collect the profits.

3. If one writer is signed to a publisher and the other is not, will the one who isn't signed be able to handle instances in which an important artist agrees to do a song only if he can keep publishing rights and the team has to reject the record?

4. If a song doesn't succeed, will one writer or the other have the

power to take his lyric or melody back and find another writer to put fresh music or words to it?

I've had students who said to me, "We began with a 50–50 split, but I've contributed more to the song. Don't you think it's fair that the percentages be amended to 60–40 or 75–25?" My answer is an emphatic "No!" In an ideal partnership, there should be no list-making, no toting up of scores of who did less or more. In a long run, the contributions even out, and a you-did-this–I-did-that attitude will only create anger and undermine the effectiveness of the team.

One arrangement that should never be made with a collaborator in the first place is agreeing to pay him or her to put words or music to your material. True partners share royalties and operate on an equal basis. A similar situation may occur with a record company, where the writer, or writer/artist, pays for his own session and pressing costs. Reliable, trustworthy labels don't function that way; if they like your work, they'll shoulder the investment.

INSPIRATION FROM ACROSS THE OCEAN

When writers think of finding collaborators, their minds are usually locked into a local framework. It wasn't until we had a chance to write with Charles Aznavour and see our joint efforts performed by him at Carnegie Hall and around the world that we realized what long-distance partnerships could mean to a career. Far away, in countries like France, Spain, Holland, Japan, Portugal, etc., brilliant tunes are being composed, and are in need of American lyrics.

Many Euro/American collaborations have resulted in hits and standards. "Volare" (Migliacci/Modugno/Parish) has been a hit three times! "My Way" (Anka/François/Revaux/Thibault), first popularized by Frank Sinatra, stands as the ultimate declaration of self-belief and confidence. "You're My World" (Sigman/Bindi/Paoli) broke through internationally for Cilla Black, and then accomplished the same magic for Helen Reddy.

There's something about the phrase "writing lyrics for foreign melodies" that sounds alien, limiting and even stuffy to a young writer, but in fact the canvas of possibilities is wide. "Yesterday When I Was Young" (Aznavour/Kretzmer), a reflective lament of lost youth, is much different in mood from "Strangers in the Night" (Kaempfert/Singleton/Snyder), a story of romance just beginning. "Never on Sunday" (Towne/Hadjidakis) cheerfully recounts a prostitute's love for her work. It is joyously rhythmic, unlike the lush ballad "More" (Newell/Ciociolini/ Oliviero/Ortolani).

Writing to foreign melodies allows the imagination a chance to stretch beyond conventional bounds. The flavor of different countries is a powerful influence. Music from Greece may inspire your thinking a certain way, music from Paris another. We all have images and impressions of exotic places, whether we've visited them or not, and these impressions will shape how we react to melodies from different shores.

Certain lyricists have practically based their entire career on this approach. The name Carl Sigman ("Losing You," a hit for Brenda Lee in 1964, "You're My World" and "What Now My Love") is synonymous with across-the-ocean songwriting. Al Stillman, Buddy Kaye, Norman Gimbel and Rod McKuen recognized the value of foreign collaboration early.

From a practical standpoint, songs like these are frequently "covered" (re-recorded over and over again by artists in albums). Generally, they're already hits in their country of origin, and this increases their chances of acceptance in the United States, on both an artist and radio level.

Sometimes European material comes to an American lyricist with words already written in a different language. Two things may happen: (a) the American writer may be asked to adhere, verse by verse, to the ideas in that lyric, or (b) he may be granted freedom to conceive entirely new ones. The European writer generally indicates a preference. Creating something altogether new is less restricting, but the alternative has advantages. It's difficult to follow a foreign lyric line by line, word by word, so you, as an author, must find fresh and interesting ways of making the meanings come alive in your native tongue. This is a challenge that will sharpen your tools as a lyricist.

Your image as a writer will be enhanced if you succeed in the foreign-song area. You'll gain an international reputation, rather than just a domestic one, opening vistas in your career you might not otherwise have had. Artists from all over the world will be aware of your work and seek it out. You may wind up working in foreign films, or on the stage abroad.

Realistically, you can't latch on to melodies of this superior caliber at the start. Certain publishers are known to specialize in the American/foreign arena. These include Chappell, United Artists Music, Southern, Leeds, E. H. Morris and Ivan Mogull Music, among others. A publisher may assign you a foreign melody that hasn't gained prominence overseas, or isn't the work of a well-known writer. Put words to it anyway, if you think it has merit. Acquire experience in the new medium, until you can set words to the sometimes tricky rhythms and syncopations of a different culture and make them sound totally relaxed and natural. When your skill becomes evident to a publisher, he'll hand you a plum from the catalogue of a Charles Aznavour, a Gilbert Bécaud or a Jacques Brel, and you'll be on your way.

THINGS TO REMEMBER

1. Try to find a partner with goals and philosophies similar to yours.

2. Agree in advance on working habits and hours.

3. In searching for a partner, be organized. Speak to musicians and performers you know. Advertise in your local paper or in *Songwriter* magazine.

4. Befriend secretaries and make allies of them. They are the key to the boss.

5. Write with producers and artists whenever possible.

6. Agree on basic business policy.

7. Write English lyrics to foreign melodies. This is an excellent way of finding new collaborators.

26

Joining ASCAP, BMI or SESAC

There are three performing-rights societies: ASCAP, BMI and SESAC. The societies log performances of all music, and collect their license fees from radio and TV stations, nightclubs, airlines and wherever else music is performed for profit. These outlets, known as music users, must obtain licenses from ASCAP, BMI or SESAC to acquire the right to broadcast or perform any of the music in their three catalogues.

When composer Stephen Foster died penniless, it was discovered that he had never received financial compensation for the performances of his works despite their popularity and acclaim. ASCAP was formed in 1914 by his friends Victor Herbert and John Philip Sousa as a reaction against that injustice. The organization was determined to protect other successful composers from a similar fate.

ASCAP, a nonprofit organization, is owned by its writer and publisher members. After subtracting operating costs, it pays the remainder of its revenue in equal shares to its publisher and writer affiliates. ASCAP distributes income four times a year, and has 17,800 composers and 4,800 publishers in its membership.

BMI, formed by some 480 broadcasters, is also a nonprofit organization, with a membership approaching 40,000 writers and 20,000 publishers. Like ASCAP, it pays all of its money to affiliates, after operating costs are deducted.

SESAC, presently the smallest of the three societies, was created before BMI—in 1931—by Paul Heinecke. It represents all music from classical to concert to pop and rock, and has a large gospel catalogue.

HOW THE LOGGING IS DONE

ASCAP's method is to use a random-sampling system. It has people all over the country taping radio stations. They switch from station to station, taping six-hour segments. The tapes are sent to New York, and other people make note of every song performed, after which performances are logged and writers and publishers given credit. Each performance credit has a cash value for the writer and the publisher, a cash value that alters with every quarter. The figure is based on the total amount of money available for distribution. ASCAP also employs network programming logs (cue sheets) to keep track of its catalogue.

BMI uses a select group of radio stations in its logging system. It monitors 300 stations—out of a U.S. total of about 7,000—on a rotating basis. A different group of 300 stations is monitored every month. During the course of two years, the vast majority of stations are covered. A statistical determination is then made of the larger picture. To log national TV, BMI, like ASCAP, receives cue sheets of music used every week by the networks. Both ASCAP and BMI use *TV Guide* to do the bulk of their logging of local television.

SESAC differs from ASCAP and BMI in that it represents mechanical and synchronization rights as well as performance royalties. ASCAP and BMI deal strictly with income from airplay. SESAC works from trade charts and pays four times a year on a quarterly basis. It licenses about 8,000 radio and TV stations in the country, along with thousands of

hotels, nightclubs, stadiums, concert halls and airlines. Most SESAC affiliates are country and gospel music writers and publishers.

To become a full member of ASCAP, you must have a song published or recorded, or get it performed on the air. Having print music for
sale or material in a stage show also makes you eligible. ASCAP charges
a yearly membership fee of $50. BMI requires its new members to have
a song recorded, with a release date on a record label, and has a $25
application fee for new publisher affiliates. There is no fee for writers.

ASCAP was originally the granddaddy of the societies. Such ge-
niuses as Irving Berlin, Jerome Kern and Rodgers and Hammerstein
contributed to its catalogue. Thus, for many years ASCAP had a theater
and motion-picture image, and BMI was thought of purely in terms of
rock and roll.

Those divisions have blurred or disappeared. ASCAP has acquired
dozens of market-oriented writers such as Carole King, Neil Diamond
and the Motown group. BMI, on the other hand, has signed the majority
of television and motion-picture scorers (John Williams of *Star Wars* and
Jerry Goldsmith are among the giants who belong).

BMI has always had a less strict advance policy with new writers,
but ASCAP is loosening up considerably in that area.

I'm an ASCAP writer; Joel belongs to BMI. Our two Academy
Award–winning songs, "The Morning After" and "We May Never Love
like This Again," are split between the two societies, as is all our work
after 1972 including the score of *Pete's Dragon*. At the beginning people
would say, "Aha, *now* you'll compare checks and see who's getting
more." We did, with some trepidation, but I'm glad to report that we
were satisfied and relieved. The specifics may vary from quarter to quarter, but the overall amounts are generally the same, and we feel we've
been treated with complete fairness by both organizations.

The new writer should have meetings with all the societies, get to
know the people personally and express his needs and aspirations. It's a
matter of personal communication, which society believes more strongly
in his work, and which one is willing to offer the advance he seeks. The

contracts are for different periods of time. ASCAP has an agreement that runs in 10-year periods, but gives its members the opportunity to resign if they send written notice prior to September 30 of each year. BMI's standard writer contract is for two years, its publishing agreement five. SESAC's contract is for three years.

All the societies are helpful and encouraging. They will suggest co-writers and direct you to publishers and producers. The addresses of the three organizations are as follows:

ASCAP

New York

> One Lincoln Plaza
> New York, N.Y. 10023

> *President:* Stanley Adams
> *Director of Membership:* Paul Adler
> *Managing Director:* Paul Marks

Hollywood

> 6430 Sunset Boulevard
> Hollywood, Calif. 90028

> *West Coast head:* John Mahan

Nashville

> 2 Music Square West
> Nashville, Tenn. 37203

> *Nashville head:* Ed Shea

BMI

New York

> 40 West 57th Street
> New York, N.Y. 10019

President: Edward Cramer
Senior Vice President: Thea Zavin
Assistant Vice President, Writer Relations: Stanley Catron

Hollywood

6255 Sunset Boulevard, Suite 1527
Los Angeles, Calif. 90069

Vice President: Ron Anton
Vice President: Neil Anderson

Nashville

10 Music Square East
Nashville, Tenn. 37203

Vice President: Frances Preston

BMI also has offices in Chicago, Montreal, Toronto, Vancouver, Miami and San Francisco.

SESAC

New York

10 Columbus Circle
New York, N.Y. 10019

President: Norm Weiser
Owner: Paul Heinecke

THINGS TO REMEMBER

1. Join one of the three performing-rights societies (ASCAP, BMI or SESAC), so that the airplay of your songs can be logged.
2. If the societies believe in your talent, they may give you an advance against future earnings.
3. BMI and ASCAP conduct workshops for writers.

27

The Anatomy of a Hit

We're now going to analyze five songs, pointing out the ways in which they have fulfilled the twin requirements of craftsmanship and commerciality. As you'll see, they incorporate the principles described in this book, and can be taken as models of professionalism.

"Rhinestone Cowboy"

by Larry Weiss

I've been walkin' these streets so long
Singin' the same old song
I know every crack on these dirty sidewalks of Broadway

Where hustle's the name of the game
And nice guys get washed away like the snow
And the rain

There's been a load of compromisin'
On the road to my horizon
But I'm gonna be where the lights are shinin' on me

Like a rhinestone cowboy
Riding out on a horse in a star-spangled rodeo

Rhinestone cowboy
Gettin' cards and letters from people I don't even know
Offers coming over the phone

Well, I really don't mind the rain
And a smile can hide all the pain
But you're down when you're riding a train
That's taking the long way

But I dream of the things I'll do
With a subway token and a dollar tucked
Inside my shoe

There's been a load of compromisin'
On the road to my horizon
But I'm gonna be where the lights are shinin' on me

(Like a rhinestone cowboy . . .) (to chorus and fade) *

"Rhinestone Cowboy" opens with an introduction that is repeated later on. This is a case in which the intro becomes an instrumental figure as well.

The first line, "I've been walkin' these streets so long," is visual, and hints at exhaustion and despair. This hint is confirmed with the next line, "Singin' the same old song," and explained by "I know every crack on these dirty sidewalks of Broadway."

The excellent prosody dramatizes this mood. The melody moves in loping eighths; it "walks" as the hero sings, as though to convey the loneliness of beating the pavement day after day. On a level of writing technique, it employs the alliteration "Singin' the same old song" and maintains its vivid use of imagery with "I know every crack on these dirty sidewalks of Broadway."

The title "Rhinestone Cowboy" sets an intriguing mood. It creates curiosity about the protagonist. We don't know yet what a rhinestone cowboy is—whether the image is meant to be real or symbolic—but there's a glittering ambiguity about it that makes the listener want to know more.

The melody is neatly and unobtrusively sequential. The first theme, in bars 1 through 5,

is answered a fourth step up in bars 9 through 12.

There's a faintly acrid tone in lines like "Nice guys get washed away like the snow and the rain," but this tone is never so cynical and bitter that listener identification breaks down, because Weiss says, "I'm gonna be where the lights are shinin' on me." The complexities of the character are highlighted—his realistic appraisal of possible failure, coupled with an overriding optimism that says, "I can do it!" This optimism gives hope to people sharing the cowboy's experience vicariously through the record.

Skillful use of prosody continues with "There's been a *load* of compromisin'," and on the word "load" the melody stretches a third. The sequence builds another step on its rhyme word, "road." We can feel the increasing excitement of the character, and in the line leading to the hook, "I'm gonna be where the lights are shinin' on *me*," the word "me" is high and sustained, a declaration of self-confidence and pride.

All the lines "talk" dramatically. In one rhyme, "compromisin' " and "horizon," the author flirts with slickness, but knows when to restrain himself. These colorful words add just the right amount of seasoning—more would have threatened the naturalistic fabric of the piece. They don't sound self-consciously arty, an amazingly hard thing to do when you're walking that thin line between ordinary speech and hipness.

The song has a steady feeling of build, and explodes when it gets to the hook. This is only appropriate when you have such expansive lines as "Like a rhinestone cowboy . . . Riding out on a horse in a star-spangled rodeo." The protagonist gives full vent to his fantasy with "Gettin' cards and letters from people I don't even know," and trails off reflectively with "Offers comin' over the phone." This prosody is particularly noteworthy, because it so perfectly meshes with the characterization. "Offers comin' over the phone" is no longer pure fantasy—it has daily reality about it, and facing that reality partially punctures the emotional balloon. To capture that, the tune drops down on "over the phone."

"Rhinestone Cowboy" is not cluttered with excessive chords. The melody has great freedom, daringly unexpected leaps like the drop of a sixth on "cowboy"; the rhythm moves unrestricted, but the chords are simple—6 bars of C, 2 of G, 4 of F, 2 of C again and so on. It basically moves back and forth between C, G and F, with occasional dashes of color. A complicated progression would possibly have made the tune too polished and "easy listening" in tone, whereas in its present state it has shadings of country and pop, and proved equally popular in both markets.

Another melodic figure appears in the hook, immediately following the title, and when the title appears a second time, this figure reappears with it.

Associative adjectives are employed throughout, words such as "Broadway," "shining lights," "riding a train" and "subway token." These evoke the atmosphere of New York.

"Rhinestone Cowboy" has a relatively wide range (an octave and 6, which is somewhat more than the usual pop song), but it still keeps within comfortable boundaries. The tune is logical, not given to erratic leaps that are the sign of an amateur. As for false rhymes, it uses only one: "game" and "pain." This, however, is conscious, not an artistic oversight, because every other rhyme in the song is perfect. Composer Weiss obviously felt that this rhyme was more soulful than a slicker alternative, and opted for that emotional truth rather than empty craftsmanship.

Larry Weiss's greatest achievement in this song is presenting a universal truth—the pursuit of success—in a way that can be readily felt by millions. There's nothing in "Rhinestone Cowboy" that locks it into a time frame. It has no limiting "now" expressions. For these reasons, it's unlikely to become dated, and will take its place as a lasting standard.

"Shop Around"

Words and music by Berry Gordy, Jr. and Bill "Smokey" Robinson

When I became of age, my mother called me to her side
She said, "Son, you're growing up now
Pretty soon you'll take a bride"

And then she said, "Just because you've become a young man now
There's still some things that you don't understand now
Before you ask some girl for her hand now
Keep your freedom for as long as you can now."
My mama told me, "You'd better shop around
Woh, yeah, you'd better shop around."

Ah ha, there's some things that I want you to know now
Just as sure as the wind's gonna blow now
The women come and the women gonna go now
Before you tell 'em that you love 'em so now

My mama told me, "You'd better shop around
Woh, yeah, you'd better shop around."

Try to find yourself a bargain, son
Don't be sold on the very first one
Pretty girls come a dime a dozen
Try to find one who's gonna give you true loving

Before you take a girl and say, "I do—now"
Make sure she's in love with you now
Make sure that her love is true now
I hate to see you feeling sad and blue now

My mama told me, "You'd better shop around
Woh, yeah, you'd better shop around." *

"Shop Around," though a rhythmic song, opens with a leisurely, ad-lib introduction. Ad-lib introductions are effective in setting up a lyric, but beyond that, they provide an effective contrast for the "A" section that follows. Their gentle mood only makes the next part seem more explosive and driving.

The song's first line, "When I became of age, my mother called me to her side," has the ring of a story unfolding, and immediately raises the question "What is his mother going to say?" With each line, the character's mother emphasizes her point and embellishes it, and the format of four rhymes in a row gives it a building intensity and continuity.

The title "Shop Around" is a title that writes itself. More than just establishing a mood, it signals the listener about the general direction the song will take. We don't know what the hero is shopping for, but it's a safe bet that what he wants won't be found in a department store, that he's after a human relationship.

The rhythmic pattern subtly and effectively alters on the hook line, "You'd better shop around." Up until then, it alternated between eighth and quarter notes:

Now the passage is completely eighth notes. The acceleration dramatizes the message and also spotlights it:

The hook contains a verbal and instrumental figure, "Woh, yeah, you'd better shop around"—a figure that repeats every time the hook does.

The chord pattern (C F⁷ C F⁷ C F⁷) is simple, as it was in "Rhinestone Cowboy," so the tune can move fluidly. All the finest writers know that simplicity is the key to communication on a wide level.

There's a conversational sense of prosody throughout "Shop Around," and it's well demonstrated by the hook line, "My mama told me," to stress the importance of Mama's lesson. The whole line climbs and then climaxes on "me." "You'd better shop around" drops from that point, rather than building to a fever pitch. This is a logical melodic decision, since the statement must sound like dialogue, like advice.

Associative lines include "Try to find yourself a bargain," "Pretty girls come a dime a dozen," and "Don't be sold on the very first one." This department-store imagery ties in neatly with the title.

Also in a conversational context, the line "Just as sure as the wind's gonna blow now" incorporates imagery—not artsy-craftsy imagery, but what I call "conversational pictures." And the use of prosody is strikingly evident with the raised fourth on "true" in the line "Make sure that her love is *true* now," since that word is the summation, the point of the entire song.

Like "Rhinestone Cowboy," "Shop Around" is a standard, because its theme too is relevant to any generation. There will always be young people facing first love and turning to experienced elders for direction. "Shop Around," in addition, has a pleasingly positive feeling about it. The advice is not given in the form of dark, ominous warnings, and there's an unstated but clearly conveyed implication that true love will turn up if those words of guidance are followed.

"I Feel the Earth Move"

by Carole King

I feel the earth move under my feet
I feel the sky tumblin' down
I feel my heart start to tremblin'
Whenever you're around

Ooh, Baby, when I see your face
Mellow as the month of May
Oh, darlin'—I can't stand it
When you look at me that way

I feel the earth move under my feet
I feel the sky tumblin' down
I feel my heart start to tremblin'
Whenever you're around

Ooh, darlin'—when I'm near you
And you tenderly call my name
I know that my emotions
Are something I just can't tame
I just got to have you, Baby
Aah! Aah! Yeah, I feel the earth move *

"I Feel the Earth Move," like "Shop Around," is a title that writes itself. The listener knows immediately that the phrase is a metaphorical description of love and lust. The sexual undercurrents are clear, imaginatively projected without need for overt, pop-pornographic references. The song opens with a throbbing, insistent piano figure that captures the flavor of the title, then begins, "I feel the earth move under my feet, I feel the sky tumbling down." A mood both sexual and romantic is conjured up. Musically, the use of downward-curving eighth notes on "under my feet" further conveys the shaking earth, and the prosody of "I feel the sky tumbling down" is appropriate—the intervals tumble down along with the phrase.

Equally effective emotional prosody marks "I feel my heart start to tremblin' Whenever *you're around*." "You're around" not only goes up, but is also sustained, because that thought is the basis for the romantic and sexual tremors being described. The words "heart" and "start" are neatly inner-rhymed, side by side, attesting to Carole King's technical skill. The line "*Mellow as the month of May*" features a triple alliteration, and its imagery adds character dimension, implying that the protagonist's reactions have poetic as well as physical elements.

The chords (Cm^7 F Cm^7 F Cm^7 F) of King's lively and prominently featured hook are simple, as in our two previous examples. There is no overabundance of words used throughout the song either, because rhythm is the keynote. The hook and verse section alternate in an A B A B arrangement, and there's no bridge at all. The main point is to hammer home the title thought, and superfluous words would only get in the way.

As one of our most commercial composers, Carole King makes sure she employs a figure—an "Aah! Aah! Yeah!"—that stresses the character's feelings, almost as though the heroine found words inadequate and had to resort to sounds to convey the depth of her emotion. And the prosody of "I've just *got* to have you, Baby," with its sudden raised minor third, dramatically summarizes her attitude.

King does what Larry Weiss did—she uses a false rhyme because it suits her purpose, in this case "down" and "around," but displays her ability to rhyme carefully on words like "name" and "tame." Like Weiss, she is in conscious control, choosing her effects with her heart rather than only with her head.

"I Feel the Earth Move" is a standard because it has all the commercial components. It speaks of love, musically and lyrically, in a direct, honest manner. The tune has the kind of simplicity and syncopation that makes it attractive to instrumental and jazz artists.

"Don't Rain on My Parade"

From the musical production *Funny Girl*
Music by Jule Styne
Lyrics by Bob Merrill

Don't tell me not to fly, I've simply got to
If someone takes a spill it's me and not you
Don't bring around a cloud to rain on my parade

Don't tell me not to live, just sit and putter
Life's candy and the sun's a ball of butter
Who told you you're allowed to rain on my parade

I'll march my band out
I'll beat my drum
And if I'm fanned out
Your turn at bat, sir
At least I didn't fake it
Hat, sir
I guess I didn't make it

But whether I'm the rose of sheer perfection
Or freckle on the nose of life's complexion
The cinder or the shiny apple of its eye

I gotta fly once, I gotta try once
Only can die once, right, sir?
Ooh, love is juicy, juicy and you see
I gotta have my bite, sir

Get ready for me, love, cause I'm a "comer"
I simply gotta march, my heart's a drummer
Don't bring around a cloud to rain on my parade

I'm gonna live and live now!
Get what I want, I know how!
All that the law will allow!

One roll for the whole sheband!
One throw, that bell will go clang!
Though I'm alone I'm a gang!
Eye on the target and wham!
One shot, one gun shot and bam!
Hey, world, here I am!

Get ready for me, love, cause I'm a "comer"
I simply gotta march, my heart's a drummer
Nobody, no, nobody is gonna rain on my parade

The first line, "Don't tell me not to fly, I've simply got to," defines
the conflict: a heroine locked into a rigid pattern and ready to burst free.
The words are stubbornly emotional and passionate, and the rhythmic,
intense melody highlights those feelings. Jule Styne's syncopations are
fast, almost breathless, on "I've simply got to," as though the character
is clenching her fists with determination.

Musically, the sequence introduced in the first two bars is repeated
in the third and fourth, familiarizing listeners with the basic tune. The
prosody is excellent. On the word "fly" there is a dramatic leap of a
fourth, from G to C. This leap repeats on "spill," and when the sequence
begins a third time in the fifth bar, the leap to "cloud" is from G to D.
The added interval stretch underscores the urgency of the heroine's
thoughts and leads powerfully into the title. The sixth measure provides
a temporary resolution, before resuming the sequence again in the second verse.

A recurring progression (C C$^+$ C^6) is set up from the start, then
utilized throughout the song. Since the notes move briskly, the anchor of
repetitive chords gives it a sense of structure. As we've seen, racing notes
and rhythms should be balanced by a minimum of chords to avoid
chaos.

"Got to" and "not you" is a double inner rhyme. This device is
effective, although it can be pretentious if overused. "Don't bring around
a cloud to rain on my parade" shows the use of associative words,
connecting "cloud" and "rain."

In the second verse we see an unusual rhyme, "putter" and "butter," and the alliteration "the sun's a ball of butter." The height of meticulous rhyming occurs with the last line of this verse, "Who told you you're allowed to rain on my parade." "Allowed" rhymes with "cloud," which appears one full verse before, on the equivalent line and in the same place.

As though following the progression of the heroine's thoughts, the next two lines are less syncopated, more sustained, spotlighting the words "I'll march my band out, I'll beat my drum." These visual images are tonally consistent with the "parade" image of the title. Dramatically, they work on a double level: as the character's declaration to the world and a declaration to herself.

The unusual rhymes continue with "band out" and "fanned out," as well as "bat, sir" and "hat, sir." The tempo picks up on "bat, sir," quickening like a heartbeat, as excitement and enthusiasm overwhelm the heroine again.

Although the lyrics of "Don't Rain on My Parade" are dazzlingly clever, they also "talk," demonstrating that craft doesn't necessarily destroy the illusion of conversational speech. The genuine emotionalism of the words gives them reality: "Your turn at bat, sir, At least I didn't fake it," or "Who told you you're allowed to rain on my parade?"

More original, fresh imagery follows: "But whether I'm the rose of sheer perfection or freckle on the nose of life's complexion" supplies an important clue to the heroine's personality. On the one hand she sees herself as unattractive, and on the other she imagines herself beautiful. This ambivalence is further developed with the line "The cinder or the shiny apple of its eye."

The words "I gotta fly once, I gotta try once, Only can die once, right, sir?" point out just how hell-bent the character is on finding love. This is underscored with "Ooh, love is juicy, juicy and you see I gotta have my bite, sir."

The next section is totally different from the rest of the song in chords, rhythm and mood, as the heroine sums up her overall philosophy: "I'm gonna live and live now, Get what I want, I know how, All that the law will allow." The verse modulates a step up, but continues the same melody and rhythmic feeling, then modulates again, culminating in the cry "Hey, world, Here I am." The alliteration on "hey" and "here" gives the climactic message additional force.

Since the development of this melody has been so unrelentingly explosive and driving, a big ending is a must. Styne and Merrill provide that ending with "Nobody, no, nobody is gonna rain on my parade." The word "parade" is held for several bars with a high C.

"Don't rain on My Parade" has several hooks: the memorably sequential tune, constantly repetitive chord progression and the use of the title after nearly every verse. It is so strikingly free of clichés that we can see, and appreciate, the efforts of the composers to be original. The subject is one that invites universal identification, dealing as it does with the pursuit of love and identity and the need to live fully. Most of all, we can see the emotional investment of the writers. Their involvement is so obvious that the song is irresistibly stirring to listeners and theater goers everywhere.

"Just the Way You Are"

by Billy Joel

> Don't go changing to try and please me
> You never let me down before
> Mm mm
> Don't imagine you're too familiar
> And I don't see you anymore
> I would not leave you—in times of trouble
> We never could have come this far
> Mm mm
> I took the good times
> I'll take the bad times
> I'll take you just the way you are
> Don't go trying some new fashion

Don't change the color of your hair
Mm mm
You always have my unspoken passion
Although I might not seem to care

I don't want clever conversation
I never want to work that hard
Mm mm
I just want someone that I can talk to
I want you just the way you are

I need to know that you will always be
The same old someone that I knew
Oh, what will it take till you believe in me
The way that I believe in you

I said I love you and that's forever
And this I promise from the heart
Mm mm
I could not love you any better
I love you just the way you are *

Another song that can serve as a textbook of composing skill is Billy Joel's "Just the Way You Are."

Musically the tune opens with a sequential pattern that imprints the melody in the listener's mind right way. The first two measures establish a theme, and the next measure answers it:

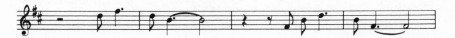

This ask-and-answer pattern is maintained throughout the piece, in bars 9–10 and 11–12, 17–18 and 19–20, and again later when these sections reappear.

The composer's flair for first lines is illustrated here with the immediately provocative "Don't go changing to try and please me." It gives complexity and dimension to the relationship by suggesting that the woman involved is trying to alter her personality to please her lover. It also makes the hero an understanding person when he urges his girl-friend to be herself. Since the characters are such recognizable human beings, you want to listen further.

Prosody is smoothly employed with the line "You never let me down before," in which the music curves downward to match the phrase "let me down." This combination of melody and lyric gives the thought poignancy.

Alliteration is used with "in times of trouble" and "We never could have come this far." These words are simple, not flashy or flamboyant, but they flow effortlessly because of the graceful alliteration.

Commercially speaking, the use of "Mm mm" in bars 8, 24, 38 and elsewhere is effective, not because it's a figure, a gimmick that adds repetition (although that's also true), but because it has a quality of tenderness which adds to the feeling of reassurance being con-veyed. The way the sound is musically curled heightens the emotional effect.

A word like "passion," misused, can seem overblown, especially in a love song as gentle as this one, but the phrase "unspoken passion" has a freshness that projects sensitivity and sincerity. It's safe to assume that the word "unspoken" was arrived at only with a good deal of thought, thought enriched by the songwriter's instinctive taste. The rhyme of "fashion" and "passion" is a unique one.

The line "Although I might not seem to care" is a line of character-ization, which slides by quietly but defines the protagonist. In those words, he implies that he is sometimes thoughtless, involved in other things, and doesn't give his lover the emotional security she needs, there-fore justifying and explaining why she feels anxious. The lyric goes way below the surface and makes the listener aware of the people involved, not merely the specifics of their dilemma. Further characterization is supplied by the brilliantly original lines "I don't want clever conversa-tion—I never want to work that hard." These lines are also modern in that they carry psychological weight, rather than expressing a one-level feeling.

In popular music, a commercially surefire approach is to have the hero pedestalize his girl. Females who buy records like to hear the singer enumerate his girl's outstanding attributes, and the title "Just the Way You Are" furnishes that dream fulfillment. We all long to be loved and accepted without reservation, for just what we are, without any need for pretense, and this song speaks for that hunger.

Today the emphasis is on rhythm, and a slow, dreamy ballad has a harder time breaking through on Top 40 formats. As a result, only what *Billboard* refers to as a "rhythm ballad" seems to gain instant acceptance with program directors, and this is a good example of one. There's an underlying pulse, a sense of syncopation, so that people are tapping their feet while absorbing the low-key subtleties of the words.

The bridge is short and doesn't wander. It starts calmly but then, when Billy Joel sings, "Oh, what will it take till you believe in me" the melody rises with corresponding dramatic energy to make its ultimate point and underline the hero's plea for understanding.

The lifeblood of hit songs is hooks, as we've seen, and the title "Just the Way You Are" is repeated after each section of the tune. Unlike "I Feel the Earth Move," it doesn't pound away, but nevertheless, when you finish hearing the record for the first time, that key phrase is permanently committed to memory. The instrumental figure (which opens the record) threads its way through the production and gives it added vitality.

The major triumph of "Just the Way You Are" is the way it blends its effects. There's a self-effacing quality of understatement; the best art or drama is always a whole, consistent tapestry, without the injection of bizarrely theatrical touches that beg for attention but detract from the overall mood. But the fact that this song seems straightforward and simple doesn't mean it is. The first four chord changes, for example (D Bm⁶ Gma⁷ Bm) are offbeat, even odd, but repetition makes them appear simple and easy to follow. That quality of inventiveness is present in every note and word of "Just the Way You Are" and offers an inspiring lesson: that experimentation and imagination are possible beyond obvious and clichéd chords, as long as the result makes sense, as long as it's logical and tuneful.

"Just the Way You Are" is a work of consummate professionalism. All the commercial devices are in it, yet the listener isn't aware of them because the material is so flawlessly constructed.

We can conclude, after placing these songs under microscopic examination, that they all possess the following: excellent prosody, conscious control of rhyme, strong hooks, visual imagery, recurring figures and intriguing first lines that set up their themes. The themes are universal, from the success-seeking Rhinestone Cowboy to the young man first discovering love and being warned to "shop around."

The registers of all five songs are comfortably within the range of any professional singer, and the musical patterns are logical and sequential, without erratic, awkward jumps that tax a vocalist and mark the melody writer an amateur. The story resolutions are all emotionally satisfying, and the melodies build from beginning to end. There are clever inner rhymes and alliterations, along with metaphors that are colorful but never pretentious.

Elements that ensure communication transcend any specific genre. "Rhinestone Cowboy" is country pop, "Shop Around" is R & B, "Don't Rain on My Parade" Broadway show music, "Just the Way You Are" middle-of-the-road pop and "I Feel the Earth Move" pop with jazz and R & B flavorings. The differences don't matter. In the most important, basic ways they are alike.

The next time you listen to hit songs on the radio and want to say, "I could have written that garbage," listen again. *There's a reason why every record breaks through and climbs the national charts.* Subjective analysis is useless and harmful. New writers are prey to it more than experienced ones, but we all take a superior, critical attitude now and then. We tend to dismiss what we don't like, automatically declaring it worthless, rather than trying to learn what it has that holds appeal for other people. Your tastes, as eclectic as they may be, can't encompass everything; in some respects they have to be narrow, and your job is to step outside those prejudices and forget what *you* enjoy. If you can do that, you'll see why the preceding songs, and thousands of others, have succeeded, and understand what you have to do to write material that will achieve comparable fame.

•

Epilogue

During a low period, when Joel and I weren't getting many records, we submitted a song to Kate Smith's producer. With no criticism intended of Miss Smith's talent, she wasn't what you'd call "hot" at the time. The producer listened to our tune and slowly shook his head. "It's not the direction she wants to go in." Joel turned red and burst out, "What direction *does* she want to go in?" as though we were losing the chance to write a three-record set for the Eagles. I had been feeling equally anxious, until the absurdity of it struck me. We were going to pieces over a Kate Smith record! Joel and I burst into hysterical laughter, and by seeing humor in the situation, we ended the depression that had been plaguing us for days.

When you feel similarly tired and discouraged, remember that there isn't a composer alive who hasn't felt just as suicidal, and that the spell will pass. Remember, too, that the music business is richer with opportunity than it has been in years.

Until recently, commercial music was divided into trends—psychedelic, bubble-gum, the California sound, the British sound, and when these trends predominated, they acted as replacements, rather than additions, to the trends that had preceded them. Now, for the first time, there is no clear-cut trend, no pressure that forces a writer to conform to a particular pattern. The only trend seems to be variety and quality.

Newcomers are breaking into the Top 10 nearly as often as established stars. Productions from small labels get heavy airplay. There is much less automatic programming of records based on the size of the label or the former successes of the singer. The record itself must impress program directors, or it won't be played.

A look at recent best sellers confirms this. "You Light Up My Life" is a beautiful ballad and deserves its acclaim, but the artist, Debby Boone, is a comparative newcomer with no previous chart history. The song is extremely slow, is a waltz and is produced in a mellow style. Writer Joe Brooks's achievements were all in the advertising area, yet programmers took a chance because of the song's merit.

"Short People," by Randy Newman, is a completely offbeat item, an odd, tongue-in-cheek piece of material, part sing-along, part blues. It conforms to no mold, but is rich in imagination and originality.

"Send In the Clowns" is a ballad, but it's also a work of sophistication, bittersweet and adult in its treatment. The artist, Judy Collins, admittedly a warm and sensitive singer, has rarely been found on the Top 40.

Instrumentals are more prevalent than ever, as witness "Star Wars" and "Close Encounters of the Third Kind," by John Williams, and a study of *Billboard*'s list of 1977 smashes shows that the only link between any of the recordings—ranging from Kenny Nolan's "I Like Dreamin' " to Peter McCann's "Do You Wanna Make Love"—is quality. "Lucille" is a leisurely country song, markedly different from the sexual "I'm So into You." "Telephone Line" mixes old and new rock influences, combining country, '50s rock and electronic sounds. There are Stevie Wonder's vivid tribute to Duke Ellington, "Sir Duke," and the delightfully danceable "Lido Shuffle." Representing the genre of Euro/American collaboration, there's the popular new version of "You're My World" by Helen Reddy.

Radio is allowing the songwriter unlimited freedom. You can open your mind and tap hidden areas without the accompaniment of that tense inner voice, "Only R & B is happening . . . disco is making it this year . . . it's country or nothing." It can be anything, as long as your music has the power to make people laugh or cry or get angry.

As long as it inspires them to feel.

Glossary of Musical Terms

Acetate   An individually cut record (as opposed to multiple pressings).

Administration   The handling by a publisher of all copyright and contractual aspects of a song or full catalogue.

Advance   "Up front" money against royalties.

AFM   American Federation of Musicians.

AFTRA   American Federation of Television and Radio Artists.

AGAC   American Guild of Authors and Composers. A protective association for songwriters.

A & R   Artists and Repertoire. An A & R man is responsible for finding material and developing talent.

ASCAP   American Society of Authors, Composers and Publishers. Logs the performances of writers and publishers and pays them.

BMI   Broadcast Music, Inc. Like ASCAP, BMI logs the performances of writers and publishers and pays them.

Bridge   The middle section of a song, appearing between the second and last verses. Also known as the release.

Bullet   Chart notation which indicates a strong rising movement of the record.

Casting   Knowing what artists are available and what kind of music they favor, so that the material can be slanted accordingly.

Casting Director   A writer who analyzes the musical trade journals (*Billboard, Cash Box, Record World* and *Songwriter*) to see what artists are available and what kind of music they favor, so that he can slant the material accordingly.

Charts   Weekly listings of best-selling records in the country, pop, soul, gospel and jazz fields. Magazines featuring weekly charts are *Cash Box, Billboard,*

Record World and *Variety*. *Songwriter* magazine carries a monthly chart, and this chart indicates, with asterisks, those artists who don't compose their own material and are open to contributions by the free-lance writer.

Chorus The portion of a song that repeats—the hook.

Click track A perforated sound track that produces click sounds, enabling the orchestrator or arranger to hear a predetermined beat in synchronization with a TV or theatrical film.

CMA Country Music Association. An organization that promotes and supports the growth of country music.

Composer Creator of music.

Co-publishing When two or more publishers publish one copyright jointly.

Copyright To copyright a song is to secure protection by filing registration forms with the Copyright Office in Washington, D.C.

Cover When artists other than the person who records the original version of a song do their versions, they are "covering" a song.

Crossover A song that gets played in one market and then receives airplay and sales in another (e.g., a pop hit that starts to click on the country or soul charts).

Cut To record.

Demo A demonstration recording of a song, either an acetate dub or a 7½-ips 4-track tape, for evaluation by producers and artists.

Distributor A company that handles the sale of record products to jobbers and retail outlets in specified territories.

Engineer Individual who operates studio equipment during a record session.

Folio A collection of songs for sale by one writer, or a collection of material by a group of writers.

Freeze To put a "freeze" on a song is to hold it exclusively.

Gold album Certified by the RIAA as having sold over 500,000 units.

Gold single Certified by the RIAA as having sold one million units.

Harry Fox Agency Organization for collecting mechanical income.

Heads (heads out) Describing a tape wound with the loose end at the beginning.

Hold When an artist or producer is holding a song for evaluation.

Hook The repetitive section of a song, whether it be melody, lyric or rhythm. The "hit" part, most identified with the record.

Leader White tape which separates one selection on a tape from another.

Lead sheet Words and music of a song notated on manuscript paper.

License Legal permit to use.

Lyric sheet The lyrics of a song.

Master The completed recording of a song, one that is ready to be pressed and sent to radio stations and stores.

Mechanicals Moneys paid to publisher by record company for sales of records and tapes of the publisher's songs, or moneys paid by publisher to writer for sales of the songwriter's material.

Mix   The blending of different tracks on a record to get a desired overall sound.

Modulation   The change from one key to another.

MOR   Middle-of-the-road music, also known as "easy listening"—sweet and mellow, softer than rock and roll.

Moviola   A projection machine that shows film on a tiny screen.

Overdub   The addition of instrumental and vocal touches to preexisting tracks.

Platinum album   One million units.

Platinum single   Two million units.

Producer   The man who oversees all aspects of a record session, and works along with the engineer on mixing and editing.

Professional manager   Publishing employee who finds songs and places them with artists.

Program director   The record-station executive who chooses songs to be included on the station's playlist.

Prosody   The comfortable and logical blending of words and music.

Public domain   Status of a composition whose copyright has expired.

R & B   Rhythm and blues.

RIAA   Record Industry Association of America.

Royalty   Payment made to publishers, writers and performers for each copy sold of their work, and to publishers and writers for every performance of their work.

SASE   The abbreviation for a self-addressed stamped envelope.

Self-contained artist   One who performs and writes his or her own songs.

SESAC   Society of European Stage Authors and Composers. Unlike BMI and ASCAP, it handles both performances and mechanicals.

Song shark   Someone who deals unethically with songwriters.

Soul   Rhythm and blues.

Spec   Speculation. When a writer composes "on spec," he does so without pay.

Split publishing   The division of publishing rights between two or more people.

SRS   Song Registration Service.

Staff writer   Salaried, exclusive writer for one publishing firm.

Standard   A song that has gained permanent popularity.

Subpublisher   When an American publisher gives a song to a foreign publisher to represent and promote in his area, the foreign representative is called the subpublisher.

Sweetening   The addition of parts to rhythm and vocal tracks, generally referring to strings and horns.

Synchronization   Putting music to film.

Tails (tails out)   Describing a tape wound with the loose end at the end.

Take   Doing a take is putting down a track or vocal and then listening back to it.

Track   Portion of a recording tape that can be individually recorded in the studio, then mixed into a finished master copy.

Trades   The music-industry publications: *Billboard, Cash Box, Record World, Songwriter, Variety.*

Verse   The section of a song that precedes the chorus. In an A B A B C A B format, the verse would be A, the chorus B and the bridge C.

Work   To push and promote a song.

Important Industry Contacts

INDEPENDENT RECORD PRODUCERS

Aerosmith
c/o Contemporary Communications
   Corp.
65 West 55th Street
New York, N.Y. 10019
Phone: (212) 765-2600

Ambrosia
c/o Rubicon Management
8319 Lankershim Boulevard
North Hollywood, Calif. 91605
Phone: (213) 767-4522

Punch Andrews
567 Purdy
Birmingham, Mich. 48009
Phone: (313) 642-0910

Peter Asher
644 North Doheny Drive
Los Angeles, Calif. 90069
Phone: (213) 273-9433

Gil Askey
c/o Curtom Records
5915 North Lincoln
Chicago, Ill. 60659
Phone: (312) 769-4676

Jon Astley
c/o Trinifold
112 Wardour Street
London W15 3LD
England
Phone: 01-439-8411

Chet Atkins
RCA Records Inc.
806 17th Avenue South
Nashville, Tenn. 37203
Phone: (615) 244-9880

Roy Ayers
c/o Polydor Inc.
810 Seventh Avenue
New York, N.Y. 10019
Phone: (212) 399-7100

Randy Bachman
Bruce Allen Talent Promotion
68 Water Street, Suite 406
Gastown, Vancouver, B.C. V68 1A5
Canada
Phone: (604) 688-7274

Roy Thomas Baker
c/o John Reid Enterprises, Ltd.
40 South Audley Street
London
England
Phone: 01-491-27-77
    or
c/o Rocket
211 South Beverly Drive
Beverly Hills, Calif. 90212
Phone: (213) 550-0144

Steve Barri
c/o Warner Brothers Records
3300 Warner Boulevard
Burbank, Calif. 91505
Phone: (213) 846-9090

Jeff Barry
9100 Sunset Boulevard, Suite 200
Los Angeles, Calif. 90069
Phone: (213) 550-8280

Fred Bauer
c/o Epic Records
51 West 52nd Street
New York, N.Y. 10019
Phone: (212) 975-4321

John Beecher
c/o MCA
100 Universal City Plaza
Universal City, Calif. 91608
Phone: (213) 985-4321

Mike Belkin and Carl Maduri
c/o Sweet City Records
Woodmere, Ohio 44122
Phone: (216) 464-5990

Thom Bell
2214 Fourth Avenue
Seattle, Wash. 91821
Phone: (206) 682-5287
    or
309 South Broad Street
Philadelphia, Pa. 19107
Phone: (215) 985-0900

Pete Bellotte
c/o Joyce Bogart
Casablanca Records
8255 Sunset Boulevard
Los Angeles, Calif. 90060
Phone: (213) 650-8300

Phil Benton
c/o Bang Records
2107 Faukner Road, N.E.
Atlanta, Ga. 30324
Phone: (404) 325-9810

Steve Bernstein
1307 Vine Street
Philadelphia, Pa. 19107
Phone: (215) 922-6640

Kurt Borusiewicz
Queens Village Recording Studios
800 South Fourth Street
Philadelphia, Pa. 19147
Phone: (215) 463-2200

Jerry Bradley
RCA Records Inc.
806 17th Avenue South
Nashville, Tenn. 37203
Phone: (615) 244-9880

Michael Brovsky
c/o Free Flow Productions
1209 Baylor
Austin, Texas 78703
Phone: (512) 474-6926

Lindsey Buckingham
c/o Seedy Management
1420 North Beechwood Drive
Los Angeles, Calif. 90028
Phone: (213) 461-7421
 (213) 464-1186

Buddy Buie
3864 Oakcliff Industrial Court
Doraville, Ga. 30340
Phone: (404) 449-5142

Larry Butler Productions
6 Music Circle North
Nashville, Tenn. 37023
Phone: (615) 254-3444

Ken Caillat
c/o Penguin Productions
1420 North Beechwood Drive
Los Angeles, Calif. 90028
Phone: (213) 461-7421
 464-1186

Charles Calello
c/o Radio Band of America
666 Fifth Avenue
New York, N.Y. 10019
Phone: (212) 687-4800

Tony Camillo
121 Meadowbrook Drive
Somerville, N.J. 08876
Phone: (201) 359-2157

Eric Carmen
944 South Center Road
Mayfield Village, Ohio 44143
Phone: (216) 473-0089

John Carter
c/o Capitol Records
1750 North Vine Street
Los Angeles, Calif. 90028
Phone: (213) 462-6252

Harry Wayne Casey
T.K. Productions
495 South East 10th Court
Hialeah, Fla. 33010
Phone: (305) 888-1685

Cashman and West
40 West 55th Street
New York, N.Y. 10019
Phone: (212) 752-3033

Boomer Castleman
P.O. Box 12723
Nashville, Tenn. 37212
Phone: (615) 356-1209

Michael Chapman
Chinnychap, Inc.
947 North La Cienega, Suite H
Los Angeles, Calif. 90069
Phone: (213) 657-8585
 or
Chinnychap, Ltd.
5 Clarges Street
London W1
England
Phone: 01-493-1409

Steve Clark
Studio One
3864 Oakcliff Industrial Court
Atlanta, Ga. 30340
Phone: (404) 447-9492

Tony Clarke
c/o Nick Massey
Threshold Records
53–55 Height Street
Gobham, Surrey
England
Phone: 09-326-4142

Julien Colbeck
c/o Janus Records
8776 Sunset Boulevard
Los Angeles, Calif. 90069
Phone: (213) 659-6444

Tom Collins
P.O. Box 40984
Nashville, Tenn. 37204
Phone: (615) 320-7800

The Commodores
c/o Benny Ashburn
39 West 55th Street
Penthouse South
New York, N.Y. 10019
Phone: (212) 246-7385

Chick Corea
New Ace Management
2214 Canyon Drive
Hollywood, Calif. 90068
Phone: (213) 463-2303

Don Costa
c/o Don Costa Productions
9229 Sunset Boulevard, Suite 311
Los Angeles, Calif. 90069
Phone: (213) 550-8542

David Crosby
c/o Hartman and Goodman
6665 West Sunset
Los Angeles, Calif. 90028
Phone: (213) 461-3461

The Crusaders
c/o George Grief
8467 Beverly Boulevard
Los Angeles, Calif. 90048
Phone: (213) 653-4780

Ron Dante
c/o Richard Rosenthal
445 Park Avenue, Suite 303
New York, N.Y. 10022
Phone: (212) 758-0809

Richard Dashut
c/o Penguin Promotions
1420 North Beechwood Drive
Los Angeles, Calif. 90028
Phone: (213) 461-7421

Ray D. Davies
c/o Mickey Shapiro
315 South Beverly Drive, Suite 210
Beverly Hills, Calif. 90212
Phone: (213) 553-1601

Don Davis
c/o Groovesville Music
15855 Wyoming Street
Detroit, Mich. 48238
Phone: (313) 861-2363

Hal Davis
c/o Jobete Music
6255 Sunset Boulevard
Los Angeles, Calif. 90028
Phone: (213) 468-3500

Bert deCoteaux
c/o CBS
51 West 52nd Street
New York, N.Y. 10019
Phone: (212) 975-4321

Sean Delaney
c/o Aucoin Management
645 Madison Avenue
New York, N.Y. 10022
Phone: (212) 826-8800

Joel Diamond
220 Central Park South
Penthouse A
New York, N.Y. 10019
Phone: (212) 586-3535

Denny Diante
c/o United Artists
6920 Sunset Boulevard
Los Angeles, Calif. 90028
Phone: (213) 461-9141

Jeff Dixon
c/o Jefkey Productions Ltd.
663 Fifth Avenue
New York, N.Y. 10022
Phone: (212) 757-6454

Jack Douglas
c/o Waterfront Productions
140 West 86th Street
New York, N.Y. 10024
Phone: (212) 873-8563

Jimmy Douglas
c/o Jefkey Productions Ltd.
663 Fifth Avenue
New York, N.Y. 10022
Phone: (212) 757-6454

Tom Dowd
c/o Atlantic Records
75 Rockefeller Plaza
New York, N.Y. 10019
Phone: (212) 484-6000

Lamont Dozier
8467 Beverly Boulevard, Suite 200
Los Angeles, Calif. 90048
Phone: (213) 653-4780

Daryl Dragon
c/o B & B Associates
9454 Wilshire Boulevard, Suite 309
Beverly Hills, Calif. 90212
Phone: (213) 273-7020

Gus Dudgeon
Magnet Records
22 York Street
London W1H 1FD
England
Phone: 01-935-4049

Walter Egan
c/o Leber Krebs
65 West 55th Street
New York, N.Y. 10019
Phone: (212) 765-2600
    or
Craig Lewerke
Jet Records
2049 Century Park East
Los Angeles, Calif. 90067
Phone: (213) 553-6801

Ahmet Ertegun
Atlantic Records Inc.
75 Rockefeller Plaza
New York, N.Y. 10019
Phone: (212) 484-6000

Charlie Fach
Mercury Records, Inc.
110 West 57th Street
New York, N.Y. 10019
Phone: (212) 645-6300

Bruce Fairbairn
c/o Bruce Allen Talent
12 Water St., Suite 108
Gastown, Vancouver, B.C. V6B 1A5
Canada
Phone: (604) 688-7272

Jack Faith
Mighty Three Productions
309 South Broad Street
Philadelphia, Pa. 19107
Phone: (215) 546-3510

Jim Farrar
c/o Gormley Management
14 Upper Harley Street
London NW1
England
Phone: 01-486-4182
    or
Katz-Gallin-Cleary
9255 Sunset Boulevard
Los Angeles, Calif. 90069
Phone: (213) 273-4210

Bob Ferguson
RCA Records, Inc.
806 17th Avenue South
Nashville, Tenn. 37203
Phone: (615) 244-9880

Richard Finch
T.K. Productions
495 S.E. 10th Court
Hialeah, Fla. 33010
Phone: (305) 888-1685

Fleetwood Mac
c/o Penguin Productions
1420 North Beechwood Drive
Los Angeles, Calif. 90028
Phone: (213) 461-7421

Mike Flicker
c/o Albatross Management
P.O. Box 66558
Seattle, Wash. 98166
Phone: (206) 246-9400

Dan Fogelberg
c/o Front Line Management
8380 Melrose Avenue, Suite 307
Los Angeles, Calif. 90069
Phone: (213) 658-6600

Jim Foglesong
ABC Records, Inc.
2409 21st Avenue South
Nashville, Tenn. 37212
Phone: (615) 385-0840

Bruce Foster
c/o CAM, U.S.A.
489 Fifth Avenue
New York, N.Y. 10017
Phone: (212) 682-8400

David Foster
c/o Ned Shankman
Thompson, Shankman and Band
9200 Sunset Boulevard
Los Angeles, Calif. 90069
Phone: (213) 273-4660

Fred Foster
Monument Records, Inc.
719 16th Avenue South
Nashville, Tenn. 37203
Phone: (615) 244-6565

Kim Fowley
c/o Jeff Wald Associates
9120 Sunset Boulevard
Los Angeles, Calif. 90069
Phone: (213) 273-2192
           or
6000 Sunset Boulevard, Suite 209
Los Angeles, Calif. 90028

Peter Frampton
c/o Dee Anthony
554 Madison Avenue
New York, N.Y. 10022
Phone: (212) 758-2122

Harvey Fugua
405 Bellevue
Oakland, Calif. 95610
Phone: (415) 839-3474

Jerry Fuller
Moonchild Productions
13216 Bloomfield Street
Sherman Oaks, Calif. 91423
Phone: (213) 872-1854

Lewis Futterman
135 Central Park West
New York, N.Y. 10023
Phone: (212) 873-2403

Albhy Galuten
c/o Criteria Recording Studios
1755 N.E. 149th Street
Miami, Fla. 33161
Phone: (305) 947-5611

Kenneth Gamble
Gamble-Huff Productions
309 South Broadway
Philadelphia, Pa. 19107
Phone: (215) 985-0900

Snuff Garrett
c/o Snuff Garrett Productions
6255 Sunset Boulevard
Hollywood, Calif. 90028
Phone: (213) 467-2181

David Gates
c/o Al Schlesinger
6255 Sunset Boulevard
Los Angeles, Calif. 90028
Phone: (213) 462-6011

Bob Gaudio
c/o Four Seasons Productions
204 South Beverly Drive
Beverly Hills, Calif. 90212
Phone: (213) 278-7344

Phil Gernhard
Tony Scotti
9229 Sunset Boulevard
Los Angeles, Calif. 90069
Phone: (213) 550-6262

Steve Gibson
c/o Creative Workshop
2804 Azalea Place
Nashville, Tenn. 27204
Phone: (615) 385-0670

Marc Gilutin
c/o Ganes Productions Ltd.
Box 46503, Station G
Vancouver, B.C.
Canada
Phone: (604) 987-5157

Jeff Glixman
c/o Budd Carr
BNB Associates
9454 Wilshire Boulevard, Suite 309
Beverly Hills, Calif. 90212
Phone: (213) 938-6204

Jack Gold
c/o CBS Records
1801 Century Park West
Los Angeles, Calif. 90067
Phone: (213) 556-4720

Steve Gold
c/o Far Out Productions
7417 Sunset Boulevard, Suite 905
Los Angeles, Calif. 90046
Phone: (213) 874-1300

Wally Gold
c/o Don Kirshner Entertainment
1370 Avenue of the Americas
New York, N.Y. 10019
Phone: (212) 489-0440

Jerry Goldstein
c/o Far Out Productions
7417 Sunset Boulevard
Los Angeles, Calif. 90046
Phone: (213) 874-1300

Steve Goodman
c/o Bill Siddons
9660 Heather Road
Beverly Hills, Calif. 90210
Phone: (213) 273-6065

Leo Graham
2131 South Michigan Avenue
Chicago, Ill. 60605
Phone: (312) 326-3510

Ron Haffkine
P.O. Box 4115
Madison, Tenn. 37115
Phone: (615) 868-4090
        or
Grapefruit Productions
106 Montague Street
Brooklyn, N.Y. 11201
Phone: (212) 858-5056

Lew Hahn
c/o Atlantic Records
75 Rockefeller Plaza
New York, N.Y. 10019
Phone: (212) 484-6000
        or
9229 Sunset Boulevard
Los Angeles, Calif. 90069
Phone: (213) 278-9230

Marvin Hamlisch
171 West 81st Street, Apt. E
New York, N.Y. 10024
Phone: (212) 873-6750

Jeff Hana
Aspen Recording Company
P.O. Box 1915
Aspen, Colo. 81611
Phone: (303) 925-1645

Bill Henderson
Ganes Productions, Ltd.
P.O. Box 46503
Station G
Vancouver, B.C.
Canada
Phone: (604) 987-5157

Wayne Henderson
At Home Productions
7033 Sunset Boulevard, Suite 320
Los Angeles, Calif. 90028
Phone: (213) 461-2914

Monk Higgins
c/o ICA
226 Massachusetts Avenue
Washington, D.C. 20002
Phone: (202) 547-4477

Rupert Holmes
712 Fifth Avenue
New York, N.Y. 10019
Phone: (212) 765-3850

Leon Huff
Gamble & Huff Productions
309 South Broad Street
Philadelphia, Pa. 19107
Phone: (215) 985-0900

Jimmy Ienner
Millennium Records
3 West 57th Street
New York, N.Y. 10019
Phone: (212) 759-3901

Isley Brothers
c/o Kelly, Isley
1650 Broadway
New York, N.Y. 10019
Phone: (212) 582-5432

Clayton Ivey
P.O. Box 2631
Wishbone Recording Studios
Muscle Shoals, Ala. 35660
Phone: (205) 381-1455

Chuck Jackson
Marvin Yancy
c/o Jay Enterprises
441 North La Salle Street
Chicago, Ill. 60610
Phone: (312) 644-2044

Millie Jackson
Keishval Enterprises
1650 Broadway, Suite 1105
New York, N.Y. 10019
Phone: (212) 757-7890
　　　or
Roy Rifkind
161 West 54th Street
New York, N.Y. 10019
Phone: (212) 581-5398

Felton Jarvis
c/o Col. Thomas A. Parker
MGM Studios
10202 West Washington Boulevard
Culver City, Calif. 90230
Phone: (213) 870-3311

Waylon Jennings
c/o Media Consulting
54 Main Street
Danbury, Conn. 06810
Phone: (203) 792-8880

Glyn Johns
Trinifold
112 Wardour Street
London W1V 3LD
England
Phone: 01-439-8411

Frank Jones
Capitol Records
38 Music Square East
Nashville, Tenn. 37203
Phone: (213) 462-6252

Quincy Jones
1416 North La Brea
Los Angeles, Calif. 90028
Phone: (213) 469-2411

Lonnie Jordan
c/o Far Out Productions
7417 Sunset Boulevard
Los Angeles, Calif. 90046
Phone: (213) 874-1300

Andy Kahn
Queens Village Recording Studio
800 South 4th Street
Philadelphia, Pa. 19147
Phone: (215) 463-2200

Jerry Kasenetz
c/o Super K. Management
323 East Shore Road
Great Neck, N.Y. 11023
Phone: (516) 482-5930

Al Kasha
200 South Roxbury Drive
Beverly Hills, Calif. 90212
Phone: (213) 553-8760

Gary Katz
c/o Warner Brothers
3300 Warner Boulevard
Burbank, Calif. 91505
Phone: (213) 846-9090

Jeff Katz
c/o Super K. Management
323 East Shore Road
Great Neck, N.Y. 11023
Phone: (516) 482-5930

Monty Kaye
9229 Sunset Boulevard
Los Angeles, Calif. 90069
Phone: (213) 278-7975

Charles Kipps
c/o Roy Radin Assocs.
P.O. Box MMM
Southampton, N.Y. 11968
Phone: (516) 283-9100

Don Kirshner
c/o Don Kirshner Entertainment
　　Corporation
1370 Avenue of the Americas
New York, N.Y. 10019
Phone: (212) 489-0440

Gary Klein
6430 Sunset Boulevard, Room 803
Los Angeles, Calif. 90028
Phone: (213) 466-6127
    or
The Entertainment Company
40 West 57th Street
New York, N.Y. 10019
Phone: (212) 586-3600

John Klemmer
c/o Bill Siddons
9660 Heather Road
Beverly Hills, Calif. 90210
Phone: (213) 273-6065

Skip "Wizard" Konte
c/o CAM—U.S.A.
489 Fifth Avenue
New York, N.Y. 10017
Phone: (212) 682-8400

Charles Koppelman
c/o The Entertainment Company
40 West 57th Street
New York, N.Y. 10019
Phone: (212) 586-3600

Eddie Kramer
c/o Record Plant
321 West 44th Street
New York, N.Y. 10036
Phone: (212) 581-6505
    or
Electric Lady Studios
52 West 8th Street
New York, N.Y. 10011
Phone: (212) 477-7500

Jon Landau
c/o Michael Tannen
36 East 61st Street
New York, N.Y. 10021
Phone: (212) 752-2276

Robert John Lange
8 Rowland Gardens
London SW7
England
Phone: 01-370-2929

Sylvester Levay
Global Music
8 München 19
Nederlinger Strasse 21
Germany
Phone: 941-521-5019

Stewart Levine
Outside Productions
1880 Century Park East, Suite 600
Los Angeles, Calif. 90067
Phone: (213) 553-6370

Jack Lewis
c/o Little David Records
9229 Sunset Boulevard, Suite 901
Los Angeles, Calif. 90069
Phone: (213) 278-7981

Ramsey Lewis
9615 Brighton Way, Suite 212
Beverly Hills, Calif. 90210
Phone: (213) 274-8071

Henry Lewy
6005 Paseo Canyon
Malibu, Calif. 90265
Phone: (213) 457-2035

Michael Lloyd
c/o Mike Curb Productions
6363 Wilshire Boulevard, Suite 420
Los Angeles, Calif. 90048
Phone: (213) 655-9934
    or
905 Beverly Drive
Beverly Hills, Calif. 90210

George Lucas
c/o 20th Century–Fox Studios
10201 Pico Boulevard
Los Angeles, Calif. 90035
Phone: (213) 277-2211

Jeff Lynne
Jet Records
Contact: Don Arden
44 Park Side
Wimbledon, London SW19
England
Phone: 01-947-5505
    or
2049 Century Park East
Los Angeles, Calif. 90067
Phone: (213) 553-6801

Tony Macaulay
No. 1 Carlton Hill
London NW
England
Phone: 01-328-4428

Brent Maher
c/o Creative Workshop
2804 Azalea Place
Nashville, Tenn. 37204
Phone: (615) 385-0670

David Malloy
c/o David Malloy
1496 Woodmont Boulevard
Nashville, Tenn. 37215
Phone: (615) 383-2388

Chuck Mangione
c/o Gates Music
270 Midtown Plaza
Rochester, N.Y. 14604
Phone: (716) 232-2490

Barry Manilow
c/o Miles Lourie
250 West 57th Street
New York, N.Y. 10019
Phone: (212) 586-1010

Arif Mardin
c/o Atlantic Records
75 Rockefeller Plaza
New York, N.Y. 10019
Phone: (212) 484-6000

Mitch and Phil Margo
Amron, Halpren and Margo
221 West 57th Street
New York, N.Y. 10019
Phone: (212) 582-4200

Bob Marley & The Wailers
c/o Stu Weintraub
Associated Booking Corporation
445 Park Avenue
New York, N.Y. 10022
Phone: (212) 754-9800

Bobby Martin
c/o Tentmakers
6367 West 6th Street
Los Angeles, Calif. 90048
Phone: (213) 937-6650

George Martin
c/o Air Recording
108 Park Street
London SW1
England
    or
Chrysalis Records
9255 Sunset Boulevard
Los Angeles, Calif. 90069
Phone: (213) 550-0170

Harry Maslin
c/o Barbara DeWitt
6430 Sunset Boulevard, Suite 1502
Los Angeles, Calif. 90028
Phone: (213) 467-2104

David Matthews
c/o CTI
1 Rockefeller Plaza
New York, N.Y. 10020
Phone: (212) 489-6120

Paul McCartney
c/o Capitol Records
1750 North Vine Street
Los Angeles, Calif. 90028
Phone: (213) 462-6252
    or
MPL Communications
39 West 54th Street
New York, N.Y. 10019
Phone: (212) 581-1330

Mathew McCauley
c/o McCauley Music
16 Overbank Crescent
Don Mills, Ont.
Canada
Phone: (416) 447-9523
    or
Finkelstein and Fiedler
98 Queen Street East
Toronto, Ont.
Canada
Phone: (416) 364-6040

Van McCoy
Contact: Roy Radin Associates
P.O. Box MMM
Southampton, N.Y. 11968
Phone: (516) 283-9100

Clarence McDonald
c/o Cavello-Ruffalo
9615 Brighton Way, Suite 212
Beverly Hills, Calif. 90210
Phone: (213) 274-8071

William McKuen
P.O. Box 1915
Aspen, Colo. 81611
Phone: (213) 273-6251

Leon S. Medica
c/o Aspen Presentations
1145 Sunset Vale
Los Angeles, Calif. 90069
Phone: (213) 273-6251

Ronnie Milsap
c/o Don Reeves
41 Music Square East
Nashville, Tenn. 37203
Phone: (615) 256-7575

Fred Mollin
c/o McCauley Music
16 Overbank Crescent
Don Mills, Ont.
Canada
Phone: (416) 447-9253
    or
Finkelstein and Fiedler
98 Queen State East
Toronto, Ont.
Canada
Phone: (416) 364-6040

Giorgio Moroder
Say Yes Productions
8 München 81
Arabellahaus 139
Germany
    or
c/o Joyce Bogart
Casablanca Records
8255 Sunset Boulevard
Los Angeles, Calif. 90069
Phone: (213) 650-8300

Larry Morton
c/o CBS Records
51 West 52nd Street
New York, N.Y. 10019
Phone: (212) 975-4321

Graham Nash
c/o Hartmann & Goodman
6665 West Sunset
Los Angeles, Calif. 90028
Phone: (213) 641-3461

Ron Nevison
c/o Barry K. Rothman
9200 Sunset Boulevard
Los Angeles, Calif. 90069
Phone: (213) 550-6166

Stevie Nicks
c/o Seedy Management
1420 North Beachwood Drive
Los Angeles, Calif. 90028
Phone: (213) 461-7421
              464-1186

Ohio Players
c/o Creative Direction
233 East Ontario Street
Chicago, Ill. 70611
Phone: (312) 664-0300

Eddie O'Laughlin
c/o Midland International
1650 Broadway
New York, N.Y. 10019
Phone: (212) 541-0100

Eugene Organ
c/o Janus Records
8776 Sunset Boulevard
Los Angeles, Calif. 90069
Phone: (213) 659-6444

Dolly Parton
c/o Katz-Gallin-Cleary
9255 Sunset Boulevard, Suite 1115
Los Angeles, Calif. 90069
Phone: (213) 273-4210

Gregg Perry
c/o Dolly Parton
811 18th Avenue South
Nashville, Tenn. 37203
Phone: (615) 659-1222

Richard Perry
Richard Perry Productions
5505 Melrose Avenue
Los Angeles, Calif. 90038
Phone: (213) 466-4306

Jerry Peters
6363 Sunset Boulevard
Los Angeles, Calif. 90028
Phone: (213) 461-4958

J. C. Phillips
c/o Jason Cooper
9465 Wilshire Boulevard
Beverly Hills, Calif. 90212
Phone: (213) 876-3696

Fred Piro
8319 Lankershim Boulevard
Hollywood, Calif. 91605
Phone: (213) 674-3522

Poco
c/o Hartmann & Goodman
6665 West Sunset
Los Angeles, Calif. 90028
Phone: (213) 461-3461

Norbert Putnam
c/o Quadrafonic Sound Studio
1802 Grand Avenue
Nashville, Tenn. 37212
Phone: (615) 327-4568

Phil Ramone
36 East 61st Street
New York, N.Y. 10021
Phone: (212) 759-6948

Genya Ravan
c/o Twin Management
641 Lexington Avenue
New York, N.Y. 10022
Phone: (212) 421-6249

Carl Richardson
c/o Criteria Recording Studios
1755 N.E. 149th Street
Miami, Fla. 33161
Phone: (305) 947-5611

Johnny Rivers
c/o Don Kelley Org.
1474 North Kings Road
Los Angeles, Calif. 90069
Phone: (213) 656-4787

Paul H. Rothchild
8728 Lookout Mountain Avenue
Los Angeles, Calif. 90046
Phone: (213) 654-3393
    or
300 Windsor Road
Englewood, N.J. 07631
Phone: (201) 567-6877

Al Rubins
1307 Vine Street
Philadelphia, Pa. 19107
Phone: (215) 922-6640

David Rubinson & Friends
827 Folsom Street
San Francisco, Calif. 94107
Phone: (415) 777-2930

Todd Rundgren
c/o Eric Gardner
184 Ninth Avenue
Brooklyn, N.Y. 11215
Phone: (212) 499-6384

Jim Rutledge
P.O. Box 12723
Nashville, Tenn. 37212
Phone: (615) 356-1209

Carole Bayer Sager
c/o John Reid
211 South Beverly Drive, Suite 200
Beverly Hills, Calif. 90212
Phone: (213) 275-5221
    or
c/o Begonia-Unichappell
810 Seventh Avenue
New York, N.Y. 10019
Phone: (212) 399-7100

Skip Scarborough
c/o Relmarc Productions
11620 Wilshire Boulevard
Los Angeles, Calif. 90025
Phone: (213) 479-3944

Tom Scholz
Pure Productions
1289 North Crescent Hills
Los Angeles, Calif. 90046
Phone: (213) 656-9464

Duane Scott
c/o Leber-Krebs
65 West 55th Street
New York, N.Y. 10019
Phone: (212) 765-2600

Bob Seger
567 Purdy
Birmingham, Mich. 48009
Phone: (313) 642-0910

Scott Shannon
c/o Ariola Records
8671 Wilshire Boulevard, Suite 5
Beverly Hills, Calif. 90211
Phone: (213) 659-6530

Brad Shapiro
c/o Spring Records
161 West 54th Street
New York, N.Y. 10019
Phone: (212) 581-5398

Louie Shelton
724 North Huntington
San Fernando, Calif. 91340
    or
Contact: Day 5 Productions
216 Chatsworth Drive
San Fernando, Calif. 91340
Phone: (213) 365-9371

Bruce Springsteen
c/o Michael Tannen
35 East 51st Street
New York, N.Y. 10022
Phone: (212) 752-2262

Jack Stack-A-Track
c/o Casablanca Records
8255 Sunset Boulevard
Los Angeles, Calif. 90046
Phone: (213) 650-8300

Cat Stevens
c/o BKM Productions
9200 Sunset Boulevard
Los Angeles, Calif. 90069
Phone: (213) 271-6265

Stephen Stills
P.O. Box 44282
Panorama City, Calif. 91402
Phone: (213) 785-4284

Louis St. Louis
c/o Bill Oakes
Paramount Pictures
5451 Marathon Street
Los Angeles, Calif. 90038
Phone: (213) 463-0100

John Stronach
c/o Record Plant
8456 West 3rd Street
Los Angeles, Calif. 90048
Phone: (213) 653-0240

Styx
c/o Derrick Sutton
Stardust Entertainment
2615 Glendower Avenue
Los Angeles, Calif. 90027
Phone: (213) 660-2553

Supertramp
c/o Dave Margereson
216 Pico Boulevard
Santa Monica, Calif. 90405
Phone: (213) 392-1774

Michael Sutton
c/o Motown
6255 Sunset Boulevard
Los Angeles, Calif. 90028
Phone: (213) 468-3500

Sweet 2
c/o Ed Leffler
El Management
9229 Sunset Boulevard
Los Angeles, Calif. 90069
Phone: (213) 550-8802

Sylvester
405 Bellevue
Oakland, Calif. 94610
Phone: (415) 839-3474

Homer Talber for
Fountain Productions
500 North Michigan Avenue
Chicago, Ill. 60312
Phone: (312) 467-5377

Chris Thomas
c/o Chrysalis (England)
388–396 Oxford Street
London W1
England
Phone: 01-408-2355

Terry Thomas
c/o Chalice Productions
8467 Beverly Boulevard
Los Angeles, Calif. 90048
Phone: (213) 658-7002

Russ Titelman
c/o Warner-Reprise
3300 Warner Boulevard
Burbank, Calif. 91505
Phone: (213) 846-9090

Rof Turney
Ganes Productions
P.O. Box 46503
Vancouver, B.C.
Canada
Phone: (604) 987-5157

Lenny Waronker
c/o Warner Reprise
3300 Warner Boulevard
Burbank, Calif. 91505
Phone: (213) 846-9090

Kent Washburn
c/o Glen Glenn Enterprises
6255 Sunset Boulevard
Los Angeles, Calif. 90028
Phone: (213) 468-3429

Bruce Welch
c/o John Reid
211 South Beverly Drive, Suite 200
Beverly Hills, Calif. 90212
Phone: (213) 275-5221
        or
16 Harley House
Marlebone Road
London
England
Phone: 01-486-4182

Tom Werman
c/o Epic Records
51 West 52nd Street
New York, N.Y. 10019
Phone: (212) 975-4321

Jerry Wexler
c/o Atlantic Records
75 Rockefeller Plaza
New York, N.Y. 10019
Phone: (212) 484-6000
        or
9229 Sunset Boulevard
Los Angeles, Calif. 90028
Phone: (213) 278-9230

Maurice White
Contact: Cavallo-Ruffalo
9615 Brighton Way, Suite 212
Los Angeles, Calif. 90210
Phone: (213) 274-8071

Norman Whitfield
Whitfield Records
8719 Santa Monica Boulevard
Los Angeles, Calif. 90069
Phone: (213) 652-5860
              846-9090

Frank Wilson
c/o Ray Tisdale
5900 Wilshire Boulevard
Los Angeles, Calif. 90036
Phone: (213) 937-3100

Woody Wilson
17565 Stoepel Street
Detroit, Mich. 48221
Phone: (313) 861-2770

Terry Woodford
Wishbone Recording Studios
P.O. Box 2631
Muscle Shoals, Ala. 35660
Phone: (205) 381-1455

UNITED STATES MUSIC PUBLISHERS

LOS ANGELES

ABC Dunhill Music
8255 Beverly Boulevard
Los Angeles, Calif. 90048

Almo/Irving Music
1416 North La Brea
Los Angeles. Calif. 90028

American Broadcasting Music
11538 San Vicente Blvd.
Los Angeles, Calif. 90049

April Blackwood Music
1801 Century Park West
Los Angeles, Calif. 90067

Ariola American Publishing Company
8761 Wilshire Blvd.
Beverly Hills, Calif. 90211

Arista Music Company
1888 Century Park East
Los Angeles, Calif. 90067

ATV Music
6255 Sunset Boulevard
Los Angeles, Calif. 90028

Audio Arts Publishing Company
5617 Melrose Avenue
Los Angeles, Calif. 90038

Barton Music Company
9220 Sunset Boulevard
Los Angeles, Calif. 90069

Beechwood Music Company
1750 North Vine Street
Hollywood, Calif. 90028

Berdoo Music Company
P.O. Box 3851
Los Angeles, Calif. 90028

Bicycle Music Company
8756 Holloway Drive
Los Angeles, Calif. 90069

Bourne Music Company
6381 Hollywood Boulevard
Hollywood, Calif. 90028

Braintree Music Company
5505 Melrose Avenue
Los Angeles, Calif. 90038

Budd Music Corporation
15831 Wells Drive
Tarzana, Calif. 91356

Glen Campbell Music Company
10920 Wilshire Boulevard
Los Angeles, Calif. 90024

Caribou Management Corporation
573 Westbourne Street
Los Angeles, Calif. 90069

Casablanca Music
8255 Sunset Boulevard
Los Angeles, Calif. 90046

Chappell Music Company
6255 Sunset Boulevard
Hollywood, Calif. 90028

Claridge Music Company
6381 Hollywood Boulevard, #318
Hollywood, Calif. 90028

Don Costa Productions
9229 Sunset Boulevard
Los Angeles, Calif. 90069

Criterion Music Corporation
6124 Selma Avenue
Hollywood, Calif. 90028

Mike Curb Productions
6363 Wilshire Boulevard
Beverly Hills, Calif. 90048

Walt Disney Music Company
350 South Buena Vista Street
Burbank, Calif. 91521

Entertainment Company Music Group
6430 Sunset Boulevard, Suite 803
Los Angeles, Calif. 90028

Equinox Music Company
9920 Sunset Boulevard, #224
Los Angeles, Calif. 90069

Famous Music Corporation
6430 Sunset Boulevard
Hollywood, Calif. 90028

Far Out Music Company
7417 Sunset Boulevard
Hollywood, Calif. 90046

Fermata International Melodies
6290 Sunset Boulevard, #616
Hollywood, Calif. 90028

Filmways Music Company
1800 Century Park East, #300
Century City, Calif. 90067

First Artists
3300 Warner Boulevard
Burbank, Calif. 91503

Four Star Music Company
9220 Sunset Boulevard, #312
Los Angeles, Calif. 90069

Frank Music Corp.
(See April Blackwood)

Fullness Music Company
13216 Bloomfield
Sherman Oaks, Calif. 90028

Al Gallico Music Corp.
6255 Sunset Boulevard
Hollywood, Calif. 90028

Garrett Music Entertainments
6255 Sunset Blvd., #1019
Hollywood, Calif. 90028

Hall of Fame Music Company
P.O. Box 921
Beverly Hills, Calif. 90213

T. B. Harms Music Company
100 Wilshire Boulevard
Santa Monica, Calif. 90401

Island Music Company
7720 West Sunset Boulevard
Los Angeles, Calif. 90046

Interworld Music Group
6255 Sunset Boulevard, Suite 709
Los Angeles, Calif. 90028

Invador Music Company
8961 Sunset Boulevard
Los Angeles, Calif. 90069

Jack and Bill Music Company
100 Wilshire Boulevard
Santa Monica, Calif. 90401

Dick James Music Company
6430 Sunset Boulevard
Hollywood, Calif. 90028

Jobete Music Company
6255 Sunset Boulevard
Hollywood, Calif. 90028

Joyfully Sad Music Company
9100 Wilshire Boulevard, #454
Beverly Hills, Calif. 90212

MCA Music Company
100 Universal City Plaza
Universal City, Calif. 91608

Open End Music Company
824 North Robertson Boulevard
Los Angeles, Calif. 90069

Peer-Southern Music Organization
6922 Hollywood Boulevard
Los Angeles, Calif. 90028

Playboy Music Publishing
8560 Sunset Boulevard, #400
Los Angeles, Calif. 90069

Respect Music Company
1159 South La Jolla Avenue
Los Angeles, Calif. 90035

Rondor Music Company
1416 North La Brea Avenue
Hollywood, Calif. 90028

Screen Gems Columbia Music
    Company (EMI)
7033 Sunset Boulevard
Hollywood, Calif. 90028

Larry Shayne Music Company
6290 Sunset Boulevard
Hollywood, Calif. 90028

Skyhill Music Publishing
5112 Hollywood Boulevard
Los Angeles, Calif. 90027

20th Century Music Corp.
8544 Sunset Boulevard
Los Angeles, Calif. 90069

United Artists Publishing Group
6920 Sunset Boulevard
Los Angeles, Calif. 90028

Valgroup Music (U.S.A.) Company
7033 Sunset Boulevard
Los Angeles, Calif. 90028

Venice Music Company
8300 Santa Monica Boulevard
Hollywood, Calif. 90069

Warner/Tamerlane Music Company
9200 Sunset Boulevard, #222
Los Angeles, Calif. 90069

NEW YORK

Allied Artists Music Company
15 Columbus Circle
New York, N.Y. 10023

American Broadcasting Music
1330 Avenue of the Americas
New York, N.Y. 10019

April Blackwood Music
1350 Avenue of the Americas
New York, N.Y. 10019

Arc Music Corporation
110 East 59th Street
New York, N.Y. 10022

ATV Music Corporation
115 East 57th Street
New York, N.Y. 10022

Belwin-Mills Publishing Corporation
16 West 61st Street
New York, N.Y. 10023

Big Seven Music Corporation
1790 Broadway
New York, N.Y. 10019

Bourne Music Company
1212 Avenue of the Americas
New York, N.Y. 10036

Brut Music Publishing
1345 Avenue of the Americas
New York, N.Y. 10019

Buddah Music Company
1350 Avenue of the Americas
New York, N.Y. 10019

Burlington Music Corporation
539 West 25th Street
New York, N.Y. 10001

CAM-U.S.A. Music Company
489 Fifth Avenue
New York, N.Y. 10017

Chappell Music Company
810 Seventh Avenue
New York, N.Y. 10019

Chrysalis Music Corporation
115 East 57th Street
New York, N.Y. 10022

Cotillion Music Company
75 Rockefeller Plaza
New York, N.Y. 10019

Famous Music Corporation
One Gulf & Western Plaza
New York, N.Y. 10023

Fania Publishing Company
888 Seventh Avenue
New York, N.Y. 10019

Fort Knox Music Company
1619 Broadway
New York, N.Y. 10019

Fourth Floor Music Company
75 East 55th Street, #505
New York, N.Y. 10022

Al Gallico Music Corporation
126 East 56th Street
New York, N.Y. 10022

Gil Music Corporation
1650 Broadway
New York, N.Y. 10019

T. B. Harms Music Company
200 West 57th Street, #807
New York, N.Y. 10019

Hudson Bay Music Company
1619 Broadway
New York, N.Y. 10019

Interworld Music Group
25 West 57th Street
New York, N.Y. 10019

Dick James Music Company
119 West 57th Street
New York, N.Y. 10019

Jobete Music Company
157 West 57th Street
New York, N.Y. 10019

Don Kirshner Music Company
1370 Avenue of the Americas
New York, N.Y. 10019

Edward B. Marks Music Group
1790 Broadway
New York, N.Y. 10019

MCA Music Company
445 Park Avenue
New York, N.Y. 10022

Robert Mellin Music Publishing Group
1841 Broadway
New York, N.Y. 10023

Midsong Music International, Ltd.
1650 Broadway
New York, N.Y. 10019

Peer-Southern Music Organization
1740 Broadway
New York, N.Y., 10019

Robert Stigwood Organization (RSO)
135 Central Park West, #2N
New York, N.Y. 10023

Screen Gems Columbia Music
   Company
1370 Avenue of the Americas
New York, N.Y. 10019

Shapiro Bernstein & Company
10 East 53rd Street
New York, N.Y., 10022

Silver Blue Music Company
220 Central Park South
New York, N.Y. 10019

Star Spangled Music Company
405 Park Avenue
New York, N.Y. 10022

The Richmond Organization (TRO)
10 Columbus Circle
New York, N.Y. 10019

Track Music Company
200 West 57th Street
New York, N.Y. 10019

Trio Music Company
1619 Broadway
New York, N.Y. 10019

United Artists Music Publishing
   Corporation
729 Seventh Avenue
New York, N.Y. 10019

Warner Brothers Music Company
75 Rockefeller Plaza
New York, N.Y. 10019

NASHVILLE

Acoustic Music Inc.
49 Music Square East
Nashville, Tenn. 37203

Acuff-Rose Publications
2510 Franklin Road
Nashville, Tenn. 37204

American Broadcasting Music
2409 21st Avenue South
Nashville, Tenn. 37212

American Cowboy Music
11 Music Circle South
Nashville, Tenn. 37203

April Blackwood Music
31 Music Square West
Nashville, Tenn. 37203

ATV Music Corp.
45 Music Square West
Nashville, Tenn. 37203

Earl Barton Music Company
1307 Division Street
Nashville, Tenn. 37212

Beechwood Music Company
1014 17th Avenue, South
Nashville, Tenn. 37212

Blue Echo Music Company
P.O. Box 15203
Nashville, Tenn. 37215

Buckhorn Music Publishers
1007 17th Avenue, South
Nashville, Tenn. 37212

Buzz Cason Music Publishing
2804 Azalea Place
Nashville, Tenn. 37204

Cedarwood Music Publishing Company
39 Music Square East
Nashville, Tenn. 37203

Chappell Music Company
10 Music Circle South
Nashville, Tenn. 37203

Coal Miners Music Company
7 Music Circle North
Nashville, Tenn. 37203

Combine Music Corporation
35 Music Square East
Nashville, Tenn. 37203

Contention Music Company
P.O. Box 824
Nashville, Tenn. 37202

Danor Music Company
1802 Grand Avenue
Nashville, Tenn. 37212

Famous Music Corporation
2 Music Circle South
Nashville, Tenn. 37203

Forrest Hills Music Company
1609 Hawkins Street
Nashville, Tenn. 37203

Four Star Music Company
901 17th Avenue South
Nashville, Tenn. 37212

Al Gallico Music Corporation
50 Music Square West
Nashville, Tenn. 37203

Ray Griff Enterprises
P.O. Box 15203
Nashville, Tenn. 37215

T. B. Harms Music Company
P.O. Box 1026
Nashville, Tenn. 37202

House of Gold Music Company
P.O. Box 50338
Belle Meade Station
Nashville, Tenn. 37205

House of Bryant Publications
P.O. Box 12618
Nashville, Tenn. 37212

Ironside Music Company
P.O. Box 40923
Nashville, Tenn. 37204

Music Mill Publishing Company, Inc.
1111 17th Avenue South
Nashville, Tenn. 37212

Newkeys Music Inc.
29 Music Square East
Nashville, Tenn. 37203

Owepar Publishing Company
811 18th Avenue South
Nashville, Tenn. 37203

Passkey Music Inc.
808 17th Avenue South
Nashville, Tenn. 37203

Peer-Southern Organization
7 Music Circle North
Nashville, Tenn. 37203

Pi-Gem Music Inc.
1225 16th Avenue South
Nashville, Tenn. 37212

Prima-Donna Music Company
P.O. Box 15385
Nashville, Tenn. 37215

Marty Robbins Music Enterprises
713 18th Avenue South
Nashville, Tenn. 37203

Sawgrass Music Publishers Inc.
1722 West End Avenue
Nashville, Tenn, 37203

Screen Gems–EMI Music Inc.
1207 16th Avenue South
Nashville, Tenn. 37212

Shade Tree Music Inc.
50 Music Square West, Suite 300
Nashville, Tenn. 37203

Shelby Singleton Music Inc.
3106 Belmont Blvd.
Nashville, Tenn. 37212

Stallion Music Company
8 Music Square West
Nashville, Tenn. 37203

Tannen Music Company
1207 16th Avenue South
Nashville, Tenn. 37212

Tree Publishing Company Inc.
8 Music Square West
Nashville, Tenn. 37203

Twitty Bird Music Publishing Company
8 Music Square West
Nashville, Tenn. 37203

United Artists Music
1013 16th Avenue South
Nashville, Tenn. 37212

Vector Music
1107 18th Avenue South
Nashville, Tenn. 37212

Hank Williams Jr. Music Company
38 Music Square East
Nashville, Tenn. 37203

Window Publishing Company Inc.
809 18th Avenue South
Nashville, Tenn. 37203

Faron Young Music
1300 Division Street, Room 103
Nashville, Tenn. 37203

OTHER MAJOR CITIES

Abnak Music Enterprises
825 Olive at Ross
Dallas, Texas 75201

Alkatraz Corner Music Company
P.O. Box 3316
San Francisco, Calif. 94114

Arcade Music Company
2733 Kensington Ave.
Philadelphia, Pa. 19134

Augsburg Publishing House
426 South 5th Street
Minneapolis, Minn. 55415

Earl Barton Music Inc.
1121 South Glenstone
Springfield, Mo. 65804

Beachtime Music
P.O. Box 32044
San Jose, Calif. 95152

Bellboy Music
309 South Broad Street
Philadelphia, Pa. 19107

Ben Peters Music
900 Old Hickory Boulevard
Route 6
Brentwood, Tenn. 37027

Blue Book Music
1225 North Chester Avenue
Bakersfield, Calif. 93308

Cherry Lane Music Company
P.O. Box 4247
50 Holly Hill Lane
Greenwich, Conn. 06830

Conquistador Music
15855 Wyoming
Detroit, Mich. 48238

Country Star Music
439 Wiley Avenue
Franklin, Pa. 16323

Crazy Cajun Music
5626 Brock
Houston, Texas 77023

Crescendo Music Sales Company
P.O. Box 395
8 Bunting Lane
Naperville, Ill. 60540

Dawn Productions
P.O. Box 535
Bel Air, Md. 21014

Eden Music Corporation
P.O. Box 325
Englewood, N.J. 07631

Fame Publishing Company
603 East Avalon Avenue
Muscle Shoals, Ala. 35660

Groovesville Productions
15855 Wyoming
Detroit, Mich. 48238

Jim Halsey Company, Inc.
329 Rockland Road
Hendersonville, Tenn. 37075

House of Cash Inc.
P.O. Box 508
Hendersonville, Tenn. 37075

Jamie Music Publishing Company
919 North Broad Street
Philadelphia, Pa. 91923

Le Bill Music Inc.
P.O. Box 11152
Fort Worth, Texas 76110

Leigh Group Inc.
1650 Oak Street
Lakewood, N.J. 08701

Van McCoy Music Inc.
6901 Old Keene Mill Road, Suite #500
Springfield, Va. 22150

Muscle Shoals Sound Publishing
   Company Inc.
3614 Jackson Highway
Sheffield, Ala. 35660

Nor Va Jak Music Inc.
1321 West 7th Street
Clovis, N.M. 88101

David Rubinson & Friends Inc.
827 Folsom Street
San Francisco, Calif. 94107

Sherlyn Publishing Company
495 S.E. 10th Court
Hialeah, Fla. 33010

Singspiration Inc.
1415 Lake Drive, S.E.
Grand Rapids, Mich. 49506

Web IV Music Inc.
2107 Faulkner Road, N.E.
Atlanta, Ga. 30324

UNITED STATES RECORD COMPANIES

LOS ANGELES

ABC Records Inc.
8255 Beverly Boulevard
Los Angeles, Calif. 90048

Alshire International
1015 Isabel Street
Burbank, Calif. 91502

A & M Records Inc.
1416 North La Brea
Los Angeles, Calif. 90028

Amherst Records
9229 Sunset Boulevard
Los Angeles, Calif. 90069

Ariola Records
8671 Wilshire Boulevard
Beverly Hills, Calif. 90210

Arista Records Inc.
1888 Century Park East, #1510
Los Angeles, Calif. 90067

Atlantic Recording Corp.
9229 Sunset Boulevard, #710
Los Angeles, Calif. 90069

Barnaby Records
816 North La Cienega Boulevard
Los Angeles, Calif. 90069

Brother Records Inc.
10880 Wilshire Boulevard South
Los Angeles, Calif. 90024

Butterfly Records Inc.
9000 Sunset Boulevard, #617
Los Angeles, Calif. 90069

Cadet Records Inc.
510 South Normandie Avenue
Los Angeles, Calif. 90044

Capitol Records Inc.
1750 North Vine Street
Los Angeles, Calif. 90028

Capricorn Records Inc.
4405 Riverside Drive
Burbank, Calif. 91521

Caribou Records
573 Westbourne Avenue
Los Angeles, Calif. 90069

Casablanca Records and Film Works
8255 Sunset Boulevard
Los Angeles, Calif. 90069

CBS Records
1801 Century Park West
Century City, Calif. 90067

Chrysalis Records
9255 Sunset Boulevard, Suite 212
Los Angeles, Calif. 90069

Cream Records Inc.
8025 Melrose Avenue
Los Angeles, Calif. 90046

Crossover Records Company
2107 West Washington Boulevard
Los Angeles, Calif. 90028

Daybreak Distributing Corporation
6725 Sunset Boulevard, Suite 402
Los Angeles, Calif. 90028

Disneyland/Vista Records
350 South Buena Vista Street
Burbank, Calif. 91521

Elektra/Asylum/Nonesuch Records
962 North La Cienega Boulevard
Los Angeles, Calif. 90069

Epic/CBS Records
1801 Century Park West
Century City, Calif. 90067

Everest Record Group
10920 Wilshire Boulevard
Los Angeles, Calif. 90024

Fantasy/Prestige/Milestone/Stax
6363 Sunset Boulevard
Los Angeles, Calif. 90028

GNP Crescendo Records
8560 Sunset Boulevard, Suite 603
Los Angeles, Calif. 90069

Haven Records Inc.
9220 Sunset Boulevard, Suite 306
Los Angeles, Calif. 90069

Jet Records Inc.
2049 Century Park East, Suite 414
Los Angeles, Calif. 90067

Lifesong Records Inc.
9229 Sunset Boulevard, Suite 818
Los Angeles, Calif. 90069

Little David Records Company Inc.
9229 Sunset Boulevard, Suite 901
Los Angeles, Calif. 90069

MCA Records Inc.
100 Universal City Plaza
Universal City, Calif. 91608

Motown Record Corporation
6255 Sunset Boulevard
Los Angeles, Calif. 90028

Mums Records
9225 Sunset Boulevard
Los Angeles, Calif. 90048

Mushroom Records Inc.
8833 Sunset Boulevard, Suite 400
Los Angeles, Calif. 90069

Original Sound Records
7120 Sunset Boulevard
Hollywood, Calif. 90046

Parachute Records
8255 Sunset Boulevard
Los Angeles, Calif. 90046

Playboy Records Inc.
8560 Sunset Boulevard
Los Angeles, Calif. 90069

Ranwood Records
8776 Sunset Boulevard
Hollywood, Calif. 90069

RCA Records
6363 Sunset Boulevard
Los Angeles, Calif. 90028

Robert Stigwood Organization (RSO)
9200 Sunset Boulevard
Los Angeles, Calif. 90069

The Rocket Record Company
211 South Beverly Drive, Suite 200
Beverly Hills, Calif. 90212

Springboard International Records Inc.
8295 Sunset Boulevard
Los Angeles, Calif. 90069

Shelter Recording Company Inc.
5112 Hollywood Boulevard
Los Angeles, Calif. 90027

20th Century–Fox Record Corp.
8544 Sunset Boulevard
Los Angeles, Calif. 90069

United Artists Music & Records Group
 Inc.
6920 Sunset Boulevard
Los Angeles, Calif. 90028

Warner/Curb Records
3300 Warner Boulevard
Burbank, Calif. 91503

Wooden Nickel Records Inc.
9465 Wilshire Boulevard, Suite 820
Beverly Hills, Calif. 90212

NEW YORK

AA Records
250 West 57th Street
New York, N.Y. 10019

ABC Records Inc.
1414 Avenue of the Americas
New York, N.Y. 10019

A & M Records Inc.
595 Madison Avenue
New York, N.Y. 10022

Arista Records Inc.
6 West 57th Street
New York, N.Y. 10019

Atlantic Recording Corp.
75 Rockefeller Plaza
New York, N.Y. 10019

Audiofidelity Ents. Inc.
221 West 57th Street
New York, N.Y. 10019

Bearsville Records Inc.
75 East 55th Street
New York, N.Y. 10022

Buddah Records Inc.
1350 Avenue of the Americas
New York, N.Y. 10019

Capitol Records Inc.
1370 Avenue of the Americas
New York, N.Y. 10019

CBS Records
51 West 52nd Street
New York, N.Y. 10019

Elektra/Asylum/Nonesuch Records
655 Fifth Avenue
New York, N.Y. 10022

Ember Records
747 Third Avenue
New York, N.Y. 10019

Epic/CBS Records
51 West 52nd Street
New York, N.Y. 10019

Fania Records Inc.
888 Seventh Avenue
New York, N.Y. 10019

Fiesta Recording Company Inc.
1619 Broadway
New York, N.Y. 10019

Folkways Records and Service Corp.
43 West 61st Street
New York, N.Y. 10023

Island Records Inc.
444 Madison Avenue
New York, N.Y. 10022

Don Kirshner Entertainment Corp.
1370 Avenue of the Americas
New York, N.Y. 10019

Laurie Records Inc.
20 F. Robert Pitt Drive
Monsey, N.Y. 10952

London Records Inc.
539 West 25th Street
New York, N.Y. 10001

Mainstream Records Inc.
175 Great Neck Road
Great Neck, N.Y. 11021

MCA Records Inc.
445 Park Avenue
New York, N.Y. 10022

Monitor Recordings Inc.
156 Fifth Avenue
New York, N.Y. 10010

Musicor Records Inc.
870 Seventh Avenue, Suite 348
New York, N.Y. 10019

Phonogram Inc/Mercury Records
810 Seventh Avenue
New York, N.Y. 10019

Private Stock Records Ltd.
40 West 57th Street
New York, N.Y. 10019

RCA Records
1133 Avenue of the Americas
New York, N.Y. 10036

Roulette Records Inc.
1790 Broadway
New York, N.Y. 10019

Sire Records Inc.
165 West 74th Street
New York, N.Y. 10023

Spring Records Inc.
161 West 54th Street
New York, N.Y. 10019

Creed Taylor Inc.
One Rockefeller Plaza
New York, N.Y. 10020

Total Sound Inc.
1133 Avenue of the Americas
New York, N.Y. 10036

United Artists Records
729 Seventh Avenue
New York, N.Y. 10019

Vanguard Recording Society Inc.
71 West 23rd Street
New York, N.Y. 10010

Warner Brothers Records Inc.
3 East 54th Street
New York, N.Y. 10022

NASHVILLE

The Benson Company
365 Great Circle Road
Nashville, Tenn. 37228

Capitol Records Inc.
38 Music Square East
Nashville, Tenn. 37203

CBS Records
49 Music Square West
Nashville, Tenn. 37203

Dial Records Inc.
P.O. Box 1273
Nashville, Tenn. 37202

Elektra/Asylum/Nonesuch Records
1216 17th Avenue South
Nashville, Tenn. 37212

Epic/CBS Records
49 Music Square West
Nashville, Tenn. 37203

4 Star Records Inc.
49 Music Square West
Nashville, Tenn. 37203

Hickory Records
2510 Franklin Road
Nashville, Tenn. 37204

MCA Records
27 Music Square East
Nashville, Tenn. 37203

Monument Record Corp.
21 Music Square East
Nashville, Tenn. 37203

Music City Workshop Inc.
1013 16th Avenue South
Nashville, Tenn. 37212

Nu-Sound Records
4701 Trousdale Drive
Nashville, Tenn. 37220

Playboy Records Inc.
1300 Division Street
Nashville, Tenn. 37203

RCA Records
806 17th Street
Nashville, Tenn. 37203

Spark Records
7 Music Circle North
Nashville, Tenn. 37203

United Artists Records
50 Music Square West
Nashville, Tenn. 37203

Warner Brothers Records
P.O. Box 12646
Nashville, Tenn. 37212

OTHER MAJOR CITIES

All Platinum Record Company Inc.
96 West Street
Englewood, N.J. 07631

Capricorn Records Inc.
535 Cotton Avenue
Macon, Ga. 31201

Crescendo Records
37–25 Crescent Street
Long Island City, N.Y. 11101

Curtom Record Company Inc.
5915 North Lincoln Avenue
Chicago, Ill. 60659

Fantasy/Prestige/Milestone/Stax
Stax Records
Mid Memphis Tower, Suite 600
1407 Union
Memphis, Tenn. 38104

Fraternity Recording Corp.
3744 Applegate Avenue
Cincinnati, Ohio 45211

Jewel Record Corp.
728 Texas Street
Shreveport, La. 71163

K-tel International
11311 K-tel Drive
Minnetonka, Minn. 55343

Ovation, Inc.
1249 Waukegan Road
Glenview, Ill. 60025

Philadelphia International Records
309 South Broad Street
Philadelphia, Pa. 19107

Savoy Records Inc.
625 Pennsylvania Avenue
Elizabeth, N.J. 07201

Springboard International Records Inc.
947 U.S. Highway 1
Rahway, N.J. 07065

TK Productions Inc.
495 S.E. 10th Court
Hialeah, Fla. 33010

Westbound Records Inc.
19631 West Eight Mile Road
Detroit, Mich. 48219

Word Inc.
4800 West Waco Drive
Waco, Texas 76703

FOREIGN MUSIC PUBLISHERS

ARGENTINA

Calmex SrL
Ciudad de la Paz 2506, 3rd floor
1428 Buenos Aires

Edami SrL (Ed Argentina de Musica
   Int'l)
Lavalle 1494
Buenos Aires

Edifon SrL
Lavalle 1454, 5th floor, No. 18
Buenos Aires

Melograf SrL (CBS Music Publishing)
Suipacha 476
Buenos Aires

Parnaso Eds. Musicales
Corrientes 1904–1906
1045 Buenos Aires

AUSTRALIA

Allans Music Australia Ltd.
P.O. Box 513J
Melbourne 3001
   or
276 Collins Street
Melbourne, Vic.

April Music Pty. Ltd.
15 Blue Street North
Sydney, NSW 2060

Associated Music Pty. Ltd.
11 Khartoum Road
North Ryde, NSW

Bellbird Music Publishing Company Pty.
   Ltd.
28 Cross Street
Brookvale, NSW 2100

Castle Music Pty. Ltd. (APRA)
2 Northcote Street
St. Leonards
Sydney, NSW

Chappell & Co. (Australia) Pty. Ltd.
   (APRA)
GPO Box 1486
Sydney 2001
   or
225 Clarence Street, 7th floor
Sydney, NSW 2000

Festival Music Pty. Ltd.
Festival House, 1 Bulwara Road
Pyrmont
Sydney, NSW 2009

Leeds Music Pty. Ltd.
Universal House
23 Pelican Street
Darlinghurst
Sydney, NSW 2010

Rondor Music (Australia) Pty. Ltd.
    (APRA)
104–108 Mount Street
North Sydney, NSW 2060

A. Schroeder Music (Australia) Pty. Ltd.
    (APRA)
ADC House, 12th floor
99 Elizabeth Street
Sydney, NSW 2000

Tumbleweed Music Pty. Ltd. (APRA)
155 Clarendon Street
South Melbourne, Vic. 3205

Warner Brothers Music (Australia) Pty.
    Ltd. (APRA)
319B Penshurst Street
Willoughby
Sydney, NSW, 2068

Woomera Music Co. (APRA)
17–19 Radford Road
Reservoir, Vic. 3073

BRAZIL

Alvorada (grupo Ed.)
Rua dos Gusmoes 235
01212 São Paulo

Editora de Musica Brasileira &
    Internacional SA (EMBI)
Rua Teofilo Otoni 135, 3rd floor
Rio de Janeiro, G.B.

Intersong Ltda. (Eds.)
Avenida Rio Branco 277
Grupo 710
Rio de Janeiro

ITAIPU Eds. Musicais Ltda. (UBC)
Caixa Postal 2752, ZCOO
Rua Mena Barreto 151
Botafogo
Rio de Janeiro ZC-02

MCA do Brasil Ed. Musical Ltda.
Rua Aurora 964
01209 São Paulo

Mundo Musical Ltda. (Ed) (div. of CBS)
Rua Buenos Aires 2, 16th floor
20000 Rio de Janeiro

Shark Music (SICAM)
Caixa Postal 13030
01000 São Paulo

Sigem (Sistema Globo de Edicões
    Musicais)
Rua João Afonso 15
Botafogo
Rio de Janeiro

Victor Ltda. (Ed. Musical) (UBC)
Rua Dona Veridiana 203, 4th floor
01000 São Paulo

CANADA

AME Ltd. (American Metropolitan Ents.
    Ltd.)
(PRO, CAPAC)
3896 Bathurst Street, Suite B-3
Downsview, Ont. M3H 3N5

April Music (Canada) Ltd., (CAPAC)
1121 Leslie Street
Toronto, Ont. M3C 2J9

Attic Publishing Group
98 Queen Street
East Toronto, Ont. M5C 156

BJC Music Mgmt. Ltd.
1912-A Avenue Road
Toronto, Ont. M5M 4A1

Burlington Music of Canada Ltd.
  (CAPAC)
6265 Côte de Lièsse
St. Laurent, P.Q. H4T 1C3

Chappell & Co. Ltd. (PRO, CAPAC)
14 Birch Avenue
Toronto, Ont. M4V 1C9

Cirrus Music (PRO)
(Div. of Nimbus 9 Productions Ltd.)
39 Hazelton Avenue
Toronto, Ont. M5R 2E3

Corinth Music (PRO)/Tarana Music
  (CAPAC)
(Divs. of GRT of Canada Ltd.)
3816 Victoria Park Avenue
Willowdale, Ont. M2H 3H7

Crea Sound Ltd.
5275 Rue Berri
Montreal, P.Q. H2J 257

Deer Park Music (CAPAC)
2 Saint Clair Avenue West
Toronto, Ont. M4V 1L6

Dunbar Music Canada Ltd. (PRO)
101 Duncan Mill Road, Suite 305
Don Mills, Ont. M3B 1Z3

Empire Music Co. (PRO)
934 12th Street
New Westminster, B.C. V3L 4Y6

Foxy Lady Music (CAPAC)
1180 Forestwood Drive, Suite 304
Mississauga, Ont. L5C 1H8

Leeds Music (Canada) (CAPAC)
(div. of MCA Canada Ltd.)
MCA Bldg.
2450 Victoria Park Avenue
Willowdale, Ont. M2J 4A2

Lonesome Polecat Music (PRO)
P.O. Box 1052, Station C
Scarborough, Ont. M1H 2Z4

Manna Music (ASCAP)
P.O. Box 6900
Vancouver, B.C. V6B 4B5

Midnight Blue Music (PRO)
42 Brahms Avenue
Willowdale, Ont. M2H 1H4

Brian Millan Music Corp. (CAPAC)
P.O. Box 1322, Station B
Montreal, P.Q. H3B 3K9

Morning Music Ltd. (CAPAC)
1343 Matheson Boulevard West
Mississauga, Ont. L4W 1R1

Northern Light Music Publishers (PRO)
1414 Hillside Avenue, Suite 101
Victoria, B.C. V8T 2B8

Palas House Publishers (PRO)
Box 7, RR 1, Beaverbank Road
Lower Sackville, N.S. B4C 2S6

Peer-Southern Organization (Canada)
  Ltd.
(PRO, CAPAC)
4 New Street, Suite 107
Toronto, Ont. M5R 1P6

Quality Music Publishing Ltd. (PRO)
38 Yorkville Avenue
Toronto, Ont. M4W 1L5

SMCL Inc. (Les Productions)
450 E. Beaumont Avenue
St. Bruno, P.Q. J3V 2R3

Springwater Productions Ltd. (CAPAC)
56 Clinton Street
Guelph, Ont. N1H 5G5

Frank Swain Music (PRO)
P.O. Box 9
Mount Albert, Ont. L0G 1M0

Gordon V. Thompson Ltd. (CAPAC)
29 Birch Avenue
Toronto, Ont. M4V 1E2

UA Music (Canada) Ltd (CAPAC)
6 Lansing Square, Suite 208
Willowdale, Ont. M2J 1T8

DENMARK

Stig Anderson Musikforlag A/S
Vesterbrogade 6D,
DK-1620 Copenhagen V

EMI Music Publishing (Denmark) A/S
Ny Oestergade 10
DK-1101 Copenhagen K

Wilhelm Hansen (Ed.)
Gothersgade 9–11
DK-1123 Copenhagen K

Kleinerts Musik Forlag A/S
Christian IX's Gade 7
DK-1111 Copenhagen K

Moerks Musikforlag A/S
Christian IX's Gade 7
DK-1111 Copenhagen K

Multitone A/S
Bogholder Alle 40
DK-2720 Vanloese

Otkav Music
Helleruplund Alle 4
DK-2900 Hellerup-Copenhagen

Sonet/Dansk Musik
Jydeholmen 15
DK-2720 Vanloese

SteepleChase Music
Rosenvaengets Alle 5
DK-2100 Copenhagen O

FRANCE

Allo Music
17 Rue Ballu
75009 Paris

April Music
3 Rue Freycinet
75016 Paris

April Music Europe
35 Avenue Franklin D. Roosevelt
75008 Paris

Arabella SarL (Eds. Musicales)
18 Rue Beffroy
92200 Neuilly sur Seine

Bagatelle SA (SACEM)
10 Rue Washington
75008 Paris

Eddie Barclay (Nouvelles Eds.)
44 Rue de Miromésnil
75008 Paris

Chappell SA
12 Rue de Penthièvre
75008 Paris

Criterion de Paris
6 Rue Ruhmkorff
75017 Paris

Walt Disney Productions France
44 Avenue des Champs-Elysées
75008 Paris

Francis Dreyfus Music/Ed. Labrador
26 Avenue Kléber
75116 Paris

Du Levain (Eds. Musicales)
1 Rue de l'Abbé Grégoire
75006 Paris

Emilhenco Music Co.
88 Rue du Faubourg St.-Martin
75010 Paris

Max Eschig (Eds.)
48 Rue de Rome
75008 Paris

Louis Gaste (Eds.)
5 Rue du Bois de Boulogne
75116 Paris

Gwenaelle Music
20 Rue Ballu
75009 Paris

Hexagon (Eds.) (SACEM)
19 Rue Galilée
75016 Paris

L'illustration Musicale SarL
6 Rue Léon Bonnat
75016 Paris

Isabelle Musique
122 Boulevard Exelmans
75016 Paris

Jobert SA (Société des Eds.)
44 Rue du Colisée
75008 Paris

Michel Legrand Productions
252 Rue du Faubourg St.-Honoré
75008 Paris

Marouani (Les Eds.)
10 Avenue Franklin D. Roosevelt
75008 Paris

MCA Music
1 Rue Lamennais
75008 Paris

Le Minotaure (Ed.) (SACEM, SDRM)
21 Rue Jean Mermoz
75008 Paris

Francis O'Neill Organization (FONO)
71 Rue de Provence
75009 Paris

PECF (Productions & Editions
Cinématographiques Françaises)
  (SACEM)
18 Rue Troyon
75017 Paris

Claude Pascal (Eds. Musicales)
5 Rue Denis Poisson
75017 Paris

Pathé Marconi
(Editions & Productions Musicales)
19 Rue Lord Byron
75008 Paris

RCA Publishing Dept
9 Avenue Matignon
75008 Paris

Le Rideau Rouge
24 Rue de Longchamp
75116 Paris

SEMI
(Société d'Editions Musicales
  Internationales)
5 Rue Lincoln
75008 Paris

A. Schroeder
(Editions Musicales) SarL
37 Rue Violet
75015 Paris

United Artists Music (France)
48 Avenue Victor Hugo
75783 Paris

GERMANY

Accord GmbH (Ed.)
Maarweg 130
D-5000 Cologne 41

Acuff-Rose Musikverlag KG
Heinrich Barth Strasse 30
D-2000 Hamburg 13

April Musikverlag GmbH
An der Alster 83
D-2000 Hamburg 1

Paul C. R. Arends Verlag (GEMA)
Hoehenweg 36
D-8211 Rimsting/Chiemsee

Bellver Music, Riedel & Co. KG
Mainzer Landstrasse 87–89
D-6000 Frankfurt/Main

Rolf Budde Musikverlage
Hohenzollerndamm 54A
D-1000 Berlin 33

Burlington Musikverlag GmbH (GEMA)
Hoehenweg 36
D-8211 Rimsting/Chiemsee

Chappell & Co. GmbH
Heinrich Barth Strasse 30
D-2000 Hamburg 13

Cyclus Musikverlage GmbH
Hallerstrasse 76
D-2000 Hamburg 13

ERP Musikverlag Eckart Rahn (GEMA)
Habsburgerplatz 2/2
D-8000 Munich 40

Finger Music-Verlage
Im oberen Ficht 10
D-8183 Rottach-Weissach

Hans Gerig (Musikverlage)
Drususgasse 7–11
D-5000 Cologne 1

Intersong International Musikverlag
  GmbH
Hallerstrasse 40
D-2000 Hamburg 13

Melodie der Welt
J. Michel KG Musikverlag
Grosse Friedbergerstrasse 23–27
D-6000 Frankfurt/Main

Musik Unserer Zeit Verlag GmbH
Leopoldstrasse 38B
D-8000 Munich 40

Peer Musikverlag GmbH (GEMA)
Muehlenkamp 43
D-2000 Hamburg 60

A. Schroeder Musikverlage GmbH
Wittelsbacherstrasse 18
D-1000 Berlin 31

Rudolf Slezak Musikverlage GmbH
  (GEMA)
Harvestehuder Weg 21
,D-2000 Hamburg 13

United Artists Musik GmbH
P.O. Box 201
Herzog Rudolfstrasse 3
D-8000 Munich 22

GREECE

Blackwood Music Publishing Company
   Ltd.
P.O. Box 2533
19 Syngrou Ave.
Makriyanni
Athens 403

Grecophon (Editions Musicales)
3 Karagiorgi Servias Street
Athens 126

Intersong Hellas Ltd.
296 Massoghion Avenue
Cholargos
Athens 142

Select Publishers
13 Eptanissou Kypseli
Athens

HONG KONG

Burlington-Palace Music Orient Ltd
(subsidiary of Burlington-Palace in UK)
1112 Star House
3 Salisbury Road
Kowloon

Pathé Publications (Far East) Ltd.
11 Fa Po Street
Yau Yat Tsuen
Kowloon

IRELAND

Celtic Songs
97A Talbot Street
Dublin 1

Emerald Music
Dublin Industrial Estate, 106-B
Finglas
Dublin 11

Emma Music Ltd.
5/6 Lombard Street
Dublin 2

Raglan Music
J. F. Kennedy Estate
Naas Road
Dublin 12

Sally Ann Songs/Pintz Music
53 Dartmouth Square South
Dublin 6

Squirrel Music
IMS House
Lombard Street
Dublin 2

ISRAEL

April Music Ltd. (ACUM)
P.O. Box 681
Tel Aviv 61000
      or
50 Thon Street
Industrial Zone
Holon 58811

Illanot Music Publishing
P.O. Box 4292
11 Herzl Street
Haifa

Israeli Music Publications Ltd. (ACUM)
P.O. Box 6011
105 Ben Yehuda Street, Tel Aviv

Israel Music Institute (IMI)
P.O. Box 11253
6 Chen Boulevard
Tel Aviv

Musicor Ltd.
11 Rozanis Street
Tel Baruch
Tel Aviv

Subar Music Publishing Company Ltd.
   (ACUM)
21 Any Ma'amin Street
Ramat-Hasharon 47212

ITALY

Alfiere/Esedra Ed. Musical SrL
(Intersong Italiana SrL)
Via Meravigli 14
20123 Milan

April Music SrL
Via Amadei 9
20123 Milan

Bongiovanni (Ed. Musicali)
Via Rizzoli 28
40125 Bologna

CAM (Creazioni Artistiche Musicali),
   SpA (SIAE)
Via Virgilio 8
00193 Rome

Chappell (Ed.) SpA (SIAE)
Via Meravigli 12
20123 Milan

Decca Ed. Musicali SrL (SIAE)
Via Brisa 3
20123 Milan

Durium (Ed. Musicali) (SIAE)
Via Manzoni 40/42
20121 Milan

Franton Music SrL (SIAE)
Via Manin 111
30174 Venice/Mestre

Dott. Gallazzi (Ed. Musicali) (SIAE)
Piazza del Liberty 2
20121 Milan

Jump Ed. Musicali (SIAE)
Galleria del Corso 2
20122 Milan

Numero Uno SpA (SIAE)
Galleria del Corso 2
20122 Milan

Pickwick SrL (Ed. Musicali)
Corso Europa 5
20122 Milan

RCA SpA (SIAE)
Via San Alessandro 7
Rome

G. Ricordi & C. SpA (SIAE)
Via Berchet 2
20121 Milan

Ri-Fi Music SrL (SIAE)
Corso Buenos Aires 77
20124 Milan

A. Schroeder Music (Italy) SrL (Ed.)
Via Quintiliano 40
20138 Milan

Senza Fine SrL (Ed.)
Piazzetta Pattari 2
20122 Milan

Southern Music (SIAE)
Piazza del Liberty 2
20121 Milan

Sugarmusic Group (SIAE)
Via Quintiliano 40
20138 Milan

Suono Ed. Musicali (SIAE)
Via Manin 111
30174 Venice/Mestre

United Artists (Italy) SrL (Ed. Musicali)
Corso Europa 5/7
20122 Milan

La Voce del Padrone
Galleria del Corso 2
20122 Milan

JAMAICA

Ivan Mogull Caribbean Ltd.
c/o Norman E. Wright
9–11 Church St.
Kingston

Record Specialists Ltd.
1 Torrington Road
Kingston W1

Sheila Music Corp. Ltd. (BMI)
15 Bell Road
Kingston 11

Woodwater Music Ltd.
220 Marcus Garvey Drive
Kingston 11

JAPAN

ABC Sounds Inc.
Nikko Bldg, No. 614
1-4-26 K Takanawa
Minato-ku
Tokyo 108

April Music Inc. (Japan)
P.O. Box 17
Tokyo Airport Station
Minato-ku
Tokyo

Arrow Music Corp.
4-11-10 Roppongi
Minato-ku
Tokyo 106

Walt Disney Ents. of Japan Ltd.
Horaiya Bldg.
5-2-1 Roppongi
Minato-ku
Tokyo 106

High Note Publishing Company Ltd.
(Jasrac)
TBS Second Building
5-3-50 Akasaka
Minato-ku
Tokyo 107

Intersong KK (Jasrac)
Horaiya Building, 5th floor
5-2-1 Roppongi
Minato-ku
Tokyo 106

Japan Central Music Ltd. (JCM)
c/o Bunka Hoso
1-5 Wakaba-cho
Shinjuku-ku
Tokyo 160

Liee (Tokyo) KK
c/o Taiyo Music Inc.
Azabu P.O. Box 20
Tokyo 106

Lux Music Tokyo KK (Jasrac)
2-12 Ogawa-Machi
Kanda
Chiyoda-ku
Tokyo 101

MCA Music KK, c/o Nichion Inc.
TBS Second Building
5-3-50 Akasaka
Minato-ku
Tokyo 107

Nichion Inc. (Jasrac)
TBS Second Building
5-3-50 Akasaka
Minato-ku
Tokyo 107

Nipo-Americana Music Publishing
   Company Ltd.
Central P.O. Box 250
Tokyo 101–91

Pacific Music Publishing Company Ltd.
(Jasrac)
c/o Nippon Broadcasting System Inc.
1-9-3 Yuraku-cho
Chiyoda-ku
Tokyo 100

A. Schroeder Music (Far East) Ltd.
Sumitomo Building, Room 832
1-4-4 Marunouchi
Chiyoda-ku
Tokyo 100

Sugarmusic Japan
c/o Seven Seas Music Co. Ltd.
2-12-13 Otowa
Bunkyo-ku
Tokyo 112

Taiyo Music Inc.
Azabu P.O. Box 20
Tokyo 106

Tokyo Music Publishing Company Ltd.
Wako Bldg.
4-8-5 Roppongi
Minato-ku
Tokyo 106

Toshiba EMI Music Publishing Company
Ltd.
Makabe Building
3-4-3 Akasaka
Minato-ku
Tokyo 107

Victor Music Publishing Company Inc.
(Jasrac) Harajuki-Piazza Building
4-26-18 Jingumae
Shibuya-ku
Tokyo 150

Watanabe Music Publishing Corp.
(Jasrac)
1-6-8 Yuraku-cho
Chiyoda-ku
Tokyo 100

MEXICO

Beechwood de Mexico SA de CV
(SACM)
Rio Balsas 49
Mexico 5, D.F.

Brambila Musical Mexico SA
Av. Cuitlahuac 2305
Mexico 17, D.F.

Edimusa SA
Av. Cuitlahuac 2327
Mexico 16, D.F.

EMLASA
(Ed. Musical Latino Americana SA)
Laguna de Mayran 258, 2nd floor
Mexico 17, D.F.

EMMI
(Ed. Mexicana de Musica Int'l) SA
Mariano Escobedo 166
1st & 2nd floors
Mexico 17 D.F.

Gamma SA (Eds. Musicales)
Apdo. 7762, Zona 1
Emerson 432
Mexico 5, D.F.

Grever International
Yautepec 107
Col. Condesa
Mexico 11 D.F.

Intersong SA
Ejercito Nacional 209
3rd floor, Col. Anzures
Mexico 5, D.F.

Juventa (Ed. Musical)
Tonala 194-G
Mexico 7, D.F.

Melodias Universales SA (MUSA)
Darwin 142, 3rd floor
Mexico 5, D.F.

Mexicana de Musica SA de CV (Ed.)
  (Edim.)
Poniente 48
No. 3902, Col. Xochimanca
Mexico 16, D.F.

Mundo Musical SA
Puebla 286, 1st floor
Mexico 7, D.F.

Rimo SA (Eds. Musicales)
Emerson 150, 4th floor
Mexico 5, D.F.

NETHERLANDS

Anagon Music Publishers BV
Tulpenkade 1
Haarlem

April Music Holland BV
Stationsplein 82–84
Haarlem

Artemis Muziekuitgeverij BV
Gerrit van der Veenlaan 4
Baarn

Associated Artists International
Postbox 37
Piet Heinstraat 4
Maarssen

Dennis Music
Paesteblookstraat 11/13
Genk

Kluger Holland
Meander 967
Amstelveen

Universal Songs BV (BUMA)
Oranje Nassaulaan 25
Amsterdam 9

Veronica Music Eds. BV P.O. Box 300
Oude Enghweg 24
1200 AH Hilversum

NEW ZEALAND

Chappell and Company Ltd.
Nimmo's Building, 2nd floor
89 Willis
Wellington C1

Innovation Music Ltd. (APRA)
27 Bayside Avenue
Te Atatu
Auckland 8

Ode Music
199 Karangahape Road
Auckland

Sandy Music Co. Ltd. (APRA)
P.O. Box 1431
Wellington

Southern Music Publishing Company
  (Australasia) Pty. Ltd.
P.O. Box 656
12 Security Building
198 Queen Street
Auckland C1

Word Music (ASCAP)
Oxford Street
Levin

PANAMA

Ed. Musical de Panama SA (BIEM)
Aptdo. 3340
Calle 45
No. 46, Panama

PORTUGAL

Belter (Ed.)
Rua Constituição 74
Porto

Valetim de Carvalho Ci, SarL
Rua Nova do Almada 95–99
Lisbon 2

Costa Pinto (Ed. Musicais) Lda. (SPA)
Rua Eqa de Queroz 2Q
3rd floor
Lisbon

Musicat (Arnaldo Trindade & Ca. Lda.
  (SPA)
Rua de Campolide 103-C
Lisbon

Telectra (Eds. Musicais)
Rua Rodrigo da Fonseca 103
Lisbon 1

SOUTH AFRICA

Clan Music Publishing Company (Pty.)
  Ltd.
Craftsman Centre
288 Commissioner Saint
Johannesburg

EMI-Brigadiers Music (Pty.) Ltd.
(Dairo, NORM, SAMRO)
32 Steele Street
Steeledale
Johannesburg

Gallo Music
(Music Publishing Company of Africa
  Pty. Ltd.)
P.O. Box 6216
Gallo Centre
Kerk & Goud Streets
Johannesburg 2000

Intersong (Pty.) Ltd.
P.O. Box 10678
132 Kerk Street
Johannesburg 2000

Laetrec Music Ltd. (SAMRO)
P.O. Box 4105
Johannesburg

Leeds Music (Africa) (Pty.) Ltd.
P.O. Box 6216
Gallo Centre
Kerk & Goud Streets
Johannesburg 2000

Musicpiece Publishers (Pty.) Ltd.
(NORM, SAMRO)
Auction House, 2nd floor
111 Fox Street
Johannesburg

Reveille Music (Pty.) Ltd.
P.O. Box 9062
Silvern Centre, 3rd floor
Corner Nugget & Market Streets
Johannesburg

Southern Music Publishing Company
  (SA) (Pty.) Ltd.
62 St. Patrick's Road
Houghton
Johannesburg

Tradelius
P.O. Box 3159
Durban 4000

WEA Music (Pty.) Ltd.
16 St. Andrews Road
Parktown
Johannesburg 2001

Yackamo Music (SAMRO)
P.O. Box 626
Johannesburg 2000

SPAIN

April Music (SGAE)
Avenida Generalisimo 25
9th floor
Madrid 16

Canciones del Mundo SA
Magallanes 25
Madrid 3

Chappell Ibérica SA
Magallanes 25
Madrid 3

EGO Musical SA
Via Augusta 2 bis
4th floor
Barcelona 6

Fontana SA (Eds. Musicales)
Magallanes 25
Madrid 3

Hispavox SA (Eds. Musicales)
Torrelaguna 64
Madrid 27

Mendaur (Eds. Musicales) (SGAE)
Virgen de Aranzazu 23
Local F
Madrid 34

Notas Mágicas SA (Grupo Ed.) (SGAE)
Calle Requeros 8
Madrid 4

Penta-Music SA (SGAE)
Tierra de Barros 4
Poligono Industrial de Coslada
Madrid

RCA Española SA (Eds. Musicales)
Dr. Fleming 43
Madrid 16

Real Musical SA
Carlos III, No. 1
Madrid 13

Southern Music Española SA (SGAE)
Disputación 337
Barcelona 9

SWEDEN

Air Music Scandinavia AB
P.O. Box 27234
Oxensteirnsgatan 37
S-102 53 Stockholm

April Music AB
P.O. Box 20037
Mariehallsvagen 40
S-161 20 Bromma

EMI Music Publishing (Sweden) AB
Ynglingagatan 17
S-113 47 Stockholm

Filadelfia Forlaget AB (STIM/NCB)
Dagenhuset
S-105 36 Stockholm

Intersong-Foerlagen AB
P.O. Box 3094
Dalvagen 4
S-171 03 Solna

Multitone AB
Storaengsvaegen 27
S-115 34 Stockholm

Nordic Songs AB
P.O. Box 745
Drottninggatan 37
S-101 30 Stockholm 1

Nordiska Musikforlaget AB
P.O. Box 745
Drottninggatan 37
S-101 30 Stockholm 1

Sonet Music AB (STIM/NCB)
Atlasvaegen 1
S-181 20 Lidingoe

SWITZERLAND

Fanfan Music H & B Liechti & Cie
   (SUISA/ML) Rue de Hesse 8-10
CH-1211 Geneva 11

Hazyville (Ed.)
Im Koller 17
CH-8706 Feldmeilen

Helbling & Co.
Pfaeffikerstrasse 6
CH-8604 Volketswil

IMPACT
(International Music Publishers and
   Composers Trust) SA
Box 10
Via del Tiglio 11
CH-6900 Cassarate/Lugano

Louvin Music (ML)
Rue de la Serre 61
C-2301 La Chaux-de-Fonds

Musikvertrieb AG
Badenerstrasse 555
Ch-8048 Zurich

UNITED KINGDOM

Acuff-Rose Music Ltd.
14 St. George Street
London W1

April Music Ltd.
54 Greek Street
London

ATV Music Ltd.
24 Bruton Street
Mayfair
London W1X 7DA

Barn Publishing Ltd.
51 Upper Montagu Street
London W1

Belwin-Mills Music Ltd.
250 Purley Way
Croydon
Surrey CR9 4QD

Big Secret Music Ltd.
57 Green Street
Flat H
London W1

Margaret Brace Copyright Bureau Ltd.
9 Dean Street, 3rd floor
London W1A 4QD

Bron Organization Ltd.
100 Chalk Farm Road
London NW1 8EH

Burlington Music Co. Ltd
9 Albert Embankment
London SE1 7SW

Campbell Connelly & Co. Ltd. (PRS)
10 Denmark Street
London WC2H 8LU

Carlin Music Corp.
17 Savile Row
London W1X 1AE

Chappell & Co. Ltd.
50 New Bond Street
London W1A 2BR

Cherry Music
7 Wordle Street
London SW14

Walt Disney Productions Ltd.
68 Pall Mall
London SW1Y 5EX

Emerald Music Ltd. (PRS)
120 Coach Road
Templepatrick
Ballyclare
County Antrim BT39 OHB
Northern Ireland

EMI Music Publishing Ltd.
140 Charing Cross Road
London WC2H OLD

The Essex Music Group
Essex House
19/20 Poland Street
London W1V 3DD

Fanfare Music Co. Ltd.
27 Forest Drive
Keston
Kent

Fleetwood Music Ltd.
77 Westbourne Park Road
London W2

Gull Songs
169 High Road
Willesden
London NW10

Hansen House (London) Ltd.
64 Dean Street
London W1V 5HU

Intersong Music Ltd.
50 New Bond Street
London W1

Island Music Ltd.
47 British Grove
London W4ZN11

Dick James Music Ltd.
James House
5 Theobalds Road
London WC1X 8SE

Kassner Associated Publishers
Broadmead House
21 Panton Street
London SW1

Leeds Music Ltd.
138 Piccadilly
London W1V 9FH

Lupus Music Co. Ltd. (PRS)
14/16 Bruton Place
London W1X 7AA

MAM (Music Publishing) Ltd.
24/25 New Bond Street
London W1

Robert Mellin Ltd. (PRS)
24 Parkside
Knightsbridge
London SW1

Panache Music Ltd. (PRS)
49 Mount Street
London W1Y 5RE

Purple Music Ltd. (PRS)
25 Newman Street
London W1P 3HA

RAK Publishing Ltd.
42-48 Charlbert Street
London NW8

Red Bus Music (International) Ltd.
113/117 Wardour Street
London W1A 4PW

The Les Reed Organization
35 Soho Square
London W1

Roberton Publications
The Windmill
Wendover
Aylesbury
Bucks HP22 6JJ

Paul Robinson Music Ltd.
20 Burnthwaite Road
London SW6

Paul Rodriguez Music (MCPS, PRS)
22 Tavistock Street
London WC2

Rondor Music (London) (PRS)
Rondor House
10a Parsons Green
London SW6 4TW

RSO (The Robert Stigwood Group Ltd.)
    Publishing Ltd.
67 Brook Street
London W1Y 1YD

Shapiro, Bernstein & Co. Ltd.
37 Great Portland Street
London W1N 5DD

Sonet Productions Ltd.
121 Ledbury Road
London W11 2AQ

Southern Music Publishing Company
    Ltd.
8 Denmark Street
London WC2H 8LT

The Sparta Florida Music Group Ltd.
Carlton Tower Place, Suite 4
Sloane Street
London SW1X 9PZ

Sun-Pacific Music (London) Ltd.
  (MCPS)
P.O. Box 78
London SE19

Tincabell Music Ltd.
17 Barlow Place
Bruton Street
London W1X 7AE

United Artists Music Ltd.
Richard House
30/32 Mortimer Street
London W1A 2JL

United 2 Music Ltd.
1 Montague Street
Russell Square
London WC1B 5BS

Valentine Music Group Ltd.
7 Garrick Street
London WC2E 9AR

Virgin Music (Publishers) Ltd.
2/4 Vernon Yard
119 Portobello Road
London W11

Warner Brothers Music Ltd.
17 Berners Street
London W1P 3DD

Josef Weinberger Ltd. (PRS)
10/16 Rathbone Street
London W1P 2BJ

FOREIGN RECORD COMPANIES

ARGENTINA

CBS SAICF (Discos)
Emilio Mitre 1819
Buenos Aires

EMI-Odeon SAIC (IFPI)
Mendoza 1660
1428 Buenos Aires

Famous SrL
Anasco 1015
Buenos Aires

RCA Ltd.
(Sucursal Argentina) (IFPI)
Paroissien 3960
1430 Buenos Aires

Sicamericana (SACIFI (IFPI)
Jose E. Uriburu 40–42
Buenos Aires

AUSTRALIA

CBS Records Australia Ltd. (IFPI)
P.O. Box 941
15 Blue Street
North Sydney, NSW 2060

Crest Record Company
P.O. Box 270
122 Chapel Street, St. Kilda
Vic. 3182

EMI (Australia) Ltd. (IFPI)
301 Castlereagh Street
Sydney, NSW 2000

Festival Records, Pty Ltd.
P.O. Box 16
63–79 Miller Street
Pyrmont, NSW 2009

Phonogram Ptd. Ltd.
Westfield Towers, 2nd floor
100 William Street
Sydney, NSW 2000

RCA Ltd.
11 Khartoum Road
North Ryde, NSW 2113

WEA Records Pty. Ltd. (IFPI)
7/9 George Place
Artamon
Sydney, NSW 2064

BRAZIL

CBS Industria & Commercio Ltda.
   (Discos)
Rua Buenos Aires 2
7th Floor
20000 Rio de Janeiro

EMI-Odeon Fonográfica Industrial &
   Eletrónica SA
Rua Mena Barreto 151
20000 Rio de Janeiro

Phonogram (Companhia Brasileira de
   Discos)
Avenida Rio Branco 311
4th floor
Rio de Janeiro ZC-06

RCA Eletrónica Ltda.
Rua Dona Veridiana 203
01238 São Paulo

WEA Discos Ltda. (IFPI)
Rua Itaipava 44
20000 Rio de Janeiro

CANADA

A & M Records of Canada Ltd.
939 Warden Avenue
Scarborough, Ont. MIL 4C5

Calart Recording Studios Ltd.
1568 Angus Street
Regina, Sask. S4T 1Z1

Capitol Records–EMI of Canada Ltd.
3109 American Drive
Mississauga, Ont. L4V 1B2

CBS Records (Canada) Ltd.
1121 Leslie Street
Don Mills, Ont. M3C 2J9

Damon Productions Ltd.
6844 76th Avenue
Edmonton, Alta. T6B 0A8

Walt Disney Music Canada Ltd.
2323 Yonge Street
Toronto, Ont. M4P 2C9

GRT of Canada Ltd.
3816 Victoria Park Avenue
Willowdale, Ont. M2H 3H7

Lip Service Studio Productions Ltd.
29 Davenport Road
Toronto, Ont. M5R 1H2

MCA Records (Canada)
2450 Victoria Park Avenue
Willowdale, Ont. M2J 4A2

Mellow Man Records
1180 Forestwood Drive
Suite 304
Mississauga, Ont. L5C 1H8

Motown Records (Canada) Ltd.
1960 Ellesmere Road
Unit 9
Scarborough, Ont. M1H 2V9

Polydor Ltd.
6000 Côte de Lièsse
St. Laurent P.Q. H4T 1E3

RCA Ltd.
101 Duncan Mill Road
Suite 300
Don Mills, Ont. M3B 1Z3

WEA Music of Canada Ltd.
1810 Birchmount
Scarborough, Ont. M1P 2J1

DENMARK

CBS Records, Aps (IFPI)
Bogholder Alle 40
DK-2720 Vanlose

EMI (Electric and Musical Inds. Dansk-
    Engelsk) A/S (IFPI)
Hoeffdingsvej 18
DK-2500 Valby-Copenhagen

Wilheim Hansen
Gothersgade 9–11
DK-1123 Copenhagen K

Sonet/Dansk Grammofon A/S (IFPI)
Jydeholmen 15
DK-2720 Vanloese

Starbox ApS (IFPI)
Store Kongensgade 40
DK-1264 Copenhagen K

FRANCE

Ades SA
54 Rue St.-Lazare
75009 Paris

A & M Records Europe (IFPI)
35 Avenue Franklin D. Roosevelt
75008 Paris

Bagatelle SA
10 Rue Washington
75008 Paris

Barclay (Compagnie Phonographique
  Française)
143 Avenue Charles de Gaulle
92521 Neuilly-sur-Seine

Carabine Music
124 Rue La Boétie
75008 Paris

Carrère (Disques)
27 Rue de Surène
75008 Paris

CBS Disques (IFPI)
3 Rue Freycinet
75016 Paris

Deller Recordings SA (IFPI)
St.-Michel de Provence
04300 Forcalquier

Walt Disney Productions of France
44 Avenue des Champs-Elysées
75008 Paris

GB Productions
15 Bis Rue de Marignan
75008 Paris

Harmonia Mundi SA (IFPI)
St.-Michel de Provence
04300 Forcalquier

Kelenn Studios
Kerivin
29215 Guipavas

MPD Productions Sonores (Mirliton)
35 Avenue du Bac
94 La Varenne–St. Hilaire

Peggy Monclair (Productions Musicales)
4 Rue du Bac
78290 Croissy

Pathé Marconi EMI
19 Rue Lord Byron
75008 Paris

Nicolas Perides (Eds. & Productions
  Musicales)
44 Rue Etienne Marcel
75008 Paris

RCA SA (IFPI)
Immeuble Matignon-Mermoz
9 Avenue Matignon
75008 Paris

Salvador (Productions Artistiques &
  Musicales)
6 Place Vendôme
75001 Paris

Sibecar, Productions Musicales
99 Rue de Vaugirard
75006 Paris

Vogue PIP (Productions Internationales
  Phonographiques) (IFPI)
82 Rue Maurice Grandcoing
93430 Villetaneuse

WEA Filipacchi Music (IFPI)
70 Avenue des Champs-Elysées
75008 Paris

WIP Productions SA
50 Rue de Miromésnil
75008 Paris

GERMANY

Adler Productions
P.O. Box 400106
Burgunderstrasse 13
D-8000, Munich 40

Christian Anders Musikverlag &
    Produktion
Hoerwarthstrasse 26
D-8000 Munich 40

Bellaphon Records GmbH & Co. KG
    Tontraegergesellschaft
Mainzer Landstrasse 87–89
D-6000 Frankfurt/Main 1

CBS Schallplatten GmbH
Bleichstrasse 64–66A
D-6000 Frankfurt/Main 1

Clariphon Schallplatten & Musicassetten
    —Produktion & Vertrieb
Kaiserstrasse 58
D-4300 Essen 1

Crystal Schallplatten GmbH
Pletschmuehlenweg 70–72
D-5024 Pulheim

EMI Electrola GmbH (IFPI)
Maarweg 149
D-5000 Cologne 41

Metronome Musik GmbH (IFPI)
Ueberseering 21
D-2000 Hamburg 60

Phonogram GmbH (IFPI)
Roedingsmarkt 14
D-2000 Hamburg 11

RCA Schallplatten GmbH (IFPI)
P.O. Box 7613
Osterstrasse 116
D-2000 Hamburg 19

WEA Musik GbmH (IFPI)
Gustav Freytagstrasse 13–15
D-2000 Hamburg 76

GREECE

CBS (Diski) AEBE (IFPI)
P.O. Box 2533
19 Syngrou Avenue
Makriyanni, Athens 403

Columbia-EMI Greece SA (IFPI)
P.O. Box 287, Central Station
127 Heracliou Street
Rizopolis, Athens

Emial SA (EMI–Lambropoulos Bros.
    Ltd.) (IFPI)
26 Praxitelous Street
Athens 134

Phonogram SA (IFPI)
296 Massoghion Avenue
Cholargos, Athens

HONG KONG

Decca Orient (Pte.) Ltd.
1112 Star House
3 Salisbury Road
Kowloon

EMI (Hong Kong) Ltd. (IFPI)
11 Fa Po Street
Yau Yat Tsuen, Kowloon

Polydor Ltd.
1001 Garley Building, 10th floor
233–239 Nathan Road
Kowloon

IRELAND

CBS Records (IFPI)
111 Cork Street
Dublin 8

EMI (Ireland) Ltd. (IFPI)
Dublin Industrial Estate
130 Slaney Road
Finglas, Dublin 11

Hawk Records (IFPI)
IMS House
5/6 Lombard Street
Dublin 2

Polydor Ltd. (IFPI)
49 Middle Abbey Street
Dublin 1

ISRAEL

CBS Records Ltd.
P.O. Box 681
Tel Aviv

Hataklit Ltd. (IFPI)
P.O. Box 4292
11 Herzl Street
Haifa

Studio One
33 Allenby Road
Tel Aviv

ITALY

CAM (Creazioni Artistiche Musicali) SpA
Via Virgilio 8
00193 Rome

CBS Dischi SpA (IFPI)
Via Amedei 9
20123 Milan

Decca Dischi Italia SpA (IFPI)
Via Brisa 3
30123 Milan

Durium SpA (IFPI)
Via Manzoni 40/42
20121 Milan

EMI-Italiana SpA
Viale dell' Oceano Pacifico 46
00144 Rome

Fonit-Cetra SpA (IFPI)
Via Bertola 34
10122 Turin

PDU Italiana SpA (IFPI)
Via Senato 12
20121 Milan

Phonogram SpA (IFPI)
Via Borgogna 2
20122 Milan

RCA SpA
Via San Alessandro 7
Rome

Ri-Fi Record Company SpA (IFPI)
Corso Buenos Aires 77
20124 Milan

Sciascia SaS (Ed.) (IFPI)
Via Brodolini
20089 Rozzano (Milan)

Sidet Ed SrL
Piazzetta Pattari 2
20122 Milan

Stereomaster
Galleria del Corso 2
20122 Milan

WEA Italiana SpA (IFPI)
Via Milano (angolo via Cuneo)
Redecesio di Segrate (Milan)

JAMAICA

Dynamic Sounds Recording Company
   Ltd. (IFPI)
15 Bell Road
Kingston 11

Total Sounds Recording Company Ltd.
   (IFPI)
14 Retirement Road
Kingston 5

JAPAN

Disco Co. Ltd.
Akasaka Makabe Building
3-4-3 Akasaka
Minato-ku
Tokyo

Nippon Columbia Co. Ltd. (IFPI)
4-14-14 Akasaka
Minato-ku
Tokyo 107

Polydor KK
1-8-4 Ohashi
Meguro-ku
Tokyo 153

Queen Ongako KK
Otema Building
3-25-14 Shibuya
Shibuya-ku
Tokyo 150

Toho Records Company Ltd.
1-2-1 Yuraku-cho
Chiyoda-ku
Tokyo 100

MEXICO

CBS/Columbia Internacional SA
Avenida 16 de Septiembre 784
Naucalpán

EMI-Capitol de México SA de CV (IFPI)
Rio Balsas 49
Mexico 5, D.F.

Grever Productions SA
Yautepec 107
Mexico 11, D.F.

Polydor SA de CV
Avenida Miguel Angel de Quevedo 531
Mexico 21, D.F.

NETHERLANDS

Associated Artists International BV
P.O. Box 37
Piet Heinstrasse 4
Maarssen

Benelux Music Inds.
P.O. Box 70
Uilenweg 38
6000 AB Weert

Bosheck Grammofoonplaten
P.O. Box 53
Aerdenhout

E & E Records
P.O. Box 1525
Amsterdam

EMI Records Holland BV (IFPI)
Tulpenkade 1
Haarlem

JR Productions
Streuveislaan 12
Roosendaal

Negram BV
Bronsteeweg 49
Heemstede

WEA Records BV
Koninginneweg 49
Hilversum

Wim Wigt Productions
P.O. Box 201
Roghorst 303
6700 AE Wageningen

NEW ZEALAND

EMI (New Zealand) Ltd. (IFPI) P.O. Box
  30-369
408 Hutt Road
Lower Hutt

Festival Records (NZ) Ltd. (IFPI)
69 Carlton Gore Road
Newmarket, Auckland 2

Phonogram Ltd.
P.O. Box 3517
Wexford Road
Miramar, Wellington

WEA Records Ltd. (IFPI)
P.O. Box 2915
14–18 Federal Street
Auckland

PANAMA

Panama Radio-Samdavid SA
Aptdo. 6906
Avenida Central
Plaza 5 de Mayo
Panama 5

Sonomundi SA
Aptdo. 6-4297
Estafeta El Dorado
Panama

PORTUGAL

Phonogram Portuguesa—Musica &
  Video SarL (IFPI)
Rua Prof. Reinaldo dos Santos 12
Lisbon 4

Radio Triunfo Lda. (IFPI)
Praca General Humberto Delgado 309
Porto

SOUTH AFRICA

EMI-Brigadiers (Pty.) Ltd. (IFPI)
32 Steele Street
Steeledale, Johannesburg

Gramophone Record Company (Pty.)
  Ltd. (GRC) (IFPI)
P.O. Box 2445
132 Kerk Street
Johannesburg

David Gresham Productions (Pty.) Ltd.
P.O. Box 626
Zone 2000
30 Eloff Street
Johannesburg

WEA Records (Pty.) Ltd. (IFPI)
16 St. Andrews Road
Parktown, Johannesburg

SPAIN

CBS SA (Discos)
Avenida del Generalisimo 25
9th floor
Madrid 16

Columbia SA (Discos)
Apdo. 2299
Avenida de los Madronos 27
Parque del Conde Orgaz
Madrid 33

Compañia Fonográfica Española SA
  (IFPI)
Augusto Figueroa 39
Madrid 4

EMI-Odeon SA (IFPI)
Via Augusta 2 bis.
4th floor
Barcelona 6

Movieplay SA (IFPI)
Tierra de Barros 4
Poligono Industrial de Coslada
Madrid

Singleton Productions
Via Augusta 59
Desp. 805
Barcelona 6

SWEDEN

Amigo Musik AB (IFPI)
P.O. Box 6058
Norra Stationsgatan 91–93
S-102 31 Stockholm 6

CBS Records AB
P.O. Box 20037
Mariehallsvaegen 40
S-161 20 Bromma

EMI Svenska AB
Tritonvaegen 17
Fack
S-171 19 Solna 1

Iver Recording Company AB
Grev Turegatan 38
S-114 38 Stockholm

Phonogram AB
P.O. Box 3083
Dalvaegen 4
S-171 03 Solna 3

SWITZERLAND

CBS Schallplatten AG (IFPI)
Unter Alstadt 10
CH-6301 Zug

EMI Records (Switzerland) AG (IFPI)
Badenerstrasse 567
CH-8048 Zurich

WEA International
Chillon 16
CH-1820 Montreux

UNITED KINGDOM

Acuff-Rose Music Ltd.
14 St. George Street
London W1

Alice Records
9 Cavendish Square
London W1M ODU

A & M Records Ltd.
A & M House
136–140 New Kings Road
London SW6 4LZ

Ariola Eurodisc UK Ltd.
48 Maddox Street
London W1

Arista Records (IFPI)
49 Upper Brook Street
London W1Y 2BT

Atlantic Records
17 Berners Street
London W1P 3DD

Noel Brown Productions, Ltd. (NBP)
16 Bracklesham Close
Farnborough Hants GU14 8LR

CBS Records (IFPI)
17/19 Soho Square
London W1V 6HE

Decca Record Company Ltd.
Decca House
9 Albert Embankment
London SE1 7SW

Walt Disney Productions Ltd.
68 Pall Mall
London SW1Y 5EX

EMI Records Ltd. (IFPI)
20 Manchester Square
London W1A 1ES

Fifth Avenue Recording Company (UK)
  Ltd.
Avenue House
River Way
Templefields
Harlow
Essex CM20 2DN

Lightning Records
841 Harrow Road
Harlesden
London NW10 5NH

Magnet Records Ltd. (IFPI)
Magnet House
22 York Street
London W1H 1FD

Motown Records Ltd.
16 Curzon Street
London W1

Music World Scotland
180 Hope Street
Glasgow G2 2UE
Scotland

Phonogram Ltd. (IFPI)
129 Park Street
London W1Y 3FA

Polydor Ltd.
17/19 Stratford Place
London W1N OBL

Private Stock Records
32 Old Burlington Street
London W1X 1LB

RCA Ltd. Record Division
50 Curzon Street
London W1Y 8EU

The Les Reed Organization
35 Soho Square
London W1

Sonet Productions Ltd. (IFPI)
121 Ledbury Road
London W11 2AQ

The Robert Stigwood Organization
67 Brook Street
London W1

Thrust Records
70 Lodge Road
Coleraine
County Londonderry
Northern Ireland

Transatlantic Records
86 Marylebone High Street
London W1M 4AY

United Artists Records Ltd. (IFPI)
Mortimer House
37/41 Mortimer Street
London W1A 2JL

WEA Records Ltd.
20 Broadwick Street
London W1V 2BH

SONGWRITER/PUBLISHER ASSOCIATIONS

ASCAP
American Society of Composers, Authors and Publishers

- Songwriters and publishers
- A performing-rights society
- Owned by membership

One Lincoln Plaza
New York, N.Y. 10023

6430 Sunset Boulevard
Hollywood, California 90028

700 17th Avenue South
Nashville, Tenn. 37203

BMI
(Broadcast Music, Inc.)

- Songwriters and publishers
- A performing-rights society
- Nonprofit organization (no membership dues)

40 West 57th Street
New York, N.Y. 10019

6255 Sunset Boulevard
Hollywood, Calif. 90028

Branch Offices: Boston, Coral Gables, Hollywood, Houston, Nashville, New York, San Mateo, Skokie, Montreal, Toronto, Vancouver

SESAC
(Society of European Stage Authors and Composers)

- Songwriters and publishers
- A performing-rights society
- Only society that also handles mechanical and film-synchronization licenses
- Has heavy catalogue of gospel music
- Nonprofit organization (no membership dues)

10 Columbus Circle
New York, N.Y. 10019

1513 Hawkins Street
Nashville, Tenn. 37203

Harry Fox Agency

- Publishers only
- A mechanical-rights organization
- Largest organization of its type
- Charges percentage of mechanical royalties for collection/audit services

110 East 59th Street
New York, N.Y. 10022

Copyright Service Bureau, Ltd.

- Publishers only
- A mechanical-rights organization
- Bureau takes care of filing all copyright notices, foreign contracts and writers' royalty statements
- Charges 10 percent of gross receipts for services

221 West 57th Street
New York, N.Y. 10019

American Mechanical Rights Association (AMRA)

- Songwriters and publishers
- A mechanical-rights organization
- Also collects mechanical royalties for writers, as well as publishers
- Charges 5 percent fee for services

250 West 57th Street
New York, N.Y. 10019

American Guild of Authors and Composers (AGAC)

- Songwriters only
- Publishers can sign contract with AGAC regarding the AGAC songwriter's agreements
- A voluntary organization
- Established "Basic Minimum Songwriter's Contract," "Royalty Collection Plan," "Copyright Renewal Administration Plan."
- AGAC members have mechanical and sheet-music royalty payments (not performances) cleared by AGAC New York office
- AGAC can serve as an auditor of mechanical performances and other rightful royalty payments

40 West 57th Street
New York, N.Y. 10019

6430 West Sunset Boulevard
Hollywood, Calif. 90028

Music Publishers Association of the U.S.

- Publishers only
- A trade association consisting mainly of the large publishers
- Handles publishers with "old standards" in their catalogues

609 Fifth Avenue, 4th Floor
New York, N.Y. 10017

National Music Publishers Association

- Publishers only
- A trade association oriented toward current popular and country music publishing

110 East 59th Street
New York, N.Y. 10022

Composers and Lyricists Guild of America (CLGA)

- Songwriters only
- Film studios sign contract with CLGA regarding minimum songwriter agreements for films
- A collective-bargaining union which represents composers and lyricists employed in TV and feature films
- Membership available only to those who have at least one assignment in TV or features

270 Madison Avenue, #1410
New York, N.Y. 10016

6565 Sunset Boulevard, #420
Hollywood, Calif. 90028

Nashville Songwriters Association (NSA)

- Songwriters only
- A voluntary organization
- Unpublished writers may also join
- Active membership for songwriters with at least one song published and affiliated with ASCAP, BMI or SESAC
- Membership

811 18th Avenue South
Nashville, Tenn. 37203

Country Music Association, Inc. (CMA)

- Songwriters only
- A voluntary professional organization
- Umbrella organization for the entire country music industry
- Membership requires that at least two songs have been published, recorded and released

700 16th Avenue South
Nashville, Tenn. 37203

Songwriters Resources and Services (SRS)

- Songwriters only
- A voluntary professional organization
- Does not collect royalties
- A service for songwriters' song protection
- Seminars, forums and workshops
- Lead-sheet service
- Song evaluation (lyrics and/or music)
- Festival of new music (annual contest and show)

- Group legal services
- Monthly newsletter
- Membership dues

6381 Hollywood Boulevard, #503
Hollywood, Calif. 90028

National Academy of Recording Arts and Sciences (NARAS)

- Membership for songwriters, singers, conductors, producers, composers, recording engineers, musicians, arrangers, album-cover art directors and liner-note writers
- A voluntary professional organization
- Annual Grammy Awards
- Hall of Fame
- Issues scholarships
- Governed by national board of trustees

4444 Riverside Drive, #202
Burbank, Calif. 91505

Chapter offices in New York, Nashville and other major cities

WEEKLY TRADE PERIODICALS

UNITED STATES

Billboard
c/o Billboard Publications, Inc.
One Astor Plaza
1515 Broadway
New York, N.Y. 10036
     or
9000 Sunset Boulevard
Los Angeles, Calif. 90069

Cash Box
c/o Cash Box Publications, Inc.
119 West 57th Street
New York, N.Y. 10019
     or
6363 Sunset Boulevard
Hollywood, Calif. 90028

Record World
c/o Record World Publications, Inc.
1700 Broadway
New York, N.Y. 10019
       or
6290 Sunset Boulevard
Hollywood, Calif. 90028

Variety
c/o Variety Publications
154 West 46th Street
New York, N.Y. 10036
       or
1400 North Cahuenga Boulevard
Hollywood, Calif. 90028

FOREIGN

Music Week
c/o Morgan-Grampian House
30 Calderwood Street
London, SE18 6QH
England

Music Labo
c/o Music Labo International
Dempa Building, Bekkan 5F
11-2 Highashi-Gotanda
1-Chome
Shinagawa-Ku, Tokyo 141
Japan

MUSIC INDUSTRY MAGAZINES

GENERAL COVERAGE

Song Hits *
c/o Charleton Publications
Office of Publications
Charleton Building
Derby, Conn. 06418

Top 40, soul, C & W

Hit Parader *
c/o Charleton Publications
Office of Publications
Charleton Building
Derby, Conn. 06418

Rock, pop

Country Song Roundup *
c/o Charleton Publications
Office of Publications
Charleton Building
Derby, Conn. 06418

C & W, country/pop

Blues and Soul
c/o Farondean Ltd.
320 West 56th Street
New York, N.Y. 10019

Blues, soul

Creem
10 Pelham Parkway
Pelham Manor, N.Y. 10803

Hard rock

Down Beat
222 West Adams Street
Chicago, Ill. 60606

Jazz, jazz/rock

* *These magazines publish lyrics of hit songs, in addition to including interviews with celebrity recording artists and singer/songwriters.*

Disco World
c/o Transamerican Publishing
352 Park Avenue South, 9th Floor
New York, N.Y. 10010

Disco

New Wave Rock
c/o Whizbang Publications
211 East 43rd Street
New York, N.Y. 10017

Punk rock, heavy metal

MUSICIAN COVERAGE

Music Contact
6381 Hollywood Boulevard, Suite 323
Hollywood, Calif. 90028

Guitar Player
12333 Saratoga/Sunnyvale Road
Saratoga, Calif. 95070

Contemporary Keyboards
20605 Lazaneo Drive
Cupertino, Calif. 95014

SONGWRITER/PRODUCER
COVERAGE

Songwriter Magazine
c/o Len Latimer Organization
6430 Sunset Boulevard
Hollywood, Calif. 90028

1- 213 - 464 - 7604

*Songwriter interviews, articles on craft
and business of music, song charts*

Album Magazine
c/o American Song Festival
P.O. Box 424
Hollywood, Calif. 90028

*Songwriter interviews, backstage
profiles, record and stage reviews,
articles of current musical interest*

Recording Engineer-Producer Magazine
c/o Recording and Broadcasting
Publications
1850 Whitley Avenue
Hollywood, Calif. 90028

*Technical and creative aspects of
producing; producer interviews*

Radio Report Magazine
c/o CHRR Publishing Corporation
7011 Sunset Boulevard
Hollywood, Calif. 90028

*International station surveys, record
trend news, hit chart analysis*

Songwriter's Market
9933 Alliance Road
Cincinnati, Ohio 45242

*Articles on craft, songwriter selling
markets, writer interviews*

MUSIC TRADE NEWSPAPERS/ NEWSLETTERS

Rolling Stone
c/o Straight Arrow Publishers
745 Fifth Avenue
New York, N.Y. 10022

Rock news and celebrity interviews

Music City News
1302 Division Street
Nashville, Tenn. 37203

Nashville news

Melody Maker
Circulation Department
Surrey House, Throwley Way
Sutton, Surrey SM1 4QQ
England

European music news and record charts;
other major countries are covered

Jazz Journal International
Subscription Department
7 Carnaby Street
London W1V 1PG
England

International Jazz coverage

Soul
c/o Soul Publications, Inc.
8271 Melrose Avenue, Suite 208
Los Angeles, Calif. 90046

Soul news and celebrity interviews

MUSIC TRADE TIP SHEETS

Bill Gavin Report
One Embarcadero Center, Suite 220
San Francisco, Calif. 94111

R & R Report (Radio and Records)
c/o Bob Wilson Publishing
1930 Century Park West
Century City, Calif. 90067

Confidential Radio Report
9000 Sunset Boulevard
Los Angeles, Calif. 90069

Claude Hall Radio Report
7011 Sunset Boulevard
Los Angeles, Calif. 90028

Fred Report
c/o Fear and Loathing Publishing
P.O. Box 5546
Carmel, Calif. 93921

SONG FESTIVALS

UNITED STATES

American Song Festival

5900 Wilshire Boulevard, West Pavilion
Los Angeles, Calif. 90036

The ASF is the only international song festival of its type currently being sponsored in the United States. The festival, originated by Tad Danz, is an annual event covering both amateur and professional music categories. Within the amateur division there are these categories:

Top 40 Rock/Soul
Country
Easy Listening
Instrumental Jazz
Folk
Gospel/Inspirational
Vocal Performance
The professional division includes these categories:
Top 40 Rock/Soul
Country
Easy Listening
The songs in both the amateur and professional ranks are judged separately for noncompeting awards.

The ASF awards cash prizes to the several levels of winners (Finalists, Semifinalists, Honorable Mentions, etc.) These cash awards are split between the two judging divisions of amateur and professional.

Festival of New Music

c/o Songwriter Resource Services (SRS)
6381 Hollywood Boulevard, Suite 503
Hollywood, Calif. 90028

The FNM is a locally sponsored songwriters' festival. Although the festival is produced on a local rather than a national or international level, anyone interested may submit material.

The Festival of New Music is sponsored by SRS in association with Peter Yarrow (of Peter, Paul and Mary fame), and is held on an annual basis in the Santa Monica, California, area. Original songs are submitted by tape to the SRS, which determines the twelve best songs. There are no winners or losers among these twelve; they are publicly performed, and exposure at the festival may result, as it has in the past, in contracts with record companies. The FNM is produced in concert form before a paying audience. One half of the proceeds is split between the writers and performers.

FOREIGN

Gibraltar Song Festival

P.O. Box #52
Gibraltar

The main function of the Gibraltar Song Festival is to raise funds for various charitable organizations. The GSF is conducted under the patronage of His Lordship, The Bishop of Gibraltar.

Original songs (unreleased) are submitted to the Chairman of the GSF, and a staff of judges selects the top song. The winner receives a cash award and a trophy. The singer of the winning song receives a souvenir Golden Medallion.

The Gibraltar Song Festival reserves the right to broadcast and/or televise the show, live or on tape.

Tokyo Music Festival

c/o Tokyo Broadcasting System, Inc.
5-3-6 Akasaka
Minato-ku, Tokyo 107
Japan

The TMF is sponsored by the Tokyo Broadcasting System, the largest broadcaster in Japan. The festival is held annually on an international basis.

In 1975 Paul Williams won the festival's grand prize. American songwriters also won that year in four other categories.

In the event an applicant has no contractual arrangement with any Japanese production company, record company or music publisher, the applicant may submit material directly to the Tokyo Music Foundation, in which case the Foundation recommends an agent for the applicant.

Original songs that win in the various categories receive cash awards as well as a display trophy.

World Popular Song Festival

c/o Yamaha Music Foundation
1-1-1 Ebisu Minami
Shibuya-ku, Tokyo 150
Japan

The WPSF is an annual festival held in Tokyo and sponsored by the Yamaha Music Foundation in association with the Ministry of Foreign Affairs of Japan, The Metropolitan Government, Japan Air Lines and Nippon Gakki Ltd.

There are cash awards for Best Foreign Entry and Best Japanese Entry, as well as in several Composition categories. Grand Prize winners also receive trophies, several gold medallions and certificates of honor. There are additional awards for Performance of a Song and Its Interpretation.

International Song Festival for Peace—in Malta

Tourist Revues International
Notabile
Malta

The ISFPM is an annual festival sponsored under the jurisdiction of the International Federation of Festival Organizations and Organizers (FIDOF).

For more information, contact either the Tourist Revues International office or the FIDOF office. The address is c/o P.O.B. Split, Split, Yugoslavia.

Castlebar International Song Festival

c/o Castlebar International Relations Office
10 St. Helens Road
Booterstown, County Dublin
Ireland

The CISF is an annual event sponsored by the Castlebar Chamber of Commerce. It is an international event open to all songwriters, amateur and professional.

Cash awards and prizes are given to the winner by donation from various Irish companies, such as the famous Galway crystals. Trophies and cash awards are also given for the Best Singing Performance and the Best Interpretation. A new category for instrumental compositions has been added to the festival. The categories are Best Entry Overall, Best Irish Entry, Best Arrangement Overall.

Grand Prix de Paris International de la Chanson Song Festival

c/o Service du Grand Prix International de la Chanson
2 bis, Rue de la Baume
75008, Paris
France

The GPPIC Song Festival is conducted on an annual basis and is an international competition. Songs must be original, unpublished and never performed.

Cash awards are received in the following categories: Best Song, Best Performance, Best French Song; Maurice Chevalier Award assigned to one of the French songs.

International Federation of Festival Organizations and Organizers

c/o P.O.B. Split, Split, Yugoslavia

The FIDOF has been in operation for more than ten years, and its membership includes major song festivals in various parts of the world that sponsor international competitions.

FIDOF publishes a bulletin regarding song festivals being held throughout the world, giving past, present and future information. This organization also publishes a Calendar of National and International Events for coming song-festival competitions. This is a special service to its active membership.

Membership in the FIDOF is granted at nominal cost and entitles the subscriber to all the benefits and information circulated by the organization.

PERMISSION ACKNOWLEDGMENTS

(continued from page 4)

Index

record-company affiliation of, 223
record producers vs., 223
society affiliations of, 220, 228, 230

Queen, 29, 188, 189

Rado, James, 169, 172
Rafferty, Gerry, 101
Ragni, Gerome, 169, 172
Raksin, David, 143
Raposo, Joe, 72, 123, 179–180
record children, songwriters as, 213–214
record companies, 189–190, 222–223
    A & R heads of, 190, 216–218
record production, 211–219
    financing independent master in, 215
    growth of, 211–213
    manager's job in, 215–216
    writer/producers and, 211–215
Reddy, Helen, 121, 160–161, 162–163, 188, 237, 266
repetition principle, 22–32
    examples of, 26–28
    in hooks, 29–31
    sequences and, 86
    variations in, 24
rewriting, 181–184
    amateur's cop-outs and, 181–182
    bridges and, 182
    criticism from publisher or producer in, 183–184
    mental blocks in, 183
rhumba, rhythm of, 79
rhyme, rhyming, 45–54, 248, 254, 256–257, 260
    avoided, 46–47

"false" vs. "true," 45–47, 50–51, 52, 53, 249–250
    inner, 50, 256, 262
    in motion pictures, 52–53
    of proper names, 52
    revolution in, 45–47
    for rhyme's sake, 45–46
    in theater, 52
rhyme schemes, 48–49
rhyming dictionaries, 47, 54
rhythm, 75–83, 249, 251–252, 261
    Bo Diddley beat, 81, 101
    boogaloo, 82
    Charleston, 83
    folk/country 2, 76–77
    Latin, 78–80
    "Louie, Louie," 82
    Memphis beat, 81
    Reggae, 80
    in sequences, 86–89
    shuffle, 75–76
    "South Seas," 82
    straight four (Motown), 81
    syncopated, 75, 85, 254, 261
    waltz, (3/4 rhythm), 77–78
rhythm and blues (R & B), 78, 93, 109 137–142
    bass line in, 139
    emotions in, 137–138
    lyrics of, 139–140
    production and, 138
    progressions in, 91
Rhythm Heritage, 27
Rich, Charlie, 27
Richard, Cliff, 49
Richard, Keith, 43, 83
riffs, see figures
Rinky Dinks, 206
Rivers, Johnny, 100